REVELATION

Verse By Verse Ministry International

Taught by Stephen Armstrong

Copyright © 2022 by **Verse By Verse Ministry International**

All rights reserved. No part of this publication may be reproduced, distributed, or transmitted in any form or by any means, without prior written permission.

All Scripture quotations are taken from the New American Standard Bible ® (NASB), copyright © 1960, 1962, 1963, 1968, 1971, 1972, 1973, 1975, 1977, 1995 by The Lockman Foundation. Used by permission. www.Lockman.org.

Scripture quotations marked (NIV) are taken from the Holy Bible, New International Version. Copyright © 1973, 1978, 1984, 2011 by Biblica, Inc.® Used by permission. All rights reserved worldwide.

Renown Publishing
www.renownpublishing.com

Revelation / Verse By Verse Ministry International
ISBN-13: 978-1-952602-75-7

To our beloved friend and pastor, Stephen Armstrong, who committed his life to the teaching of God's word and lived with eyes for eternity.

May his soul rest peacefully with our Lord and Savior, Jesus Christ.

CONTENTS

GETTING STARTED — v
REVELATION 1:1–3 — 1
REVELATION 1:4–16 — 8
REVELATION 1:17–20 — 16
REVELATION 2 INTRODUCTION — 21
BACKGROUND OF THE LETTERS — 26
REVELATION 2:1–7 — 33
REVELATION 2:8–11 — 40
REVELATION 2:12–17 — 48
REVELATION 2:18–29 — 54
REVELATION 3:1–6 — 64
REVELATION 3:7–13 — 71
REVELATION 3:14–22 — 79
DANIEL 2:1–11 — 89
DANIEL 2:12–39 — 95
DANIEL 2:40–45 — 101
DANIEL 7:1–8 — 107
DANIEL 9:1–5 — 114
DANIEL 9:3–5; 20–27 — 121
REVELATION 4:1–4 — 127
APOLOGETICS FOR THE RAPTURE — 134
THE DAY OF THE LORD VERSUS THE COMING OF THE LORD — 140
REVELATION 4:5–8; 5:1–14 — 145
REVELATION 5:1–14 — 153
COVENANTS AND CONSEQUENCES — 160
SIGNS OF THE END OF THE AGE PART ONE — 166
SIGNS OF THE END OF THE AGE PART TWO — 171
REVELATION 6:1–4 — 177
REVELATION 6:5–8 — 182

- **REVELATION 6:9–17** — 187
- **REVELATION 7:1–17** — 193
- **REVELATION 8:1–7** — 200
- **REVELATION 8:8–13; 9:1–6** — 206
- **REVELATION 9:1–12** — 213
- **REVELATION 9:13–19** — 219
- **REVELATION 9:20–10:7** — 225
- **REVELATION 10:8–11** — 231
- **REVELATION 10:11–11:6** — 236
- **REVELATION 11:3–6** — 241
- **REVELATION 11:7–19** — 246
- **REVELATION 12:1–5** — 252
- **REVELATION 12:6–12** — 258
- **REVELATION 12:13–17** — 265
- **REVELATION 13:1–2** — 271
- **REVELATION 13:3–4** — 276
- **REVELATION 13:5–18** — 282
- **REVELATION 14:1–5** — 289
- **REVELATION 14:6–11** — 294
- **REVELATION 14:12–20** — 300
- **REVELATION 15:1–4** — 307
- **REVELATION 15:5–16:6** — 312
- **REVELATION 16:7–16** — 317
- **REVELATION 16:17–21** — 323
- **REVELATION 17:1–8** — 328
- **REVELATION 17:9–18** — 333
- **REVELATION 18:1–3** — 338
- **REVELATION 18:1–8** — 344
- **REVELATION 18:9–24** — 350
- **REVELATION 19:1–10** — 355
- **REVELATION 19:6–10** — 361
- **ISAIAH 29:1–7** — 368
- **STAGES ONE–THREE OF ARMAGEDDON** — 374

ISRAEL'S CONFESSION AND SALVATION	379
REVELATION 19:11–16	385
ARMAGEDDON STAGE FOUR	391
CHRIST'S FINAL VICTORY	397
RESOLUTION OF ARMAGEDDON	402
THE 75-DAY INTERVAL	406
REVELATION 20:1–4	412
REVELATION 20:5	419
THE 1,000-YEAR KINGDOM	424
CHANGES TO NATURE AND ISRAEL	430
THE STATE OF ISRAEL IN THE KINGDOM	436
DAILY LIFE AND DEATH IN THE KINGDOM	441
LIFE AND FAITH IN THE KINGDOM	446
OVERVIEW OF LIFE IN THE KINGDOM	451
THE TEMPLE IN THE KINGDOM	455
THE GLORY OF GOD	460
THE MILLENNIAL KINGDOM	466
REVELATION 20:7–9	471
THE PURPOSE OF THE WAR OF GOG AND MAGOG	476
THE RESOLUTION OF THE WAR OF GOG AND MAGOG	482
REVELATION 20:10–15	487
REVELATION 20:21	492
REVELATION 21:1–8	497
REVELATION 21:9–21	502
REVELATION 21:22–22:5	508
REVELATION 22:6–21	513
ANSWER KEY	518
ABOUT THE AUTHOR	596
ABOUT RENOWN PUBLISHING	597

INTRODUCTION

Getting Started

Video One Part One

Topical overview: Introduction to the VBVMI study method.
Learning goals: Establish how to approach the study of Revelation. Identify the golden rule of this study. Build a foundation for the rest of the study of Revelation.

LISTENING GUIDE

This session is recommended for the first meeting as an introduction to the study and as an opportunity to set norms and expectations for homework, meeting times, etc. First homework assignment (optional Digging Deeper section) assigned at this meeting.

As you watch video one part one, complete the following section. For many, reading the questions before watching the video will aid their understanding of the video content.

1. Why do we study with rigor?

_____

_____

_____

2. What is the proof that the enemy doesn't want you to study Revelation?

_____

_____

_____

3. What does 1 Corinthians 14:33, which says: "…for God is not a God of confusion but of peace, as in all the churches of the saints," teach us?

4. How is the Bible like a novel?

5. Why is Revelation the last book of the Bible?

6. What is Pastor Armstrong's job?

7. Why has this study been called a survey of the whole Bible masquerading as a study of Revelation?

8. What is the purpose of having rules of interpretation?

9. What will we *not* do?

_____
_____
_____

10. When we get to a place where we have an unanswered question, what will the answer be?

_____
_____
_____

Two Rules for Interpretation

The Golden Rule: When the plain sense of the text makes common sense, seek no further sense.

11. If you follow the golden rule of interpretation, how often will you steer clear of trouble?

_____
_____
_____

Symbols will always be interpreted by Scripture itself. You never have to guess.

12. If a symbol has significance, where will its meaning be already established?

_____
_____
_____

13. How do the rules of interpretation work?

_____
_____

14. Why do you only look backward?

15. What leads to confusion?

As you go through this study, find hope and reassurance in knowing God wants you to be able to understand His word.

DIGGING DEEPER (OPTIONAL)

Should you choose to dig deeper, complete the following Digging Deeper section. Each meeting will open with discussion of what you've learned and observed in Scripture, and this section will prepare you for that discussion.

To record what you observe in each passage and the questions you have about it, reproduce or re-create the two-column graphic organizer below. Things to look for: Who is speaking? To whom is he speaking? What does he say about God? Jesus? The church? Individual believers? What do readers of this text stand to gain?

Scripture Passage: Revelation 1:1–3

OBSERVATIONS	QUESTIONS

SESSION ONE

Revelation 1:1–3

> ***Remember the Golden Rule:*** *When the plain sense of Scripture makes common sense, we seek no other sense.*

Video One Part Two

Topic overview: Introduction to the book of Revelation and the benefits of studying it.

Learning goal: Realize the benefit of studying Revelation. Identify preconceived notions of Revelation. Establish expectations for the study. Understand what a symbol is and its literary purpose.

CORE QUESTIONS

Before finishing video one, read Revelation 1:1–3. Use the two-column graphic organizer to help you organize your thoughts. Discuss your observations as a group.

As you watch the video, complete the following section. For many, reading the questions before watching the video will aid their understanding of the video content.

The book of Revelation is a letter. Read Revelation 1:1–3.

1. What does the Greek word for Revelation teach us?

_____

_____

_____

Revelation

2. Of whom is this book said to be the direct revelation?

3. Which entities make up the "chain of custody" for this letter?

4. Why does God include this "chain of custody" information?

5. How does Jesus communicate the details of this letter (verse 1)?

6. What is this letter a testimony about (verse 3)?

7. Why are these two verbs so crucial to our understanding of Revelation?

REVELATION 1:1–3

8. What does Revelation specifically promise to those who study it?

_____
_____
_____

9. What does it mean to "heed" the teaching in Revelation?

_____
_____
_____

DISCUSSION QUESTIONS

1. What are you hoping to learn or gain from participating in this study?

_____
_____
_____

2. What do you already think you know about Revelation? What are your preconceived notions, and where did these notions come from?

_____
_____
_____

3. What is a symbol? List some symbols that come to mind, either from the Bible or from our culture in general. Why might God, through John, use symbols to convey His meaning?

_____
_____
_____

4. What do we learn in this session about who God is? Who Jesus is? Who we are?

_____

REVELATION

_____

_____

5. Does the "chain of custody" at the beginning of this book help you as a reader? Why or why not?

_____

_____

_____

6. First Corinthians 1:27 says, "but God has chosen the foolish things of the world to shame the wise, and God has chosen the weak things of the world to shame the things which are strong," and 2 Corinthians 4:3 says, "And even if our gospel is veiled, it is veiled to those who are perishing." The Bible clearly teaches that not all are meant to understand it, and the same applies to Revelation. How does this make you feel?

_____

_____

_____

7. Pastor Armstrong teaches that God truly desires His people to understand His word. This means that if you are a child of God, you already have what you need to understand His word, including Revelation. Does this encourage you? If so, how?

_____

_____

_____

8. In the space below, record your takeaway from Revelation 1:1–3 and any questions you have that remain unanswered.

_____

_____

_____

Digging Deeper (Optional)

Should you choose to dig deeper, complete the following Digging Deeper section. Each meeting will open with discussion of what you've learned and observed in Scripture, and this section will prepare you for that discussion.

In a two-column graphic organizer, record what you observe in each passage and the questions you have about it. Things to look for: Who is speaking? To whom is he speaking? What does he say about God? Jesus? The church? Individual believers? What do readers of this text stand to gain? The purpose of this portion of each session is to familiarize you with the text from which Pastor Armstrong will teach in each video. You'll have an opportunity to read it objectively, record your thoughts and questions, and then, when you watch the video, you'll be able to follow what Pastor Armstrong says more closely because you'll already be familiar with the text.

Scripture Passage: Read Revelation 1:4–16

Scripture Passage: Colossians 1:13–20

> *For He rescued us from the domain of darkness, and transferred us to the kingdom of His beloved Son, in whom we have redemption, the forgiveness of sins. He is the image of the invisible God, the firstborn of all creation. For by Him all things were created, both in the heavens and on earth, visible and invisible, whether thrones or dominions or rulers or authorities—all things have been created through Him and for Him. He is before all things, and in Him all things hold together. He is also head of the body, the church; and He is the beginning, the firstborn from the dead, so that He Himself will come to have first place in everything. For it was the Father's good pleasure for all the fullness to dwell in Him, and through Him to reconcile all things to Himself, having made peace through the blood of His cross; through Him, I say, whether things on earth or things in heaven.*

A Little Deeper…

1. What do we learn about who and what Jesus is in these two passages?

___

___

___

2. What do we learn about Jesus and His relationship with God in these two passages?

___

_____
_____

3. As we read these two passages, we see imagery of bondservants, kingdoms, dominions, etc. What is your position in the kingdom of God as you understand it? How do you fill this role?

_____
_____
_____

4. Take a moment to compare and contrast Jesus as you imagine Him to be with Jesus as He is described in this passage. Use the Venn diagram provided to organize your thoughts.

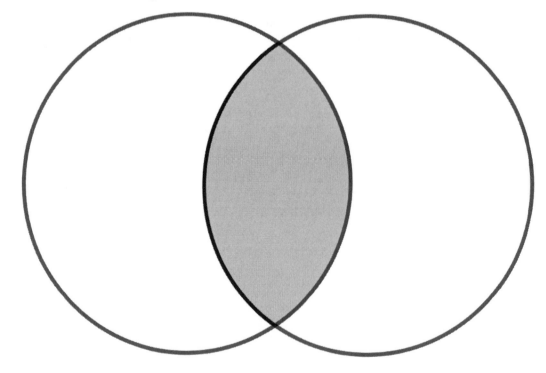

_____
_____

REVELATION 1:1–3

5. Take a minute to reread these passages. Are there any words or phrases you aren't sure about? Take the time to look up their meanings.

6. Spend some time in prayer. Ask God to help you understand His word and to prepare your heart for Session Two. Ask Him to help you truly understand both who He is and who you are in light of that.

SESSION TWO

Revelation 1:4–16

> ***Remember the Golden Rule:*** *When the plain sense of Scripture makes common sense, we seek no other sense.*

Video Two

Topical overview: Where did Revelation come from? What do those who read it stand to gain? By whom is it written? To whom is it written? What is the significance of the number seven?

Learning goals: Identify the source, structure, and influences of Revelation. Realize the benefit of studying Revelation. Catalog what this passage teaches about who God is, who Jesus is, and who we are. Practice unpacking symbolism.

CORE QUESTIONS

Before watching video two, read Revelation 1:4–16. Use the two-column graphic organizer to help you organize your thoughts. Discuss your observations as a group.

As you watch the video, complete the following section. For many, reading the questions before watching the video will aid their understanding of the video content.

Revelation 1:4–8

1. To whom does John write?

_____

_____

2. In the Bible, what does the number seven generally convey?

3. So, what is the symbolic meaning of "the seven churches of Asia?"

4. Who does John's greeting come from?

5. What do the descriptions of Jesus point to?

6. What is the book of Revelation about?

7. What it the significance of the phrase "kingdom of priests?"

Revelation 1:9–16

1. Where was John moved from when he was exiled to Patmos?

2. Who are the Church Fathers?

3. How old was John when he wrote this text?

4. How did the letter, Revelation, get off Patmos?

"Being in the Spirit on a Lordy day" means experiencing a particularly Spirit-filled time with the Lord.

5. What is John commanded to do?

6. What should a "lampstand" look like?

_____
_____
_____

7. What does a lampstand mean?

_____
_____
_____

One like a Son of Man is referring to Jesus; He's like a man, but not exactly a man.

DISCUSSION QUESTIONS

1. What do we learn in this session about who God is? Who Jesus is? Who we are?

_____
_____
_____

2. How does the application of the symbolic nature of the number seven affect your understanding of this passage?

_____
_____
_____

3. Revelation is John's verbal explanation of what he *saw* with his eyes. How does this affect your understanding of Revelation? Does it interfere with any of your preconceived notions about the book? Why or why not?

_____
_____
_____

REVELATION

4. Have you ever experienced a "brass horn" moment like John does here? A time when the Lord spoke to you so loudly and clearly there was no doubt it was Him? Describe your experience. How did you know it was the Lord?

_____

_____

_____

5. What does a "Lordy day" look like for you? How do you best commune with the Lord?

_____

_____

_____

6. Review the description of Jesus in verses 13–16. Do you recognize any symbols in this description? If so, which do you recognize, and where else in Scripture do you remember seeing them?

_____

_____

_____

7. Imagine yourself encountering the heavenly form of Jesus as described here. How might you respond? Why?

_____

_____

_____

8. What is the significance of Jesus being like a man, but not exactly a man? Do you think those of your current religious context understand the difference? Why or why not? What might change if they did?

_____

_____

_____

REVELATION 1:4–16

9. In the space below, record your takeaway from Revelation 1:4–16 and any questions you have that remain unanswered.

_____

_____

_____

DIGGING DEEPER (OPTIONAL)

Should you choose to dig deeper, complete the following Digging Deeper section. Each meeting will open with discussion of what you've learned and observed in Scripture, and this section will prepare you for that discussion.

In a two-column graphic organizer, record what you observe in each passage and the questions you have about it. Things to look for: Who is speaking? To whom is he speaking? What does he say about God? Jesus? The church? Individual believers? What do readers of this text stand to gain?

Scripture Passage: Read Revelation 1:17–20

Scripture Passage: Daniel 7:9

I kept looking until thrones were set up, and the Ancient of Days took His seat; His vesture was like white snow and the hair of His head like pure wool. His throne was ablaze with flames, its wheels were a burning fire.

Scripture Passage: Daniel 10:4–6

On the twenty-fourth day of the first month, while I was by the bank of the great river, that is, the Tigris, I lifted my eyes and looked, and behold, there was a certain man dressed in linen, whose waist was girded with a belt of pure gold of Uphaz. His body also was like beryl, his face had the appearance of lightning, his eyes were like flaming torches, his arms and feet like the gleam of polished bronze, and the sound of his words like the sound of a tumult.

Scripture Passage: Isaiah 11:1–5

Then a shoot will spring from the stem of Jesse, and a branch from his roots will bear fruit. The Spirit of the LORD will rest on Him, the spirit of wisdom and understanding, the spirit of counsel and strength, the spirit of knowledge and the fear of the LORD. And He will delight in the fear of the LORD, and He will not judge by what His eyes see, nor make a decision by what His ears hear; but with righteousness He will judge the poor, and decide with fairness for the afflicted of the earth; and He will strike the earth with the rod of His mouth, and with the breath of His lips He will slay the wicked. Also righteousness will be the belt about His loins, and faithfulness the belt about His waist.

Scripture Passage: Joshua 5:13–14

Now it came about when Joshua was by Jericho, that he lifted up his eyes and looked, and behold, a man was standing opposite him with his sword drawn in his hand, and Joshua went to him and said to him, "Are you for us or for our adversaries?" He said, "No; rather I indeed come now as captain of the host of the LORD." And Joshua fell on his face to the earth, and bowed down, and said to him, "What has my lord to say to his servant?"

Scripture Passage: Ezekiel 1:28

As the appearance of the rainbow in the clouds on a rainy day, so was the appearance of the surrounding radiance. Such was the appearance of the likeness of the glory of the LORD. And when I saw it, I fell on my face and heard a voice speaking.

Scripture Passage: Daniel 8:15, 17

When I, Daniel, had seen the vision, I sought to understand it; and behold, standing before me was one who looked like a man. ... So he came near to where I was standing, and when he came I was frightened and fell on my face; but he said to me, "Son of man, understand that the vision pertains to the time of the end."

A LITTLE DEEPER...

1. We see in these verses both a thorough description of Jesus' heavenly form and the consistent reaction of men when they see it. In the space below, create a list of every adjective describing Jesus in the passages above. As you read, highlight or underline the reaction of men when they see Him.

_____

_____

_____

2. How do you reconcile the Jesus described here with the one in your mind? Review the Venn Diagram you completed in Session One "A Little Deeper..." to help form your

response.

_____

_____

_____

SESSION THREE

Revelation 1:17–20

> ***Remember the Golden Rule:*** *When the plain sense of Scripture makes common sense, we seek no other sense.*

Video Three

Topical overview: John's response. Continued description of the heavenly form of Jesus. Decoding symbols from Session Two.

Learning goals: Identify the symbolism of the seven stars and seven lampstands. Understand how John's description of Jesus reflects His character and His relationship to us.

CORE QUESTIONS

Before watching video three, read Revelation 1:17–20. Use the two-column graphic organizer to help you organize your thoughts. Discuss your observations as a group.

As you watch the video, complete the following section. For many, reading the questions before watching the video will aid their understanding of the video content.

Revelation 1:20

1. What do the seven stars represent?

_____
_____
_____

REVELATION 1:17–20

2. What do the seven lampstands represent?

_____
_____
_____

3. What do lampstands commonly represent?

_____
_____
_____

4. What is the mission of the whole church?

_____
_____
_____

5. How does John's description of Jesus compare with that of the rest of Scripture?

_____
_____
_____

We *do not* need to guess at what the Bible means. The Bible gives us everything we need to understand it. For example, the symbols in verses 9–16 are explained:

- Belt = faithfulness, righteousness
- Robe = one in a position of authority, priesthood
- Sword coming from His mouth = breath of His lips slaying the wicked
- White hair = purity, holiness
- Burning eyes = piercing discernment
- Glowing bronze feet = judgment as He tramples out His wrath on the wicked
- Shining face = light of the truth

Revelation

Revelation 1:17–18

1. What is John's response to seeing Jesus again after 60 years?

___

2. Philippians 2:5–9 illustrates what about Jesus' incarnate form?

___

3. If you can hug your God when you see Him in His glory, what kind of god do you have?

___

4. What do we learn about Jesus here?

___

The description of Jesus in Revelation is a preview of how we will see Him in the future in His kingdom. (See Revelation 19)

5. How does Jesus describe Himself?

___

Revelation 1:19

This verse sets up the whole rest of the book.

1. What is John's task?

_____

_____

_____

2. What are the three parts of his task?

_____

_____

_____

DISCUSSION QUESTIONS

1. Review Revelation 1:9–16, Daniel 7:9, 10:4–6, and Isaiah 11:1–5. How does this description of Christ's heavenly form impact you? Return to the discussion from last week, and consider the symbolic significance of this description. Is our present understanding of Jesus accurate?

_____

_____

_____

2. How might this description of who Jesus is affect your practical theology, how your faith affects your everyday life? (The King we serve isn't the gentle, lowly, huggable man portrayed in the Gospels, but many of us live our lives as if He were. How does adjusting your view of Jesus to the one we see here in Revelation affect how you live your life?)

_____

_____

_____

3. Review the outline of the three parts of John's task (verse 19). Do you think this outline will help your understanding as the study goes on? Do any of the preconceived notions you discussed in Session One touch on the timing outlined here?

_____

_____

_____

4. In the space below, record your takeaway from Revelation 1:17–20 and any questions you have that remain unanswered.

_____

_____

_____

DIGGING DEEPER (OPTIONAL)

Should you choose to dig deeper, complete the following Digging Deeper section. Each meeting will open with discussion of what you've learned and observed in Scripture, and this section will prepare you for that discussion.

In a two-column graphic organizer, record what you observe in each passage and the questions you have about it. Things to look for: Who is speaking? To whom is he speaking? What does he say about God? Jesus? The church? Individual believers? What do readers of this text stand to gain?

Scripture Passage: Read Revelation 2–3

A LITTLE DEEPER...

1. List the seven churches and summarize Christ's message to each in a word or phrase.

_____

_____

_____

SESSION FOUR

Revelation 2 Introduction

Remember the Golden Rule: *When the plain sense of Scripture makes common sense, we seek no other sense.*

Video Four

Topical overview: Outline of Revelation. The things that *are*.

Learning goals: Understand the possible interpretations of the time periods referred to by "the times which are" in Revelation 1:19.

CORE QUESTIONS

Before watching video four, read Revelation 2. Use the two-column graphic organizer to help you organize your thoughts. Discuss your observations as a group.

As you watch the video, complete the following section. For many, reading the questions before watching the video will aid their understanding of the video content.

Remember, John is told to write what he *sees*, not what he's told. That's part of why this book is so difficult to understand

Revelation 1:19

1. The outline of Revelation includes which 3 parts?

_____

_____

_____

2. What did John see (Review Revelation chapter 1)?

_____
_____
_____

3. What is the purpose of these descriptions?

_____
_____
_____

4. Who is the "are" in the "things that are" applicable to? Who in history falls into the time period John calls "the things that are?"

_____
_____
_____

Interpreting the Letters

1. How many methods are there for interpreting the letters? What are the three methods?

_____
_____
_____

2. What might the clockwise naming of the churches indicate?

_____
_____
_____

3. The "times that are" might prophetically represent what?

_____

DISCUSSION QUESTIONS

1. How would you summarize Pastor Armstrong's explanation of the "things which are?"

2. Of the three interpretive methods through which we read Revelation (literally, universally, and prophetically), with which are you most comfortable? Why?

3. How might exploring all three of these interpretive methods enrich your understanding of Scripture?

4. At this point, we've only been introduced to Pastor Armstrong's prophetic reading of the letters to the seven churches. What are your thoughts on this topic? What questions do you have?

5. In the space below, record your takeaway from the introduction to Revelation 2 and any questions you have that remain unanswered.

DIGGING DEEPER (OPTIONAL)

Should you choose to dig deeper, complete the following Digging Deeper section. Each meeting will open with discussion of what you've learned and observed in Scripture, and this section will prepare you for that discussion.

In a two-column graphic organizer, record what you observe in each passage and the questions you have about it. Things to look for: Who is speaking? To whom is he speaking? What does he say about God? Jesus? The church? Individual believers? What do readers of this text stand to gain?

Scripture Passage: Read Revelation 2:1–7

A LITTLE DEEPER…

1. What praises does Jesus offer the Ephesian church? What criticisms?

2. What might Jesus refer to when He says they've "lost [their] first love?"

3. What are the consequences for lack of repentance?

4. What might we learn from this?

SESSION FIVE

Background of the Letters

> ***Remember the Golden Rule:*** *When the plain sense of Scripture makes common sense, we seek no other sense.*

Video Five

Topical overview: Background of the letters to the churches, apostleship, the letter to the church in Ephesus.

Learning goals: Decipher the literal and universal meanings of the letter to the church in Ephesus.

CORE QUESTIONS

Before watching video five, read Revelation 2:1–7. Use the two-column graphic organizer to help you organize your thoughts. Discuss your observations as a group.

As you watch the video, complete the following section. For many, reading the questions before watching the video will aid their understanding of the video content.

Overview

1. Prophetic reading of the letters indicates a symbolic, eschatological meaning. What does this mean?

_____

_____

_____

BACKGROUND OF THE LETTERS

2. What do chapters 2 and 3 explain?

_____

_____

_____

3. When did the first mention of a prophetic reading of the letters to the churches occur?

_____

_____

_____

    Your God is big enough to layer all three types of meaning into these letters at the same time. It's not one or the other: these letters spoke specifically to the churches to whom they're addressed, they speak specifically to churches today, and they speak prophetically of the nature of the church throughout time, all at the same time.

4. So the seven churches represent not only 100% of the church but also what?

_____

_____

_____

5. What will the church age look like?

_____

_____

_____

6. The prophetic reading of this text will reveal what two things?

_____

_____

_____

7. If there are only seven stages in the letters, what is possible?

_____

8. How does Scripture refer to Christ's second coming?

Letter to the Church in Ephesus

These letters have a highly structured, repeated form: name of a city, a salutation, Jesus will offer commendations, condemnations, exhortations, promises, and warnings.

1. What was historical Ephesus like?

2. What symbols appear in this letter, and what do they represent?

3. What is Jesus' assessment of the Ephesian church?

4. Summarize Pastor Armstrong's teaching about apostleship:

5. Who were the Nicolaitans, and what was Jesus' problem with them?

6. How can we imitate the Ephesian church?

7. These people had a history of perseverance. What does the Bible say about perseverance?

DISCUSSION QUESTIONS

1. What did you know about apostles prior to this teaching, and what have you learned?

2. What sort of discernment are we in the position to exercise today?

Revelation

3. How can we apply the instruction of this letter to the church today?

_____

_____

_____

4. In the space below, record your takeaway from Revelation 2:1–7 and any questions you have that remain unanswered.

_____

_____

_____

Digging Deeper (Optional)

Should you choose to dig deeper, complete the following Digging Deeper section. Each meeting will open with discussion of what you've learned and observed in Scripture, and this section will prepare you for that discussion.

In a two-column graphic organizer, record what you observe in each passage and the questions you have about it. Things to look for: Who is speaking? To whom is he speaking? What does he say about God? Jesus? The church? Individual believers? What do readers of this text stand to gain?

Scripture Passage: Read Revelation 2:1–7

The following verses describe the nature of the church in the first century and the reasons Jesus would use to support the consequences for its lack of repentance as outlined in the letter to the church in Ephesus. Since these scriptures serve one purpose in Session Six, use a two-column graphic organizer for your observations and questions about the following collection of verses.

Scripture Passage: James 5:11

We count those blessed who endured. You have heard of the endurance of Job and have seen the outcome of the Lord's dealings, that the Lord is full of compassion and is merciful.

Scripture Passage: Hebrews 10:35–36

Therefore, do not throw away your confidence, which has a great reward. For you have need of endurance, so that when you have done the will of God, you may receive what was promised.

Scripture Passage: 1 Corinthians 2:1–2

And when I came to you, brethren, I did not come with superiority of speech or of wisdom, proclaiming to you the testimony of God. For I determined to know nothing among you except Jesus Christ, and Him crucified.

Scripture Passage: Romans 8:9,14

However, you are not in the flesh but in the Spirit, if indeed the Spirit of God dwells in you. But if anyone does not have the Spirit of Christ, he does not belong to Him. ... For all who are being led by the Spirit of God, these are sons of God.

Scripture Passage: Ephesians 4:4–6

There is one body and one Spirit, just as also you were called in one hope of your calling; one Lord, one faith, one baptism, one God and Father of all who is over all and through all and in all.

Scripture Passage: Acts 2:41–47

So then, those who had received his word were baptized; and that day there were added about three thousand souls. They were continually devoting themselves to the apostles' teaching and to fellowship, to the breaking of bread and to prayer. Everyone kept feeling a sense of awe; and many wonders and signs were taking place through the apostles. And all those who had believed were together and had all things in common; and they began selling their property and possessions and were sharing them with all, as anyone might have need. Day by day continuing with one mind in the temple, and breaking bread from house to house, they were taking their meals together with gladness and sincerity of heart, praising God and having favor with all the people. And the Lord was adding to their number day by day those who were being saved.

REVELATION

Scripture Passage: John 17:14–18

I have given them Your word; and the world has hated them, because they are not of the world, even as I am not of the world. I do not ask You to take them out of the world, but to keep them from the evil one. They are not of the world, even as I am not of the world. Sanctify them in the truth; Your word is truth. As You sent Me into the world, I also have sent them into the world.

A LITTLE DEEPER…

1. Based on the scriptures above, how would you define "the church"?

_____

_____

_____

2. What exactly makes a person a believer?

_____

_____

_____

3. The consequences to Ephesus outlined in Revelation 2 for lack of repentance is removal of their lampstand. What might this mean?

_____

_____

_____

4. Many believers struggle with the nature of God in that He is both loving and just. What is your initial reaction to the warning Jesus gives the church in Revelation 2:5? Your reaction reveals much of your view of God. Do you notice a bias toward one aspect of His nature over the other, love or justice? Spend some time in prayer over this point. Repent if God leads you to do so, and worship God for *all* of who He is.

_____

_____

_____

SESSION SIX

Revelation 2:1–7

> ***Remember the Golden Rule:*** *When the plain sense of Scripture makes common sense, we seek no other sense.*

Video Six

Topical overview: Prophetic interpretation of the letter to the church in Ephesus.
Learning goals: Recognize the hand of God throughout history as it relates to the historic and prophetic readings of the letter to the church in Ephesus. Identify our place in this letter as we read it in its universal sense: are we self-satisfied?

CORE QUESTIONS

Before watching video six, read Revelation 2:1–7. Use the two-column graphic organizer to help you organize your thoughts. Discuss your observations as a group.

As you watch the video, complete the following section. For many, reading the questions before watching the video will aid their understanding of the video content.

Letter to the Church in Ephesus

1. How do we bring ourselves to where God is trying to bring us?

___

___

___

2. What sort of good example is Ephesus to us?

3. Jesus critiques them for leaving their first love (Jesus)—but how can this be true considering their commendations?

4. What is the remedy outlined in the letter?

5. The Ephesians were practicing "self-satisfied Christianity." How does Pastor Armstrong define this?

6. What are the marks of a modern self-satisfied Christian?

7. Christ holds being on autopilot against us. What does self-satisfaction do to spiritual growth?

There's a consequence for lack of repentance of self-satisfaction: removal. First Corinthians 2:1–2 serves as a mantra for the recovering self-satisfied (see Session Five's Digging Deeper section for the full text).

8. Historically, Ephesus the city declined. They didn't repent, and Jesus followed through with His warning. What did these historical consequences look like?

_____

_____

_____

9. Each letter ends with what?

_____

_____

_____

10. No matter what goes on in the church or the world, what is true for the individual believer?

_____

_____

_____

11. How does this letter represent the first church age?

_____

_____

_____

12. What is the biblical definition of a Christian?

_____

_____

_____

REVELATION

Toward the end of the first century, the censure at the end of the letter plays out. Jewish conversion to Christianity had largely stopped by then, and the movement was spreading among Gentiles at this point. The Gentiles brought with them their pagan influences, and they were far more willing to mix in with the surrounding cultures, unlike the Jews, who were used to being set apart.

13. How did the first century church end up?

_____

_____

_____

14. What exactly did this look like?

_____

_____

_____

The consequences for Ephesus were losing their economic position and status as a city of import. For the whole of the church, he took away the church's place of security within the Roman Empire.

14. How did Christ purify the church at the end of the first century?

_____

_____

_____

- Second Letter—Smyrna = "death"
- Ephesus = 30–100 AD (estimation)

DISCUSSION QUESTIONS

1. In Session Five's Digging Deeper section, we explored God's nature as both loving and just and our feelings about that. As Pastor Armstrong explored the literal, universal, and prophetic consequences for lack of repentance within the church, what was your emotional reaction? What does this reveal about your view of God?

2. Summarize what self-satisfied Christianity looks like. Do you see the evidence of such belief in your community? In yourself? What can you do about it?

3. Pastor Armstrong points out that each of the seven letters in Revelation 2–3 follows a form that allows us to decipher them more easily. How does knowing the structure of a text help you understand its content?

4. Now that we've walked through all three interpretive methods of Revelation—literal, universal, and prophetic—which of these methods are you most comfortable with? Most uncomfortable? Why? Do you have any questions about how these methods work? If so, what are they?

5. In the space below, record your takeaway from Revelation 2:1–7 and any questions you have that remain unanswered.

Revelation

DIGGING DEEPER (OPTIONAL)

Should you choose to dig deeper, complete the following Digging Deeper section. Each meeting will open with discussion of what you've learned and observed in Scripture, and this section will prepare you for that discussion.

In a two-column graphic organizer, record what you observe in each passage and the questions you have about it. Things to look for: Who is speaking? To whom is he speaking? What does he say about God? Jesus? The church? Individual believers? What do readers of this text stand to gain?

Scripture Passage: Read Revelation 2:8–11

Scripture Passage: Romans 2:28–29

For he is not a Jew who is one outwardly, nor is circumcision that which is outward in the flesh. But he is a Jew who is one inwardly; and circumcision is that which is of the heart, by the Spirit, not by the letter; and his praise is not from men, but from God.

Scripture Passage: 1 John 2:22–23

Who is the liar but the one who denies that Jesus is the Christ? This is the antichrist, the one who denies the Father and the Son. Whoever denies the Son does not have the Father; the one who confesses the Son has the Father also.

Scripture Passage: Matthew 5:10–12

Blessed are those who have been persecuted for the sake of righteousness, for theirs is the kingdom of heaven. Blessed are you when people insult you and persecute you, and falsely say all kinds of evil against you because of Me. Rejoice and be glad, for your reward in heaven is great; for in the same way they persecuted the prophets who were before you.

Scripture Passage: Romans 8:38–39

For I am convinced that neither death, nor life, nor angels, nor principalities, nor things present, nor things to come, nor powers, nor height, nor depth, nor any other created thing, will be able to separate us from the love of God, which is in Christ Jesus our Lord.

REVELATION 2:1–7

A LITTLE DEEPER…

1. There are several pairings of things in opposition in the letter to the church in Smyrna. Which do you observe? For example, in verse 9, the church is both poor and rich.

_____
_____
_____

2. How do you reconcile these opposing ideas? How is the church both poor and rich, etc.?

_____
_____
_____

3. The name Smyrna is associated with death. What messages do you see about death in the scriptures above?

_____
_____
_____

4. What is the church of Smyrna promised, and what is their reward?

_____
_____
_____

5. Can you think of places in the modern world that would identify with the experience of the church in Smyrna? If so, name them. Spend time praying for these Christians and these churches. Pray that they'd stay strong and remain faithful.

_____
_____
_____

SESSION SEVEN

Revelation 2:8–11

> ***Remember the Golden Rule:*** *When the plain sense of Scripture makes common sense, we seek no other sense.*

Video Seven

Topical overview: Interpretation of the letter to the church in Smyrna.
Learning goals: Recognize what this letter teaches us about the Christian experience of and approach to death and persecution; understand the historical background of Smyrna and how it affected the church.

CORE QUESTIONS

Before watching video seven, read Revelation 2:8–11. Use the two-column graphic organizer to help you organize your thoughts. Discuss your observations as a group.

As you watch the video, complete the following section. For many, reading the questions before watching the video will aid their understanding of the video content.

Overview

1. What are the three complementary interpretative methods?

_____

_____

_____

2. What does the number seven symbolize?

3. What do these seven letters represent as a unit?

4. These letters seem not to fit into the prophetic meaning, so why are these letters here?

The prophetic meaning of these letters have been designed so perfectly by God to reveal itself to only the community that most needs to know it, only in hindsight, without giving away the history of the church before it happened.

5. How do these letters give us confidence in God?

Letter to the Church in Smyrna

1. The name of each city has meaning. What is significant about Smyrna?

2. First-century Roman law mandated what sort of worship, and who was the exception?

3. Smyrna serves as a center for persecution of Christians. Which church father was martyred there?

4. Jesus assigns which element of His nature to this church?

5. What is Jesus' promise in this letter?

6. What was the cultural consequence of refusing to worship pagan gods as required by the government and workers' unions?

7. What is the "synagogue of Satan?"

REVELATION 2:8–11

8. "Children of God" is a biblical statement that refers to whom?

9. This understanding leads you to what?

10. Jesus notices their persecution and poverty. What does He *not* say?

11. What is Christ specifically reminding this church of?

12. How can the church of Smyrna make the most of their situation (verse 10)?

13. What is God's primary concern for you here on earth?

Discussion Questions

1. Have you or anyone you know personally experienced persecution? What does persecution look like in today's society, both locally and globally?

___

2. Pastor Armstrong addresses a current popular teaching: that God's primary concern for us here on earth is happiness. God's primary concern for us here is our *holiness*. Have you heard this before? What is the difference between happiness and holiness? How might the difference between these two things affect both how we pray and how we understand God's answers?

___

3. When we identify "children of God," what does this mean? Is this what society tells us today? How do we see this theme play out in the world around us?

___

4. These last two questions may seem like nitpicking or semantics, but words matter. These two false teachings are insidious and pervasive in the modern world. As we learned before, the way we combat false teaching is to hold them accountable to Scripture. How do we combat the teachings that we are "all God's children" and that God's primary concern for us is our happiness? What is the truth?

___

5. In the space below, record your takeaway from Revelation 2:8–11 and any questions you have that remain unanswered.

_____

_____

_____

DIGGING DEEPER (OPTIONAL)

Should you choose to dig deeper, complete the following Digging Deeper section. Each meeting will open with discussion of what you've learned and observed in Scripture, and this section will prepare you for that discussion.

In a two-column graphic organizer, record what you observe in each passage and the questions you have about it. Things to look for: Who is speaking? To whom is he speaking? What does he say about God? Jesus? The church? Individual believers? What do readers of this text stand to gain?

Scripture Passage: Read Revelation 2:12–17

Scripture Passage: 2 Timothy 4:7–8

I have fought the good fight, I have finished the course, I have kept the faith; in the future there is laid up for me the crown of righteousness, which the Lord, the righteous Judge, will award to me on that day; and not only to me, but also to all who have loved His appearing.

Scripture Passage: James 1:12

Blessed is a man who perseveres under trial; for once he has been approved, he will receive the crown of life which the Lord has promised to those who love Him.

Scripture Passage: 1 Corinthians 9:24–25

Do you not know that those who run in a race all run, but only one receives the prize? Run in such a way that you may win. Everyone who competes in the games exercises self-control in all things. They then do it to receive a perishable wreath, but we an imperishable.

Scripture Passage: 1 John 5:4–5

For whatever is born of God overcomes the world; and this is the victory that has overcome the world—our faith. Who is the one who overcomes the world, but he who believes that Jesus is the Son of God?

Scripture Passage: Romans 13:3–4

For rulers are not a cause of fear for good behavior, but for evil. Do you want to have no fear of authority? Do what is good and you will have praise from the same; for it is a minister of God to you for good. But if you do what is evil, be afraid; for it does not bear the sword for nothing; for it is a minister of God, an avenger who brings wrath on the one who practices evil.

A Little Deeper...

1. Notice the imagery of winning and losing in these passages. Ephesians 2:8–9 teaches us that "For by grace you have been saved through faith; and that not of yourselves, it is the gift of God; not as a result of works, so that no one may boast." Salvation is not something we can earn, so what might we be winning and losing, earning, in these verses?

___

2. The symbol of a sword appears multiple times in these verses. What might it symbolize? Share the verses that led you to this interpretation.

___

3. Who are the authorities in your life, and what are your behaviors and attitudes toward the authorities in your life? Notice the relationship between the demands of authority and Christian deeds as explained in Romans 13:3–4. What is it?

___

4. Remember previous teaching on the Nicolaitans (letter to the church in Ephesus) and notice the relationship between their teachings and that of Balaam in Numbers 22. What is Christ's criticism about the Nicolaitans in this letter? Can you extrapolate this relationship to teachings of today? If so, how do you see similar false teaching in today's society?

_____

_____

_____

SESSION EIGHT

Revelation 2:12–17

> ***Remember the Golden Rule:*** *When the plain sense of Scripture makes common sense, we seek no other sense.*

Topical overview: Interpretation of the letter to the church in Pergamum.

Learning goals: Recognize what this letter teaches us about maintaining faithfulness despite the lure of worldly wealth, privilege, and culture, and of false teachers who only tell us what we want to hear. Understand the historical background of Pergamum and how it affected the church. Identify the prophetic value of this letter.

CORE QUESTIONS

Before watching video eight, read Revelation 2:12–17. Use the two-column graphic organizer to help you organize your thoughts. Discuss your observations as a group.

As you watch the video, complete the following section. For many, reading the questions before watching the video will aid their understanding of the video content.

Overview

1. What is Jesus' goal for the church?

_____

_____

_____

REVELATION 2:12–17

2. How were Roman prisons different than our modern prisons?

3. This time period of ten days' imprisonment is consistent with what?

4. What is the symbolic significance of the number ten?

5. So what is Jesus communicating symbolically?

6. What is the key to understanding this symbolism?

7. What does faithfulness in this context refer to?

Revelation

8. What is the reward for their faithfulness?

9. What does the crown of life symbolize?

10. What is the substance of the reward the crown symbolizes?

11. How does one earn a crown of life?

12. In reference to the race imagery referenced in 1 Corinthians 9:24–25, who are you competing against to earn your heavenly crowns?

13. What promise does the letter end with?

No matter what happens to that church or how they respond to their circumstances, they will always be with Christ. Christ's faithfulness is not dependent on ours.

14. What is the prophetic value of the letter?

Letter to the Church in Pergamum

1. What does the name Pergamum signify?

2. What is the historical background of Pergamum?

3. What is the symbolic significance of a two-edged sword?

4. What was Pergamum like spiritually?

5. What is the historic significance of Balaam?

Discussion Questions

1. In the space below, record your takeaway from Revelation 2:12–17 and any questions you have that remain unanswered.

Digging Deeper (Optional)

Should you choose to dig deeper, complete the following Digging Deeper section. Each meeting will open with discussion of what you've learned and observed in Scripture, and this section will prepare you for that discussion.

In a two-column graphic organizer, record what you observe in each passage and the questions you have about it. Things to look for: Who is speaking? To whom is he speaking? What does he say about God? Jesus? The church? Individual believers? What do readers of this text stand to gain?

Scripture Passage: Read Revelation 2:18–29

A Little Deeper...

1. Create a list of the various symbols contained in the letter to the church in Thyatira. Do you recognize any of them? If so, which ones and where from?

2. Remember the pattern by which we interpret: attribute of Christ applied to the church, commendation, correction, warning, and reward. Identify these parts within this letter.

3. Christ again refers to those who overcome in this letter. What obstacle do these believers face?

SESSION NINE

Revelation 2:18–29

> ***Remember the Golden Rule:*** *When the plain sense of Scripture makes common sense, we seek no other sense.*

Video Nine

Topical overview: Interpretation of the letter to the church in Thyatira.
Learning goals: Recognize what this letter teaches us about perseverance in the faith. Understand how the contents of the letter relate to the historical experience of the church, particularly under Roman Catholic leadership.

CORE QUESTIONS

Before watching video nine, read Revelation 2:18–29. Use the two-column graphic organizer to help you organize your thoughts. Discuss your observations as a group.

As you watch the video, complete the following section. For many, reading the questions before watching the video will aid their understanding of the video content.

Overview

1. How do Peter and Jude use the phrase "the way of Balaam?"

_____

_____

_____

REVELATION 2:18–29

2. What is the "error of Balaam?"

3. In what false teachings did Pergamum's Balaams encourage the church?

4. What does the biblical phrase "tickling ears" refer to?

5. What three things are a recipe for "tickled ears?"

6. What did the Nicolaitans teach?

7. What does it mean to "make war with the word of His mouth?"

8. What is the significance of hidden manna?

9. What is the significance of the white stone?

10. What stopped the persecution of the second era of the church?

11. At that point, what powerful institution was married to the church?

12. What were the consequences of institutionalizing Christianity within the Roman government?

13. So what three things resulted from this explosive "growth" of Christianity as the state religion?

14. How does Jesus say He will respond if they don't repent?

___

15. Historically, how did Jesus "end it with a sword?"

___

Letter to the Church of Thyatira: Roman Empire Church 313–600AD

1. What is the possible meaning of "Thyatira?"

___

2. Who was the primary god worshiped in this area?

___

3. Again, what was the conflict between union work and Christians?

___

4. What is the significance of "eyes like a flame of fire" (Revelation 2:18)?

___

5. What is the significance of "feet like burnished bronze" (Revelation 2:18)?

6. Combined, what do we learn about Jesus?

7. What does Jesus have to say positively about Thyatira?

8. What's the catch with good works?

9. Who was Jezebel?

10. What was the difference between Pergamum's and Thyatira's false teachers?

11. What judgment does Christ proclaim over Thyatira?

12. What will the physical evidence of Christ's judgment (illness in Thyatira) speak of?

13. What does the morning star signify?

14. What does Jesus promise the church at the end of this letter?

15. What period of history does this letter represent?

16. This era began in AD 600 and continued for how long?

Revelation

17. How do we see a judgment of pestilence on the Roman Catholic Church?

_____

_____

_____

Discussion Questions

1. Summarize some of the ways in which the Roman Catholic church aligns with the content of the letter to the church in Thyatira.

_____

_____

_____

2. Compare and contrast the churches of Thyatira and Pergamum, in both the literal and historic and prophetic senses. What do the churches of Thyatira and Pergamum have in common? How are they different? What does the Roman Imperial Christian Church have in common with the Roman Catholic Church? How are they different?

_____

_____

_____

3. Would you agree that, in general, we have an easier time accurately attributing blessings to God's goodness and provision rather than attributing suffering to God's judgment? Why or why not?

_____

_____

_____

4. Remember Christ's declaration in Revelation 2:23—He is the one worthy to prescribe judgment, and it is to His glory when such pronouncements come to pass in this life. How does this fit with your understanding of who Christ is?

_____

_____

REVELATION 2:18–29

5. So far, the historic era symbolized by Thyatira, the Roman Catholic Church, was given the most time to repent, about 1,000 years. Why might this period of history have been allowed to go on so long?

_____

_____

_____

6. In the two prophetic interpretations discussed in this video, God has shaped the course of history using natural events and unbelieving forces to execute His will. The Old Testament clearly demonstrates His propensity for such action (see Genesis, Judges, Esther, and various writings within the major and minor prophets). On a more personal scale, have you seen the same to be true? Can you think of instances when God has used natural events and outside forces to shape your path in life? If so, share some with the group.

_____

_____

_____

7. In the space below, record your takeaway from Revelation 2:12–29 and any questions you have that remain unanswered.

_____

_____

_____

DIGGING DEEPER (OPTIONAL)

Should you choose to dig deeper, complete the following Digging Deeper section. Each meeting will open with discussion of what you've learned and observed in Scripture, and this section will prepare you for that discussion.

In a two-column graphic organizer, record what you observe in each passage and the questions you have about it. Things to look for: Who is speaking? To whom is he speaking? What does he say about God? Jesus? The church? Individual believers? What do readers of this text stand to gain?

Scripture Passage: Read Revelation 3:1–6

Scripture Passage: James 2:17, 20

Even so faith, if it has no works, is dead, being by itself. ... But are you willing to recognize, you foolish fellow, that faith without works is useless?

Scripture Passage: Ephesians 2:10

For we are His workmanship, created in Christ Jesus for good works, which God prepared beforehand so that we would walk in them.

Scripture Passage: Galatians 3:27

For all of you who were baptized into Christ have clothed yourselves with Christ.

Scripture Passage: 2 Corinthians 5:2–4

For indeed in this house we groan, longing to be clothed with our dwelling from heaven, inasmuch as we, having put it on, will not be found naked. For indeed while we are in this tent, we groan, being burdened, because we do not want to be unclothed but to be clothed, so that what is mortal will be swallowed up by life.

A LITTLE DEEPER...

1. In the letter to the church in Sardis, Christ tells the church that it is asleep. When combined with the other verses, what might "asleep" mean?

_____

_____

_____

2. Remember the symbolic nature of the number 7. What might be the symbolic nature of the stars in Revelation 3:1? Use Scripture to support your answer.

_____

_____

3. Reflect on the balance of faith and good works in your own life. How are you doing? Does your "walk" match your "talk?" Spend some time in reflection and prayer. Repent as the Spirit leads. Consider sharing what you learn in this time with a friend. Allow the sharing to hold you accountable.

SESSION TEN

Revelation 3:1–6

> ***Remember the Golden Rule:*** *When the plain sense of Scripture makes common sense, we seek no other sense.*

Video Ten

Topical overview: Literal interpretation of the letter to the church in Sardis.
Learning goals: Review previously discussed symbols and discuss new ones. Explore background of the historical city of Sardis. Extrapolate truths about general church life.

CORE QUESTIONS

Before watching video ten, read Revelation 3:1–6. Use the two-column graphic organizer to help you organize your thoughts. Discuss your observations as a group.

As you watch the video, complete the following section. For many, reading the questions before watching the video will aid their understanding of the video content.

Letter to the Church in Sardis

1. What are the three interpretive methods?

_____

_____

_____

2. What is the meaning of the name Sardis?

_____

_____

_____

3. Summarize what you learned about the historical city of Sardis.

_____

_____

_____

4. What does the number seven signify?

_____

_____

_____

5. What do the "seven spirits of God and the seven stars" of verse 1 represent?

_____

_____

_____

6. What is Christ's assessment of the historical church of Sardis?

_____

_____

_____

7. How do we fulfill the purpose of faith: glorifying the Father?

_____

_____

_____

When we lack works, our faith is still there, but it's not fulfilling its purpose.

8. Who alone is the judge of whether or not our works have met His expectations?

_____

_____

_____

If our faith remains an intellectual pursuit, we are doing nothing for the glory of Christ. Our possession of truth without action becomes cause for conviction rather than praise.

9. What was the church in Sardis satisfied with?

_____

_____

_____

10. How does Sardis compare to Thyatira?

_____

_____

_____

11. What is the whole point of good works?

_____

_____

_____

Thyatira was using works to justify heresy while Sardis was using truth to justify laziness.

12. What does Jesus mean by His admonition to "wake up" in verse 2?

_____

_____

_____

13. What is the fundamental truth of church life at work here?

14. What is Jesus' recipe for strengthening the church?

15. What is the consequence for Sardis if it doesn't awaken?

16. What is Jesus's encouragement to the individual believer?

17. What is the significance of a white garment?

18. What is the picture of the unbeliever?

19. So what, then, is the significance of soiled and unsoiled garments?

_____
_____
_____

DISCUSSION QUESTIONS

1. Pastor Armstrong hasn't entirely unpacked the significance of Sardis meaning "remnant" yet. Given what we've learned so far, how do you see the idea of a "remnant" playing out in the letter to the church in Sardis?

_____
_____
_____

2. Thyatira used proper works to justify improper theology while Sardis used proper theology to justify improper (nonexistent) works. Where on this spectrum do you see churches falling today? Justify your answer.

_____
_____
_____

3. What is the role of good works in the gospel? Use Scripture to support your answer (See Session Nine's Digging Deeper for help if needed).

_____
_____
_____

4. At this point, we're beginning to see that Christ's encouragement to the individual believer is fairly consistent among the letters. What is it, and how does this comfort you considering the state of the modern church?

_____
_____

5. Discuss the symbolism of garments and their cleanliness. Has what you learned in this session affected your understanding? If so, how? Evaluate yourself: are you symbolically clothed? How clean is your garment?

_____

_____

_____

6. In the space below, record your takeaway from Revelation 3:1–6 and any questions you have that remain unanswered.

_____

_____

_____

DIGGING DEEPER (OPTIONAL)

Should you choose to dig deeper, complete the following Digging Deeper section. Each meeting will open with discussion of what you've learned and observed in Scripture, and this section will prepare you for that discussion.

In a two-column graphic organizer, record what you observe in each passage and the questions you have about it. Things to look for: Who is speaking? To whom is he speaking? What does he say about God? Jesus? The church? Individual believers? What do readers of this text stand to gain?

Scripture Passage: Read Revelation 3:7–13

Scripture Passage: 2 John 1:8

> *Watch yourselves, that you do not lose what we have accomplished, but that you may receive a full reward.*

Scripture Passage: Read Revelation 3:14–22

A LITTLE DEEPER…

1. List the symbols you observe in these passages. What do they signify? Use Scripture to support your answer(s).

2. In both the letter to the church in Philadelphia and 2 John, we are warned to be careful so as not to lose what we've accomplished. What is this accomplishment, how do we earn it, and how might we lose it?

3. At the beginning of teaching these letters, Pastor Armstrong pointed out that as we read the letters prophetically, we search for our own time within them. So far, we've placed the letter to the church in Sardis as beginning with the protestant reformation (sixteenth century). Based on what we've learned so far, that means our current era will be represented by either the church of Philadelphia or the church of Laodicea. Which do you suspect represents our era and why?

4. At this point, we've now read all seven letters for ourselves. In the universal sense, which letter do you identify with the most and why?

SESSION ELEVEN

Revelation 3:7–13

> ***Remember the Golden Rule:*** *When the plain sense of Scripture makes common sense, we seek no other sense.*

Topical overview: Prophetic interpretation of the letter to the church in Sardis. Background and historical interpretation of the letter to the church in Philadelphia.

Learning goals: Clarify aspects of obtaining salvation. Compare and contrast the Catholic and Reformed churches. Explore the historic significance of the Peace of Westphalia. Further examine what it means to have and maintain your witness.

CORE QUESTIONS

Before watching video eleven, read Revelation 3:7–13. Use the two-column graphic organizer to help you organize your thoughts. Discuss your observations as a group.

As you watch the video, complete the following section. For many, reading the questions before watching the video will aid their understanding of the video content.

Overview

1. Summarize Pastor Armstrong's explanation of the phrase "I will not erase your name from the book of life."

_____

_____

_____

2. When does the historical era of Sardis begin?

3. What is the prophetic significance of the name Sardis (the escaping ones, the remnant)?

4. Why was the Protestant Church at this time considered the true church?

5. What is the often-overlooked consequence of the Protestant Reformation?

6. What historic event gave rise to the beginning of the denominations we know today?

7. How does Jesus' admonition to "wake up" align with church history?

8. When does the age of Sardis end?

___

Letter to the Church in Philadelphia

1. What does Philadelphia mean?

___

2. Summarize what you've learned about historic Philadelphia.

___

3. What do the attributes of Jesus in this letter point to?

___

4. What is the significance of "the key of David?"

___

5. What is true if you have a heart to reach the lost?

___

6. What is important about knowing that Christ is the only one who opens and who closes doors of gospel opportunity?

_____

_____

_____

7. What does Philadelphia best model to the church at large?

_____

_____

_____

8. It's important to note that Philadelphia, alongside Smyrna, receives none of what from Jesus?

_____

_____

_____

9. How does Philadelphia's faithfulness differ from Smyrna's?

_____

_____

_____

10. What do these churches have in common?

_____

_____

_____

REVELATION 3:7–13

DISCUSSION QUESTIONS

1. As we compare the Catholic Church's teachings with that of the Protestant Reformation, we see an example of a reactionary pendulum effect. How so? Why do you think this reactionary tendency is so prevalent within the church? Can you identify some modern examples of this effect, whether large or small?

2. When you trace the path of this reactionary pendulum effect, where, most often, does Jesus reside?

3. Evaluate your observations of today's church denominations considering what Pastor Armstrong teaches about the church historically "waking up." What remnants of this consequence do we still see today?

4. Between Smyrna and Philadelphia, we see Christ's strong desire for believers to maintain both their internal witness (integrity of Christian character) and external witness (integrity of mission and message). What does maintaining the whole of your witness look like practically in today's world?

5. How is it that the persecuted churches maintain the strongest witness? Cite Scripture to support your answer if you're able.

Revelation

6. In the space below, record your takeaway from Revelation 3:7–13 and any questions you have that remain unanswered.

Digging Deeper (Optional)

Should you choose to dig deeper, complete the following Digging Deeper section. Each meeting will open with discussion of what you've learned and observed in Scripture, and this section will prepare you for that discussion.

In a two-column graphic organizer, record what you observe in each passage and the questions you have about it. Things to look for: Who is speaking? To whom is he speaking? What does he say about God? Jesus? The church? Individual believers? What do readers of this text stand to gain?

Scripture Passage: Revelation 3:14–22

Scripture Passage: Matthew 7:21–23

Not everyone who says to Me, "Lord, Lord," will enter the kingdom of heaven, but he who does the will of My Father who is in heaven will enter. Many will say to Me on that day, "Lord, Lord, did we not prophesy in Your name, and in Your name cast out demons, and in Your name perform many miracles?" And then I will declare to them, "I never knew you; DEPART FROM ME, YOU WHO PRACTICE LAWLESSNESS."

Scripture Passage: Hebrews 2:6–8, 11

But one has testified somewhere, saying, "WHAT IS MAN, THAT YOU REMEMBER HIM? OR THE SON OF MAN, THAT YOU ARE CONCERNED ABOUT HIM? YOU HAVE MADE HIM FOR A LITTLE WHILE LOWER THAN THE ANGELS; YOU HAVE CROWNED HIM WITH GLORY AND HONOR, AND HAVE APPOINTED HIM OVER THE WORKS OF YOUR HANDS; YOU HAVE PUT ALL THINGS IN SUBJECTION UNDER HIS FEET." For in subjecting all things to him, He left nothing that is not subject to him. But now we do not yet see all things subjected to him. ... For both He who sanctifies and those who are sanctified are all from one Father; for which reason He is not ashamed to call them brethren.

Scripture Passage: 1 Timothy 4:1–3

But the Spirit explicitly says that in later times some will fall away from the faith, paying attention to deceitful spirits and doctrines of demons, by means of the hypocrisy of liars seared in their own conscience as with a branding iron, men who forbid marriage and advocate abstaining from foods which God has created to be gratefully shared in by those who believe and know the truth.

Scripture Passage: 2 Timothy 3:1–5

But realize this, that in the last days difficult times will come. For men will be lovers of self, lovers of money, boastful, arrogant, revilers, disobedient to parents, ungrateful, unholy, unloving, irreconcilable, malicious gossips, without self-control, brutal, haters of good, treacherous, reckless, conceited, lovers of pleasure rather than lovers of God, holding to a form of godliness, although they have denied its power; avoid such men as these.

Scripture Passage: 2 Timothy 4:1–4

I solemnly charge you in the presence of God and of Christ Jesus, who is to judge the living and the dead, and by His appearing and His kingdom: preach the word; be ready in season and out of season; reprove, rebuke, exhort, with great patience and instruction. For the time will come when they will not endure sound doctrine; but wanting to have their ears tickled, they will accumulate for themselves teachers in accordance to their own desires, and will turn away their ears from the truth and will turn aside to myths.

A LITTLE DEEPER...

1. A theme that rises from these passages might best be described as cultural Christianity. How would you define cultural Christianity, both in general and in your personal cultural context?

_____

_____

_____

2. What does it mean to be zealous? Should we repent and pursue Christ with zeal, how might the world receive us? Use Scripture to support your answer.

3. "Falling away" can take many forms. Explain what some of them are from your personal experience.

4. How does Scripture admonish us to interact with those who may have "fallen away?" Use Scripture to support your answer.

5. Evaluate yourself. Have you fallen prey to the misleading doctrines of our day? Do you interact with people who have done so in a godly manner? Are you zealous for the Lord? Are your eyes open to the truth? Spend some time seeking the Lord in prayer. Repent as the Spirit leads and consider sharing what you learn with a friend for the sake of accountability.

SESSION TWELVE

Revelation 3:14–22

> ***Remember the Golden Rule:*** *When the plain sense of Scripture makes common sense, we seek no other sense.*

Video Twelve

Topical overview: Prophetic interpretation of Philadelphia and all interpretations of Laodicea.

Learning goals: Absorb the truths about earning and keeping our crowns. Explore what it means to be lukewarm and unpack how this aligns with the church we know today.

CORE QUESTIONS

Before watching video twelve, read Revelation 3:14–22. Use the two-column graphic organizer to help you organize your thoughts. Discuss your observations as a group.

As you watch the video, complete the following section. For many, reading the questions before watching the video will aid their understanding of the video content.

Overview

1. What does persecution do for you?

_____
_____
_____

REVELATION

2. How will Jesus protect His church from persecution?

3. What phrase tells us that we are justified in reading Revelation prophetically?

4. What does a crown represent?

5. What does Jesus mean when He admonishes us to not let anyone steal our crowns?

6. What promise does Jesus leave the believers with?

7. Prophetically, what years does the age of Philadelphia span?

REVELATION 3:14–22

Letter to the Church in Laodicea

1. What is the significance of the name "Laodicea?"

___

2. Summarize what you learned about the historical city of Laodicea.

___

3. How does Jesus' reference to the deeds of this church differ from his references to the deeds of the other churches?

___

4. What spiritual conditions are represented by the physical conditions of verse 17?

___

The church of Laodicea is condemned by Jesus for a state of unbelief, yet they tell themselves they have everything they need.

5. What has blinded the Laodicean church to their spiritual poverty?

___

6. How can a church be unbelieving?

7. Is it possible for people to accurately determine the spiritual "state of dress" of any other person?

The presence of unrecognized unbelief in the body is the single most dangerous problem any church can have.

8. What does the presence of unbelievers in the church cause?

9. So what is the significance of hot and cold?

10. What's the problem of the lukewarm state?

11. Why does Jesus use the spitting out metaphor?

REVELATION 3:14–22

12. Jesus doesn't offer any commendation to this church. What does He offer instead?

13. So prophetically, what era does the church of Laodicea represent?

14. What does apostasy mean?

15. Is the individual or the corporate church the issue here?

16. How does the shift to an apostate church happen?

17. What are among the signs of the end times according to 1 and 2 Timothy?

18. Where did the church go wrong?

19. When does the age of Laodicea end?

DISCUSSION QUESTIONS

1. Review the symbols discussed in this lesson, particularly as they relate to a person's spiritual state.

2. Of the four symbols given to represent the unbeliever (naked, poor, blind, wretched), which would you say best describes the unbelievers in your context? Why?

3. What is apostasy, and how is it at work in the church today? (Note: if your group needs to study this concept further to fully understand it, review Judges.)

REVELATION 3:14–22

4. Have you noticed or experienced this shift within the church makeup from believer to unbeliever? If so, how? If not, praise God!

5. Review 1 Timothy 4:1–3 and 2 Timothy 3:1–5 and 4:1–4. Describe how you see these scriptures applying to the world today.

6. What is biblical criticism, and how did its influence lead to apostasy?

7. What is the "progressive" church, exactly? Know that its opposite descriptors would be fundamental or traditional.

8. What is the hope of Christ for the apostate church, and what is the role of the individual believer in achieving it?

9. In the space below, record your takeaway from Revelation 3:14–22 and any questions you have that remain unanswered.

Revelation

_____

_____

DIGGING DEEPER (OPTIONAL)

Should you choose to dig deeper, complete the following Digging Deeper section. Each meeting will open with discussion of what you've learned and observed in Scripture, and this section will prepare you for that discussion.

In a two-column graphic organizer, record what you observe in each passage and the questions you have about it. Things to look for: Who is speaking? To whom is he speaking? What does he say about God? Jesus? The church? Individual believers? What do readers of this text stand to gain?

Scripture Passage: Mark 10:29–30

Jesus said, "Truly I say to you, there is no one who has left house or brothers or sisters or mother or father or children or farms, for My sake and for the gospel's sake, but that he will receive a hundred times as much now in the present age, houses and brothers and sisters and mothers and children and farms, along with persecutions; and in the age to come, eternal life."

Scripture Passage: James 5:3

Your gold and your silver have rusted; and their rust will be a witness against you and will consume your flesh like fire. It is in the last days that you have stored up your treasure!

Scripture Passage: Hebrews 1:1–2

God, after He spoke long ago to the fathers in the prophets in many portions and in many ways, in these last days has spoken to us in His Son, whom He appointed heir of all things, through whom also He made the world.

Scripture Passage: Luke 21:23–24

Woe to those who are pregnant and to those who are nursing babies in those days; for there will be great distress upon the land and wrath to this people; and they will fall by the edge of the sword, and will be led captive into all the nations; and Jerusalem will be trampled under foot by the Gentiles until the times of the Gentiles are fulfilled.

REVELATION 3:14–22

Scripture Passage: Jeremiah 27:5–7

I have made the earth, the men and the beasts which are on the face of the earth by My great power and by My outstretched arm, and I will give it to the one who is pleasing in My sight. Now I have given all these lands into the hand of Nebuchadnezzar king of Babylon, My servant, and I have given him also the wild animals of the field to serve him. All the nations shall serve him and his son and his grandson until the time of his own land comes; then many nations and great kings will make him their servant.

Scripture Passage: Daniel 2:1–11

Now in the second year of the reign of Nebuchadnezzar, Nebuchadnezzar had dreams; and his spirit was troubled and his sleep left him. Then the king gave orders to call in the magicians, the conjurers, the sorcerers and the Chaldeans to tell the king his dreams. So they came in and stood before the king. The king said to them, "I had a dream and my spirit is anxious to understand the dream." Then the Chaldeans spoke to the king in Aramaic: "O king, live forever! Tell the dream to your servants, and we will declare the interpretation." The king replied to the Chaldeans, "The command from me is firm: if you do not make known to me the dream and its interpretation, you will be torn limb from limb and your houses will be made a rubbish heap. But if you declare the dream and its interpretation, you will receive from me gifts and a reward and great honor; therefore declare to me the dream and its interpretation." They answered a second time and said, "Let the king tell the dream to his servants, and we will declare the interpretation." The king replied, "I know for certain that you are bargaining for time, inasmuch as you have seen that the command from me is firm, that if you do not make the dream known to me, there is only one decree for you. For you have agreed together to speak lying and corrupt words before me until the situation is changed; therefore tell me the dream, that I may know that you can declare to me its interpretation." The Chaldeans answered the king and said, "There is not a man on earth who could declare the matter for the king, inasmuch as no great king or ruler has ever asked anything like this of any magician, conjurer or Chaldean. Moreover, the thing which the king demands is difficult, and there is no one else who could declare it to the king except gods, whose dwelling place is not with mortal flesh."

A LITTLE DEEPER...

1. Why might we be discussing Nebuchadnezzar before reading Revelation 4?

_____

_____

_____

REVELATION

2. Based on the descriptions here, what sort of place will the end times be?

_____
_____
_____

3. Does it give you comfort that Jesus gets the final say? Why or why not?

_____
_____
_____

4. As we see here in this lesson, God has ordained Nebuchadnezzar's kingship and domain, and He's chosen to speak to this pagan king in a prophetic dream of far-reaching import. God uses believers and unbelievers alike to bring Himself glory. He is in control of both the broad sweep, and minutiae, of history. How do you see this truth playing out in the world today?

_____
_____
_____

SESSION THIRTEEN

Daniel 2:1–11

> ***Remember the Golden Rule:*** *When the plain sense of Scripture makes common sense, we seek no other sense.*

Video Thirteen

Topical overview: background about Revelation as found in Daniel; exploring the questions raised by a prophetic reading of Revelation and finding their answers.

Learning goals: Acquire the definitions of both "age" and "last days." Identify 2 specific traits Jesus applies to the age in which we live. Explore the connection between Revelation and Daniel.

CORE QUESTIONS

Before watching video thirteen, read Daniel 2:1–11. Use the two-column graphic organizer to help you organize your thoughts. Discuss your observations as a group.

As you watch the video, complete the following section. For many, reading the questions before watching the video will aid their understanding of the video content.

Overview

1. Why did Jesus embed a prophetic meaning in Revelation 2–3 that couldn't possibly be understood for centuries?

_____

_____

REVELATION

2. Do we know when exactly the end of the Laodicean church era will end?

___

3. What does an "age" signify?

___

4. What is the significance of the term *last days*?

___

5. According to the writer of Hebrews, what event signaled our entrance into the last days?

___

6. We now have a series of questions:
What is this age called, what will it be like, and why did it start (Luke 21:24)?

___

7. So why are we reading Daniel?

___

Daniel 2:1–11

1. Summarize the context of this story in Daniel 2.

_____

_____

_____

DISCUSSION QUESTIONS

1. God's definition of and attitude toward time differs from ours. Second Peter 3:8–9 says, "But do not let this one fact escape your notice, beloved, that with the Lord one day is like a thousand years, and a thousand years like one day. The Lord is not slow about His promise, as some count slowness, but is patient toward you, not wishing for any to perish but for all to come to repentance." What does it mean to you that we are living in the latter portion of the last days?

_____

_____

_____

2. While the prophetic reading of the letters in Revelation 2–3 is not *new* revelation, it is *special* revelation intended specifically for the believers of our era in Church history. Hebrews 4:12 says, "For the word of God is living and active and sharper than any two-edged sword, and piercing as far as the division of soul and spirit, of both joints and marrow, and able to judge the thoughts and intentions of the heart." Have you ever experienced such a personal, specific message from the word of God like we find in Revelation 2–3? If so, share your experience with the group.

_____

_____

_____

3. What do you know about Nebuchadnezzar's dream and the prophetic nature of the book of Daniel? Share with your group. What do you know already, what confuses you, and what do you hope to learn from your study of Daniel in this context?

_____

4. Review what you've learned about the age of the Gentiles (Luke 21:24). What is it? What are its characteristics? When did it start? If you have one, share your hypothesis of why it started.

5. Pastor Armstrong mentioned that not only are ages significant, but the transitions between ages are themselves significant. He mentioned that the transition into the Gentile Age was marked by the full, physical revelation of Jesus Christ and the completion of the scriptural canon. There is no new revelation or ongoing creation of Scripture: Jesus is it. How is this idea received in the church today? Why is this truth so foundational to our ability to "wake up" as Jesus calls us to in Revelation 3?

6. In the space below, record your takeaway from Daniel 2:1–12 and any questions you have that remain unanswered.

DIGGING DEEPER (OPTIONAL)

Should you choose to dig deeper, complete the following Digging Deeper section. Each meeting will open with discussion of what you've learned and observed in Scripture, and this section will prepare you for that discussion.

In a two-column graphic organizer, record what you observe in each passage and the questions you have about it. Things to look for: Who is speaking? To whom is he speaking? What does he say about God? Jesus? The church? Individual believers?

What do readers of this text stand to gain?

Scripture Passage: Daniel 2:12–16, 25–39

Because of this the king became indignant and very furious and gave orders to destroy all the wise men of Babylon. So the decree went forth that the wise men should be slain; and they looked for Daniel and his friends to kill them. Then Daniel replied with discretion and discernment to Arioch, the captain of the king's bodyguard, who had gone forth to slay the wise men of Babylon; he said to Arioch, the king's commander, "For what reason is the decree from the king so urgent?" Then Arioch informed Daniel about the matter. So Daniel went in and requested of the king that he would give him time, in order that he might declare the interpretation to the king. …

Then Arioch hurriedly brought Daniel into the king's presence and spoke to him as follows: "I have found a man among the exiles from Judah who can make the interpretation known to the king!" The king said to Daniel, whose name was Belteshazzar, "Are you able to make known to me the dream which I have seen and its interpretation?" Daniel answered before the king and said, "As for the mystery about which the king has inquired, neither wise men, conjurers, magicians nor diviners are able to declare it to the king. However, there is a God in heaven who reveals mysteries, and He has made known to King Nebuchadnezzar what will take place in the latter days. This was your dream and the visions in your mind while on your bed. As for you, O king, while on your bed your thoughts turned to what would take place in the future; and He who reveals mysteries has made known to you what will take place. But as for me, this mystery has not been revealed to me for any wisdom residing in me more than in any other living man, but for the purpose of making the interpretation known to the king, and that you may understand the thoughts of your mind. You, O king, were looking and behold, there was a single great statue; that statue, which was large and of extraordinary splendor, was standing in front of you, and its appearance was awesome. The head of that statue was made of fine gold, its breast and its arms of silver, its belly and its thighs of bronze, its legs of iron, its feet partly of iron and partly of clay. You continued looking until a stone was cut out without hands, and it struck the statue on its feet of iron and clay and crushed them. Then the iron, the clay, the bronze, the silver and the gold were crushed all at the same time and became like chaff from the summer threshing floors; and the wind carried them away so that not a trace of them was found. But the stone that struck the statue became a great mountain and filled the whole earth. "This was the dream; now we will tell its interpretation before the king. You, O king, are the king of kings, to whom the God of heaven has given the kingdom, the power, the strength and the glory; and wherever the sons of men dwell, or the beasts of the field, or the birds of the sky, He has given them into your hand and has caused you to rule over them all. You are the head of gold. After you there will arise another kingdom inferior to you, then another third kingdom of bronze, which will rule over all the earth."

Scripture Passage: Jeremiah 27:5–7

I have made the earth, the men and the beasts which are on the face of the earth by My great power and by My outstretched arm, and I will give it to the one who is pleasing in My sight. Now I have given all these lands into the hand of Nebuchadnezzar king of Babylon, My servant, and I have given him also the wild animals of the field to serve him. All the nations shall serve him and his son and his grandson until the time of his own land comes; then many nations and great kings will make him their servant.

A LITTLE DEEPER...

1. Consider that God refers to Nebuchadnezzar as His servant, but Nebuchadnezzar, at this point, does not acknowledge the Lord as his God. What does this tell you about the nature of God Himself and His relationship with His creation, people?

_____
_____
_____

2. How would you characterize Daniel based on his words and actions in this passage?

_____
_____
_____

3. When you read passages like the one we find here in Daniel that are clearly symbolic, what is your response and why?

_____
_____
_____

4. List any symbols you notice in the Daniel passage. If you can think of scriptures that may point to what any of those symbols represent, list those as well.

_____
_____
_____

SESSION FOURTEEN

Daniel 2:12–39

> ***Remember the Golden Rule:*** *When the plain sense of Scripture makes common sense, we seek no other sense.*

Video Fourteen

Topical overview: Daniel's interpretation of Nebuchadnezzar's dream about the great statue.

Learning goals: Identify the ways in which the details of Nebuchadnezzar's dream, and Daniel's interpretation of it, connect to the history of ancient empires. Recognize the relationship between this dream and the age of the Gentiles.

CORE QUESTIONS

Before watching video fourteen, read Daniel 2:12–39. Use the two-column graphic organizer to help you organize your thoughts. Discuss your observations as a group.

As you watch the video, complete the following section. For many, reading the questions before watching the video will aid their understanding of the video content.

Daniel 2:25–39

1. What sort of work did Nebuchadnezzar enlist Daniel into?

_____

_____

2. What time does Nebuchadnezzar's dream tell of?

3. What pattern do we observe about the materials of which the dream statue is made?

4. What is significant about the nature of the dream and its interpretation?

5. By God's decree, what is Nebuchadnezzar's domain?

6. What do the various sections of the statue represent?

7. How do we know this dream represents the beginning of the age of the Gentiles?

DANIEL 2:12–39

8. What are the criteria for being a kingdom represented by the statue?

9. What is the second kingdom, and how is it less valuable than the first, Babylon?

10. What is the significance of the statue's crossed arms?

11. As far as God's role was concerned, how did the Medo-Persian empire differ from the Babylonian empire?

12. What is the third, bronze kingdom?

13. What is the significance of the bronze on the statue encompassing the thighs (a physical split)?

Revelation

Discussion Questions

1. Babylon is situated about 50 miles south of Baghdad, Iraq. When you think about what you know of the history of this area in conjunction with the history of Israel (specifically Jerusalem), what do you notice? What, again, are the criteria to determine the age of the Gentiles (Luke 21:24)? How do you see these things playing out in this theater of the world, even in the present day? (Remember, a Gentile is anyone who is not biologically Jewish, as in physical descendants of Abraham, Isaac, and Jacob.)

_____
_____
_____

2. Nebuchadnezzar's dream as recorded in the Bible is completely corroborated by world history. Have you learned about any of these empires before (Babylonian, Medo-Persian, Greek)? If so, share what you remember about them.

_____
_____
_____

3. Both Nebuchadnezzar's dream and its fulfillment point to a clear, fundamental truth about God: He is completely in control of the world, on both a macro and micro scale. He controls the rise and fall of pagan empires, just as much as He determines each of our steps (Proverbs 16:9). Does this comfort you or make you uncomfortable? Why?

_____
_____
_____

4. God uses pagan rulers, wars, and various other worldly motives, actions, and events to accomplish His will in such a way that He creates opportunities for His people to step into the unbelieving world and declare His glory. Notice Daniel's words in verses 27–28 (See Digging Deeper from Session Thirteen for full text). How have you seen God create opportunities for you or others to do the same? How can we learn from Daniel's example as we encounter these opportunities ourselves?

_____

5. In the space below, record your takeaway from Daniel 2:12–39 and any questions you have that remain unanswered.

DIGGING DEEPER (OPTIONAL)

Should you choose to dig deeper, complete the following Digging Deeper section. Each meeting will open with discussion of what you've learned and observed in Scripture, and this section will prepare you for that discussion.

In a two-column graphic organizer, record what you observe in each passage and the questions you have about it. Things to look for: Who is speaking? To whom is he speaking? What does he say about God? Jesus? The church? Individual believers? What do readers of this text stand to gain?

Scripture Passage: Daniel 2:40–45

Then there will be a fourth kingdom as strong as iron; inasmuch as iron crushes and shatters all things, so, like iron that breaks in pieces, it will crush and break all these in pieces. In that you saw the feet and toes, partly of potter's clay and partly of iron, it will be a divided kingdom; but it will have in it the toughness of iron, inasmuch as you saw the iron mixed with common clay. As the toes of the feet were partly of iron and partly of pottery, so some of the kingdom will be strong and part of it will be brittle. And in that you saw the iron mixed with common clay, they will combine with one another in the seed of men; but they will not adhere to one another, even as iron does not combine with pottery. In the days of those kings the God of heaven will set up a kingdom which will never be destroyed, and that kingdom will not be left for another people; it will crush and put an end to all these kingdoms, but it will itself endure forever. Inasmuch as you saw that a stone was cut out of the mountain without hands and that it crushed the iron, the bronze, the clay, the silver and the gold, the great God has made known to the king what will take place in the future; so the dream is true and its interpretation is trustworthy.

Revelation

Scripture Passage: Deuteronomy 27:5–6

Moreover, you shall build there an altar to the LORD your God, an altar of stones; you shall not wield an iron tool on them. You shall build the altar of the LORD your God of uncut stones, and you shall offer on it burnt offerings to the LORD your God....

A LITTLE DEEPER...

1. Do you have a guess of what this fourth kingdom of iron might be?

_____

_____

_____

2. Why do you suppose the statue didn't have more sections on it? (Remember the criteria for being represented on the statue.)

_____

_____

_____

3. Both of the verses above reference uncut stone. What might the significance of the uncut stones be?

_____

_____

_____

4. What other verses can you think of that use stone as a symbol? What might it represent in the case of the Daniel passage? (In the case of the Deuteronomy passage, stone isn't a symbol, just the uncut nature of the stone is.)

_____

_____

_____

SESSION FIFTEEN

Daniel 2:40–45

> *Remember the Golden Rule:* When the plain sense of Scripture makes common sense, we seek no other sense.

Video Fifteen

Topical overview: Additional unpacking of Nebuchadnezzar's dream from Daniel 2.
Learning goals: Align our understanding of history with Daniel's prophecy. Acquire new knowledge of symbols. Identify our place in history as represented by the statue.

CORE QUESTIONS

Before watching video fifteen, read Daniel 2:40–45. Use the two-column graphic organizer to help you organize your thoughts. Discuss your observations as a group.

As you watch the video, complete the following section. For many, reading the questions before watching the video will aid their understanding of the video content.

1. Why does Daniel gloss over the second and third kingdoms?

_____

_____

_____

2. How is the fourth kingdom different from the other three?

_____

REVELATION

_____

_____

3. When does the fourth kingdom begin?

_____

_____

_____

4. Why can people not single out an ending date for the Roman empire?

_____

_____

_____

5. What exactly succeeded the Roman Empire?

_____

_____

_____

6. What is the point of all of this national upheaval from a prophetic perspective?

_____

_____

_____

7. What phrase best describes the fourth kingdom?

_____

_____

_____

8. What is the last portion of Nebuchadnezzar's dream representative of?

_____

9. Why can this stone not be another Gentile nation?

10. What is an altar?

11. What is the purpose of sacrifice?

12. What is the significance of uncut stones in Deuteronomy 27?

13. When we pull together all the symbolism from the final portion of Nebuchadnezzar's dream, what conclusion can we draw? What is Daniel prophesying?

Discussion Questions

1. Pastor Armstrong mentioned a pet peeve in this video- our tendency to refer to something at the front of our sanctuaries as altars. Why is this language inaccurate? Can you think of any other biblical terms that have been misappropriated by modern usage?

_____

_____

_____

2. Summarize the symbolic significance of the composition of the statue's feet in Nebuchadnezzar's dream. How does this align with history as we know it?

_____

_____

_____

3. Throughout Scripture, God reinforces the symbolism of the uncut stone. Read Ephesians 2:8–9 and Galatians 2:15–21. How do we receive atonement? Do you struggle with believing that there is nothing *you* can do to *earn* your salvation? How does the knowledge and belief that your atonement is a free gift, not earned by any works, allow you to live?

_____

_____

_____

4. In Daniel 2:44–45, Daniel prophesies the second coming of Christ before Christ even comes the first time. He does so by the grace of and revelation from God. Does this give you comfort? How so?

_____

_____

_____

5. In the space below, record your takeaway from Daniel 2 and any questions you have that remain unanswered.

_____

_____

_____

DIGGING DEEPER (OPTIONAL)

Should you choose to dig deeper, complete the following Digging Deeper section. Each meeting will open with discussion of what you've learned and observed in Scripture, and this section will prepare you for that discussion.

In a two-column graphic organizer, record what you observe in each passage and the questions you have about it. Things to look for: Who is speaking? To whom is he speaking? What does he say about God? Jesus? The church? Individual believers? What do readers of this text stand to gain?

Scripture Passage: Daniel 7:1–10, 20–28

In the first year of Belshazzar king of Babylon Daniel saw a dream and visions in his mind as he lay on his bed; then he wrote the dream down and related the following summary of it. Daniel said, "I was looking in my vision by night, and behold, the four winds of heaven were stirring up the great sea. And four great beasts were coming up from the sea, different from one another. The first was like a lion and had the wings of an eagle. I kept looking until its wings were plucked, and it was lifted up from the ground and made to stand on two feet like a man; a human mind also was given to it. And behold, another beast, a second one, resembling a bear. And it was raised up on one side, and three ribs were in its mouth between its teeth; and thus they said to it, 'Arise, devour much meat!' After this I kept looking, and behold, another one, like a leopard, which had on its back four wings of a bird; the beast also had four heads, and dominion was given to it. After this I kept looking in the night visions, and behold, a fourth beast, dreadful and terrifying and extremely strong; and it had large iron teeth. It devoured and crushed and trampled down the remainder with its feet; and it was different from all the beasts that were before it, and it had ten horns. While I was contemplating the horns, behold, another horn, a little one, came up among them, and three of the first horns were pulled out by the roots before it; and behold, this horn possessed eyes like the eyes of a man and a mouth uttering great boasts. I kept looking until thrones were set up, and the Ancient of Days took His seat; His vesture was like white snow and the hair of His head like pure wool. His throne was ablaze with flames, its wheels were a burning fire. A river of fire was flowing and coming out from before Him; thousands upon thousands were attending Him, and myriads upon myriads were standing before Him; the court sat, and the books were opened.

"...and the meaning of the ten horns that were on its head and the other horn which came up, and before which three of them fell, namely, that horn which had eyes and a mouth uttering great boasts and which was larger in appearance than its associates. I kept looking, and that horn was waging war with the saints and overpowering them until the Ancient of Days came and judgment

was passed in favor of the saints of the Highest One, and the time arrived when the saints took possession of the kingdom. Thus he said: 'The fourth beast will be a fourth kingdom on the earth, which will be different from all the other kingdoms and will devour the whole earth and tread it down and crush it. As for the ten horns, out of this kingdom ten kings will arise; and another will arise after them, and he will be different from the previous ones and will subdue three kings. He will speak out against the Most High and wear down the saints of the Highest One, and he will intend to make alterations in times and in law; and they will be given into his hand for a time, times, and half a time. But the court will sit for judgment, and his dominion will be taken away, annihilated and destroyed forever. Then the sovereignty, the dominion and the greatness of all the kingdoms under the whole heaven will be given to the people of the saints of the Highest One; His kingdom will be an everlasting kingdom, and all the dominions will serve and obey Him.' At this point the revelation ended. As for me, Daniel, my thoughts were greatly alarming me and my face grew pale, but I kept the matter to myself."

A Little Deeper...

1. List the symbols in this passage and their significance as is revealed in the latter half of the passage.

_____

_____

_____

2. Notice Daniel's reaction to his dream in verse 28. How might you have responded in his position?

_____

_____

_____

3. Acts 2:16–18 says this of the last days: "…but this is what was spoken of through the prophet Joel: 'And it shall be in the last days,' God says, 'That I will pour forth of My Spirit on all mankind; And your sons and your daughters shall prophesy, And your young men shall see visions, And your old men shall dream dreams; Even on My bondslaves, both men and women, I will in those days pour forth of My Spirit And they shall prophesy." Have you ever received a dream you felt to be from the Lord? If so, what was it like, and what was your response? If not, that's okay. What do you imagine it would be like? How do you imagine you might feel?

_____

_____

SESSION SIXTEEN

Daniel 7:1–8

> ***Remember the Golden Rule:*** *When the plain sense of Scripture makes common sense, we seek no other sense.*

Video Sixteen

Topical overview: Daniel's vision of the four beasts.

Learning goals: Understand what each of the four beasts in Daniel's dream symbolizes. Recognize the pattern reflected in the dream. Identify how the details of the dream connect to the age of the Gentiles and to historical developments.

CORE QUESTIONS

Before watching video sixteen, read Daniel 7:1–8. Use the two-column graphic organizer to help you organize your thoughts. Discuss your observations as a group.

As you watch the video, complete the following section. For many, reading the questions before watching the video will aid their understanding of the video content.

Overview

1. Why are we reading outside of Revelation over the next several sessions?

_____

_____

_____

2. What transitional event moves us from the church age (the things that are) to the next age (the things after these things)?

3. What, again, is the age of the Gentiles?

4. What will signal the end of the age of the Gentiles?

5. What exactly will the reversal of these sanctions look like?

Daniel 7:1–10

1. What part of the dream in Daniel 2 is the focus of the dream in Daniel 7?

2. Rather than a timeline, what do these animals symbolize?

DANIEL 7:1–8

3. How does the fourth beast break the pattern?

_____
_____
_____

4. What is the historical norm of kingdoms in the world?

_____
_____
_____

5. What is the pattern we need to recognize?

_____
_____
_____

DISCUSSION QUESTIONS

1. We know that the age of the Gentiles is the period in which Israel experiences judgment on earth. Why is this judgment justified? Use Scripture to support your answer.

_____
_____
_____

2. Despite Israel gaining its sovereignty in the form of land after World War II (1947), we are still in the age of Gentiles. Review the three traits of the age of Gentiles, and discuss how Israel's current status in our world adheres to them.

_____
_____
_____

3. Pastor Armstrong highlights a pattern in which the one who comes later resembles the one who came before. This is an application of something called typology in which the former is called a type and the latter is called an antitype. Another example of this sort of symbolic relationship is the relationship between the sacrificial Passover lamb, and Jesus and His sacrificial death of atonement on the cross. The type is a shadow or a veiled representation of the clear, unveiled thing to come, the antitype. Can you think of any other typological relationships in the Bible? Share them with the group. Why might God use symbolic relationships like these to help us understand?

_____

_____

_____

4. From our perspective in history, it's becoming increasingly apparent that God's revealed word in Daniel's prophecies, while couched in symbolism, is extremely detailed and clearly aligns with what we know to be historical fact. As we begin to approach prophecy concerning things that remain in the future, how does this make you feel?

_____

_____

_____

6. So far in our study, what have you learned about who God is? Has your understanding of Him changed? How so?

_____

_____

_____

7. In the space below, record your takeaway from Daniel 2:1–8 and any questions you have that remain unanswered.

_____

_____

_____

DANIEL 7:1–8

DIGGING DEEPER (OPTIONAL)

Should you choose to dig deeper, complete the following Digging Deeper section. Each meeting will open with discussion of what you've learned and observed in Scripture, and this section will prepare you for that discussion.

In a two-column graphic organizer, record what you observe in each passage and the questions you have about it. Things to look for: Who is speaking? To whom is he speaking? What does he say about God? Jesus? The church? Individual believers? What do readers of this text stand to gain?

Scripture Passage: Daniel 9:3–10

So I gave my attention to the Lord God to seek Him by prayer and supplications, with fasting, sackcloth and ashes. I prayed to the LORD my God and confessed and said, "Alas, O Lord, the great and awesome God, who keeps His covenant and lovingkindness for those who love Him and keep His commandments, we have sinned, committed iniquity, acted wickedly and rebelled, even turning aside from Your commandments and ordinances. Moreover, we have not listened to Your servants the prophets, who spoke in Your name to our kings, our princes, our fathers and all the people of the land. Righteousness belongs to You, O Lord, but to us open shame, as it is this day—to the men of Judah, the inhabitants of Jerusalem and all Israel, those who are nearby and those who are far away in all the countries to which You have driven them, because of their unfaithful deeds which they have committed against You. Open shame belongs to us, O Lord, to our kings, our princes and our fathers, because we have sinned against You. To the Lord our God belong compassion and forgiveness, for we have rebelled against Him; nor have we obeyed the voice of the LORD our God, to walk in His teachings which He set before us through His servants the prophets."

Scripture Passage: Leviticus 26:32–34, 40–42

I will make the land desolate so that your enemies who settle in it will be appalled over it. You, however, I will scatter among the nations and will draw out a sword after you, as your land becomes desolate and your cities become waste. Then the land will enjoy its sabbaths all the days of the desolation, while you are in your enemies' land; then the land will rest and enjoy its sabbaths. ...

If they confess their iniquity and the iniquity of their forefathers, in their unfaithfulness which they committed against Me, and also in their acting with hostility against Me—I also was acting with hostility against them, to bring them into the land of their enemies—or if their uncircumcised heart becomes humbled so that they then make amends for their iniquity, then I will remember My covenant with Jacob, and I will remember also My covenant with Isaac, and My covenant with Abraham as well, and I will remember the land.

Revelation

Scripture Passage: Jeremiah 25:11–12

This whole land will be a desolation and a horror, and these nations will serve the king of Babylon seventy years. "Then it will be when seventy years are completed I will punish the king of Babylon and that nation," declares the LORD, "for their iniquity, and the land of the Chaldeans; and I will make it an everlasting desolation."

A Little Deeper...

1. The greater context of Leviticus 26 is God outlining the consequences and rewards for obeying His commands. If you review the whole chapter, you'll see they quite clearly describe Israel's history from the time of Judges onward, prophesied an entire generation and more before each and every bit came to pass. List the specific punishments outlined in the passages above, and see if you can match them with historical circumstances pertaining to the nation of Israel. Some are historically contained within the Bible, and others occur later in history.

_____

_____

_____

2. In the verses from Leviticus 26, the third paragraph begins with the word *If*. What is the Lord's condition for ending the punishment of Israel?

_____

_____

_____

3. Now review the passage from Daniel. How are Daniel 9 and Leviticus 26 related? (Remember: Leviticus comes about while the Israelites wander the desert. Daniel comes about during Israel's Babylonian exile hundreds of years later.)

_____

_____

_____

4. God clearly honored Daniel's faithfulness in an apostate world. Chapter 9 shows Daniel humbling himself in repentance on behalf of the whole of Israel. But we know from our previous study that Daniel's prayers in chapter 9 do not end the age of the Gentiles. Remember the promise to the individual believer at the end of each letter in Revelation 2–3. How do we see the same concept playing out in Daniel's life?

SESSION SEVENTEEN

Daniel 9:1–5

> ***Remember the Golden Rule:*** *When the plain sense of Scripture makes common sense, we seek no other sense.*

Video Seventeen

Topical overview: Daniel's vision of the end times.
Learning goals: Identify Christ's role in the prophetic material of Daniel. Unpack the fourth beast as it applies to modern ruling powers.

CORE QUESTIONS

Before watching video seventeen, read Daniel 9:1–5. Use the two-column graphic organizer to help you organize your thoughts. Discuss your observations as a group.

As you watch the video, complete the following section. For many, reading the questions before watching the video will aid their understanding of the video content.

Overview

1. What in Daniel 7 parallels the uncut stone in Daniel 2?

_____
_____
_____

DANIEL 9:1–5

2. What is the chief reason Daniel 7 exists?

3. What do the horns represent?

4. At the end of the world, how many rulers will there be?

5. Where else do we find this same usage of the word *time*, and what does it represent?

6. What has to happen to our present-day world for it to fulfill the prophecy we see here?

7. What is important to pull from this?

Revelation

8. How did Pastor Armstrong apply dates to the kingdom sections of his diagrams?

9. Who is the primary subject of the events of Revelation?

Daniel 9:1–2

1. By the time Daniel reaches the ninth chapter of his book, what kingdom (Daniel 2) is he living in?

2. At what point is Scripture self-evident to humanity?

3. How is Leviticus 26 connected to Jeremiah 25?

Discussion Questions

1. Pastor Armstrong illuminates that the reason Daniel 9 exists is to elaborate on the end of Daniel 2 and to preface Revelation 4–22. He also points out that Scripture is

DANIEL 9:1–5

recognized as such by its' writers' contemporaries, not centuries later (Peter and Paul, Daniel and Jeremiah). How is this knowledge useful to the believer in the modern age of deconstructing faith and decentralizing truth?

_____

_____

_____

2. Near the last third of the video, Pastor Armstrong points out a truth that applies to our understanding of much of Scripture: We want it to be about us, but more often than not, it simply isn't. In the case of the "things after the things which are," chapters 4–22 of Revelation, Pastor Armstrong points out on multiple occasions that they are directed at Israel, not the church. How do we see this same error in understanding affecting our approach to Scripture in other ways?

_____

_____

_____

3. Review what has to happen to our present-day world (as far as we know at this point) to usher in the times described in Revelation 4–22. Think about what you hear about the "End Times" in our culture... social media, educational programming, Christian leaders and teachers, etc. How does this align with what you've learned is true in this lesson, and what is your answer?

_____

_____

_____

4. Why does Pastor Armstrong assert that the times described in Revelation 4–12 are not imminent in our understanding of time? Do you agree or disagree, and why?

_____

_____

_____

5. In the space below, record your takeaways from Daniel 7 and 9 and any questions you have that remain unanswered.

_____

_____

_____

DIGGING DEEPER (OPTIONAL)

Should you choose to dig deeper, complete the following Digging Deeper section. Each meeting will open with discussion of what you've learned and observed in Scripture, and this section will prepare you for that discussion.

In a two-column graphic organizer, record what you observe in each passage and the questions you have about it. Things to look for: Who is speaking? To whom is he speaking? What does he say about God? Jesus? The church? Individual believers? What do readers of this text stand to gain?

Scripture Passage: Daniel 9:3–5, 20–27

So I gave my attention to the Lord God to seek Him by prayer and supplications, with fasting, sackcloth and ashes. I prayed to the LORD my God and confessed and said, "Alas, O Lord, the great and awesome God, who keeps His covenant and lovingkindness for those who love Him and keep His commandments, we have sinned, committed iniquity, acted wickedly and rebelled, even turning aside from Your commandments and ordinances. ..."

Now while I was speaking and praying, and confessing my sin and the sin of my people Israel, and presenting my supplication before the LORD my God in behalf of the holy mountain of my God, while I was still speaking in prayer, then the man Gabriel, whom I had seen in the vision previously, came to me in my extreme weariness about the time of the evening offering. He gave me instruction and talked with me and said, "O Daniel, I have now come forth to give you insight with understanding. At the beginning of your supplications the command was issued, and I have come to tell you, for you are highly esteemed; so give heed to the message and gain understanding of the vision. Seventy weeks have been decreed for your people and your holy city, to finish the transgression, to make an end of sin, to make atonement for iniquity, to bring in everlasting righteousness, to seal up vision and prophecy and to anoint the most holy place. So you are to know and discern that from the issuing of a decree to restore and rebuild Jerusalem until Messiah the Prince there will be seven weeks and sixty-two weeks; it will be built again, with plaza and moat, even in times of distress. Then after the sixty-two weeks the Messiah will be cut off and have nothing, and the people of the prince who is to come will destroy the city and the sanctuary. And its end will come with a flood; even to the end there will be war; desolations are determined. And he will make a firm covenant with the many for one week, but in the middle of the week he will put a stop to sacrifice and grain offering; and on the wing of abominations will come one who makes desolate, even until a complete destruction, one that is decreed, is poured out on the one who makes desolate."

DANIEL 9:1–5

Scripture Passage: Romans 11:7, 11, 25

What then? What Israel is seeking, it has not obtained, but those who were chosen obtained it, and the rest were hardened. ...

I say then, they did not stumble so as to fall, did they? May it never be! But by their transgression salvation has come to the Gentiles, to make them jealous. ...

For I do not want you, brethren, to be uninformed of this mystery—so that you will not be wise in your own estimation—that a partial hardening has happened to Israel until the fullness of the Gentiles has come in.

A LITTLE DEEPER...

1. Many if not all of us are the among the Gentiles to whom Paul refers in Romans. We see an example of how God works the enemy's plans for good. How so?

_____

_____

_____

2. The language of the passage in Romans also highlights a concept that is difficult to grasp. God is in control of both softening (Praise God!) and hardening hearts. We see this happen clearly in the story of the Exodus with Pharaoh. But God hasn't changed (Hebrews 13:8). He still softens *and hardens* hearts. How do you see this truth around you, and how does accepting it help you to walk in freedom in Christ? Have you accepted it?

_____

_____

_____

3. The latter portion of Daniel 9 is something many have tried to interpret. It's a popular topic in apocalyptic educational programming. What have you heard previously about Daniel and his prophecy of weeks? Examine the posture of your heart as you prepare to learn in the next session. What place are you coming from? Pray that God will reveal the truth of His word to you and that you will embrace His truth with obedience and acceptance.

_____

Revelation

SESSION EIGHTEEN

Daniel 9:3–5; 20–27

> ***Remember the Golden Rule:*** *When the plain sense of Scripture makes common sense, we seek no other sense.*

Video Eighteen

Topical overview: The timing and counting within Daniel 9.
Learning goals: Understand the significance of "weeks," how this counting matches up to our understanding of history, and our place in all of this.

CORE QUESTIONS

Before watching video eighteen, read Daniel 9:3–5; 20–27. Use the two-column graphic organizer to help you organize your thoughts. Discuss your observations as a group.

As you watch the video, complete the following section. For many, reading the questions before watching the video will aid their understanding of the video content.

1. How did Daniel misinterpret this period of 70 weeks?

_____
_____
_____

2. How do we know Daniel has made this misinterpretation?

_____

3. What do we learn about the Abrahamic covenant?

4. How does God correct Daniel's understanding?

5. What is "the Holy Mountain of God?"

6. What is "weeks," literally?

7. Are these "years" counted in the same way we count them?

8. What implies a break or pause in the counting?

DANIEL 9:3–5, 20–27

9. What ends the "pause" and resumes the counting?

10. Where is the church?

11. When does God's focus shift from the salvation of Gentiles to the resolution of Israel?

12. What is the purpose of the first 70 years?

13. What is the purpose of the subsequent 490+ years?

14. What is eight the number of?

REVELATION

15. What is our role in this timeline?

DISCUSSION QUESTIONS

1. In the space below, record your takeaway from Daniel 9 and any questions you have that remain unanswered.

DIGGING DEEPER (OPTIONAL)

Should you choose to dig deeper, complete the following Digging Deeper section. Each meeting will open with discussion of what you've learned and observed in Scripture, and this section will prepare you for that discussion.

In a two-column graphic organizer, record what you observe in each passage and the questions you have about it. Things to look for: Who is speaking? To whom is he speaking? What does he say about God? Jesus? The church? Individual believers? What do readers of this text stand to gain?

Scripture Passage: Read Revelation 4:1–4

Scripture Passage: Jeremiah 30:7

Alas! for that day is great, there is none like it; and it is the time of Jacob's distress, but he will be saved from it.

DANIEL 9:3–5, 20–27

Scripture Passage: 1 Thessalonians 5:2–3

For you yourselves know full well that the day of the Lord will come just like a thief in the night. While they are saying, "Peace and safety!" then destruction will come upon them suddenly like labor pains upon a woman with child, and they will not escape.

Scripture Passage: 2 Peter 3:10

But the day of the Lord will come like a thief, in which the heavens will pass away with a roar and the elements will be destroyed with intense heat, and the earth and its works will be burned up.

Scripture Passage: Galatians 3:27

For all of you who were baptized into Christ have clothed yourselves with Christ.

Scripture Passage: 2 Corinthians 5:21

He made Him who knew no sin to be sin on our behalf, so that we might become the righteousness of God in Him.

A LITTLE DEEPER...

1. This collection of Scripture can be subdivided into three categories: one (Revelation 4:1–4), two (Jeremiah 30:7; 1 Thessalonians 5:2–3, 2 Peter 3:10), and three (Galatians 3:27; 2 Corinthians 5:21). What is the subject of the scripture in each category, and how are the categories related to one another?

_____

_____

_____

2. The scene depicted in Revelation 4–5 describes John's first view of "the things which will take place after these things [which are]" (Revelation 1:19). Draw or find a picture online to help you grasp the visual this passage gives of God's throne room.

_____

3. What symbols do you notice in the Revelation passage? Include their significance if you know them.

4. The second set of passages all describe the Tribulation. What do you notice?

5. The third set of passages discuss a theological concept called *imputed righteousness*. What is the definition of *imputed*? Imputed righteousness is symbolized throughout the Bible by robes, usually white ones. Summarize all we've learned so far about imputed righteousness and its associated symbolism.

SESSION NINETEEN

Revelation 4:1–4

> ***Remember the Golden Rule:*** *When the plain sense of Scripture makes common sense, we seek no other sense.*

Video Nineteen

Topical overview: Review of what's been taught so far. Introduction to John's vision of "the things after the things that are."

Learning goals: Acquire new symbol significance. Assimilate the timelines discussed over the past few weeks into one. Explore John's vision of God the Father. Review the significance of white robes.

CORE QUESTIONS

Before watching video nineteen, read Revelation 4:1–4. Use the two-column graphic organizer to help you organize your thoughts. Discuss your observations as a group.

As you watch the video, complete the following section. For many, reading the questions before watching the video will aid their understanding of the video content.

Overview

1. What again are the three characteristics of the age of Gentiles?

___

___

___

2. How does the remainder of Revelation (chapters 4–22) relate with Daniel 9 (weeks/sevens)?

3. How should we refer to this final see, the seventieth seven?

Revelation 4:1–4

1. What is the symbolic effect of repeating something three times in Scripture?

2. In heaven there will be no doubt about what?

3. What do we know about the *when* of this scene?

4. What does chapter 4 focus on?

REVELATION 4:1–4

5. What is jasper an ancient name for?

6. What does the vision of Revelation 4–5 center on?

7. What do elders in white robes signify?

8. What is suggested by the fact that these elders do not appear in earlier visions?

DISCUSSION QUESTIONS

1. In the space below, record your takeaway from Revelation 4:1–4 and any questions you have that remain unanswered.

Digging Deeper (Optional)

Should you choose to dig deeper, complete the following Digging Deeper section. Each meeting will open with discussion of what you've learned and observed in Scripture, and this section will prepare you for that discussion.

In a two-column graphic organizer, record what you observe in each passage and the questions you have about it. Things to look for: Who is speaking? To whom is he speaking? What does he say about God? Jesus? The church? Individual believers? What do readers of this text stand to gain?

Scripture Passage: Revelation 19:8

It was given to her to clothe herself in fine linen, bright and clean; for the fine linen is the righteous acts of the saints.

Scripture Passage: Luke 22:28–30

You are those who have stood by Me in My trials; and just as My Father has granted Me a kingdom, I grant you that you may eat and drink at My table in My kingdom, and you will sit on thrones judging the twelve tribes of Israel.

Scripture Passage: Revelation 20:4

Then I saw thrones, and they sat on them, and judgment was given to them. And I saw the souls of those who had been beheaded because of their testimony of Jesus and because of the word of God, and those who had not worshiped the beast or his image, and had not received the mark on their forehead and on their hand; and they came to life and reigned with Christ for a thousand years.

Scripture Passage: 1 Corinthians 9:25

Everyone who competes in the games exercises self-control in all things. They then do it to receive a perishable wreath, but we an imperishable.

Scripture Passage: 2 Timothy 4:8

In the future there is laid up for me the crown of righteousness, which the Lord, the righteous Judge, will award to me on that day; and not only to me, but also to all who have loved His appearing.

Scripture Passage: James 5:7–9

Therefore be patient, brethren, until the coming of the Lord. The farmer waits for the precious produce of the soil, being patient about it, until it gets the early and late rains. You too be patient; strengthen your hearts, for the coming of the Lord is near. Do not complain, brethren, against one another, so that you yourselves may not be judged; behold, the Judge is standing right at the door.

Scripture Passage: John 14:1–3

Do not let your heart be troubled; believe in God, believe also in Me. In My Father's house are many dwelling places; if it were not so, I would have told you; for I go to prepare a place for you. If I go and prepare a place for you, I will come again and receive you to Myself, that where I am, there you may be also.

Scripture Passage: Daniel 7:27

Then the sovereignty, the dominion and the greatness of all the kingdoms under the whole heaven will be given to the people of the saints of the Highest One; His kingdom will be an everlasting kingdom, and all the dominions will serve and obey Him.

Scripture Passage: 1 Corinthians 15:42–53

So also is the resurrection of the dead. It is sown a perishable body, it is raised an imperishable body; it is sown in dishonor, it is raised in glory; it is sown in weakness, it is raised in power; it is sown a natural body, it is raised a spiritual body. If there is a natural body, there is also a spiritual body. So also it is written, "The first man, Adam, became a living soul." The last Adam became a life-giving spirit. However, the spiritual is not first, but the natural; then the spiritual. The first man is from the earth, earthy; the second man is from heaven. As is the earthy, so also are those who are earthy; and as is the heavenly, so also are those who are heavenly. Just as we have borne the image of the earthy, we will also bear the image of the heavenly. Now I say this, brethren, that flesh and blood cannot inherit the kingdom of God; nor does the perishable inherit the imperishable. Behold, I tell you a mystery; we will not all sleep, but we will all be changed, in a moment, in the twinkling of an eye, at the last trumpet; for the trumpet will sound, and the dead

> REVELATION

> *will be raised imperishable, and we will be changed. For this perishable must put on the imperishable, and this mortal must put on immortality.*

Scripture Passage: 1 Thessalonians 4:13–18

> *But we do not want you to be uninformed, brethren, about those who are asleep, so that you will not grieve as do the rest who have no hope. For if we believe that Jesus died and rose again, even so God will bring with Him those who have fallen asleep in Jesus. For this we say to you by the word of the Lord, that we who are alive and remain until the coming of the Lord, will not precede those who have fallen asleep. For the Lord Himself will descend from heaven with a shout, with the voice of the archangel and with the trumpet of God, and the dead in Christ will rise first. Then we who are alive and remain will be caught up together with them in the clouds to meet the Lord in the air, and so we shall always be with the Lord. Therefore comfort one another with these words.*

A LITTLE DEEPER...

1. Based on what we read in these scriptures, where will we, Gentile believers, be in God's kingdom?

___

___

___

2. What is the attitude Scripture admonishes believers to maintain as we await Christ's return?

___

___

___

3. Take a moment to assess your heart. We know the world is a scary, broken place, and it's not getting any better until Jesus comes back. But how does Scripture tell us to live in the meantime? How are you doing with that? Does your life look like, from both the inside and the outside, the life of someone who has *hope* of *Christ*? If it does, pray that those around you would know and rest in the hope of Christ. If you find that you yourself are not resting in Christ, that you yourself live as if you had no hope, take some time to pray and repent. Christ promises His people supernatural peace (John 14:27) when we walk with Him because His yoke is easy and His burden is light (Matthew

11:28–30). He promises His people soul-deep rest that springs from our hope in our eternal inheritance: Jesus Himself. This is true for all who believe, no matter what your circumstances may seem to indicate. Trust Jesus. Live with hope. If you find yourself in this place of repentance, consider sharing what you learn in this time with a trusted friend who will hold you accountable and lift you up when you're tempted to lose your hope.

_____

_____

_____

SESSION TWENTY

Apologetics for the Rapture

Remember the Golden Rule: *When the plain sense of Scripture makes common sense, we seek no other sense.*

Video Twenty

Topical overview: Apologetics for the Rapture.
Learning goals: Process Pastor Armstrong's argument for the biblical justification of the rapture. Explore the scriptures Pastor Armstrong uses to support his argument.

CORE QUESTIONS

Before watching video twenty, read Revelation 4:1–4 for review. Use the two-column graphic organizer to help you organize your thoughts. Discuss your observations as a group.

As you watch the video, complete the following section. For many, reading the questions before watching the video will aid their understanding of the video content.

1. What do the (whiteness purity) of the garments represent?

_____

_____

_____

2. What do thrones represent?

_____

3. What do the crowns represent?

4. What do the elders represent?

5. What is the significance of 24?

Seven lampstands refers to seven spirits of God, which means 100% of God's Spirit. All of it in one place at one time.

6. What is the significance of the entirety of the Holy Spirit being in God's throne room in this vision?

7. What is the conclusive proof of this being true of the end of the church age (take notes over the next several minutes as Pastor Armstrong constructs an argument for the rapture of the church)?

Revelation

The "coming of the Lord" is the day of the resurrection in the Lord, the rapture The dead ones resurrect, and the alive ones are "caught up."

Discussion Questions

1. Prior to this session, what did you know of the rapture? What was your position on it and why?

_____
_____
_____

2. As a group, walk back through Pastor Armstrong's apologetic for the rapture. (Use the outline and slides available on the VBVMI website or in the app if you need help.) How do we know that the church, the whole of those who have believed throughout the Gentile age, will be bodily present in God's throne room at the historical occurrence John describes in Revelation 4?

_____
_____
_____

3. In the space below, record your takeaway from Session Twenty and any questions you have that remain unanswered.

_____
_____
_____

Digging Deeper (Optional)

Should you choose to dig deeper, complete the following Digging Deeper section. Each meeting will open with discussion of what you've learned and observed in Scripture, and this section will prepare you for that discussion.

In a two-column graphic organizer, record what you observe in each passage and the questions you have about it. Things to look for: Who is speaking? To whom is he speaking? What does he say about God? Jesus? The church? Individual believers? What do readers of this text stand to gain?

Scripture Passage: Hebrews 11:39–40

And all these, having gained approval through their faith, did not receive what was promised, because God had provided something better for us, so that apart from us they would not be made perfect.

Scripture Passage: 1 Thessalonians 4:15

For this we say to you by the word of the Lord, that we who are alive and remain until the coming of the Lord, will not precede those who have fallen asleep.

Scripture Passage: 2 Corinthians 5:9–10

Therefore we also have as our ambition, whether at home or absent, to be pleasing to Him. For we must all appear before the judgment seat of Christ, so that each one may be recompensed for his deeds in the body, according to what he has done, whether good or bad.

Scripture Passage: 1 Corinthians 4:5

Therefore do not go on passing judgment before the time, but wait until the Lord comes who will both bring to light the things hidden in the darkness and disclose the motives of men's hearts; and then each man's praise will come to him from God.

Scripture Passage: 1 Thessalonians 2:19–20

For who is our hope or joy or crown of exultation? Is it not even you, in the presence of our Lord Jesus at His coming? For you are our glory and joy.

Scripture Passage: Revelation 22:12–13

Behold, I am coming quickly, and My reward is with Me, to render to every man according to what he has done. I am the Alpha and the Omega, the first and the last, the beginning and the end.

REVELATION

Scripture Passage: 1 Peter 1:6–7

In this you greatly rejoice, even though now for a little while, if necessary, you have been distressed by various trials, so that the proof of your faith, being more precious than gold which is perishable, even though tested by fire, may be found to result in praise and glory and honor at the revelation of Jesus Christ.

Scripture Passage: 1 Thessalonians 5:2–4, 9–10

For you yourselves know full well that the day of the Lord will come just like a thief in the night. While they are saying, "Peace and safety!" then destruction will come upon them suddenly like labor pains upon a woman with child, and they will not escape. But you, brethren, are not in darkness, that the day would overtake you like a thief. …

For God has not destined us for wrath, but for obtaining salvation through our Lord Jesus Christ, who died for us, so that whether we are awake or asleep, we will live together with Him.

Scripture Passage: 2 Thessalonians 2:1–8

Now we request you, brethren, with regard to the coming of our Lord Jesus Christ and our gathering together to Him, that you not be quickly shaken from your composure or be disturbed either by a spirit or a message or a letter as if from us, to the effect that the day of the Lord has come. Let no one in any way deceive you, for it will not come unless the apostasy comes first, and the man of lawlessness is revealed, the son of destruction, who opposes and exalts himself above every so-called god or object of worship, so that he takes his seat in the temple of God, displaying himself as being God. Do you not remember that while I was still with you, I was telling you these things? And you know what restrains him now, so that in his time he will be revealed. For the mystery of lawlessness is already at work; only he who now restrains will do so until he is taken out of the way. Then that lawless one will be revealed whom the Lord will slay with the breath of His mouth and bring to an end by the appearance of His coming.

Scripture Passage: Matthew 24:36

But of that day and hour no one knows, not even the angels of heaven, nor the Son, but the Father alone.

A LITTLE DEEPER…

1. What is "lawlessness," and how do we already see it at work?

2. The first several passages here refer to judgment, specifically that of Christ. What is Christ to judge?

3. Christ Himself taught on multiple occasions in the Gospels that it isn't the place of the believer to judge the spiritual condition of others. Paul writes of the same on several occasions as well. The temptation to do so, however, is strong. How might we resist the temptation to usurp Christ's authority by sitting in judgment on others? What does it look like when you personally are tempted to judge others? What are the effects of this particular sin in our lives?

SESSION TWENTY-ONE

The Day of the Lord Versus the Coming of the Lord

Remember the Golden Rule: When the plain sense of Scripture makes common sense, we seek no other sense.

Topical overview: The Day of the Lord and the coming of the Lord.
Learning goals: Understand the difference between the day of and the coming of the Lord. Add to your timeline of events.

CORE QUESTIONS

Before watching video twenty-one, review the Digging Deeper passages from Session Twenty. Use the two-column graphic organizer to help you organize your thoughts. Discuss your observations as a group.

As you watch the video, complete the following section. For many, reading the questions before watching the video will aid their understanding of the video content.

1. What do we learn about the resurrection from Hebrews?

___

___

___

2. What are the implications of the coming of the Lord in John 14?

___

___

3. What all happens in the same moment at the Coming of the Lord?

_____
_____
_____

4. What is the "Day of the Lord?"

_____
_____
_____

5. How do we know the Day of the Lord (Tribulation) follows the Coming of the Lord (Rapture/ Resurrection)?

_____
_____
_____

6. Why does Jesus use the metaphor of preparing a home for us to explain the waiting period before His return to claim His bride (the church)?

_____
_____
_____

7. So what is Jesus waiting for?

_____
_____
_____

DISCUSSION QUESTIONS

1. Review the timeline. Which label refers to the "Day of the Lord?" "The Coming of the

Lord?"

2. Before this session, did you recognize a difference between the *day* of the Lord and the *coming* of the Lord? Do you recognize the difference now? Take a moment to be sure your group fully understands the difference between the two.

3. What comfort do you find in this session's discussion of the coming of the Lord?

4. This session sets up a clear division between people: (group one) those who chose to serve Jesus are grouped with those who served God faithfully while waiting for Jesus, (group two) and those who did not serve God faithfully before or after Christ's earthly ministry. Where else in Scripture do we learn of this grouping? When you think about modern theology, do you think these lines are clear? Why or why not?

5. In the space below, record your takeaway from Session Twenty-One and any questions you have that remain unanswered.

DIGGING DEEPER (OPTIONAL)

Should you choose to dig deeper, complete the following Digging Deeper section. Each meeting will open with discussion of what you've learned and observed in Scripture, and this section will prepare you for that discussion.

In a two-column graphic organizer, record what you observe in each passage and the questions you have about it. Things to look for: Who is speaking? To whom is he speaking? What does he say about God? Jesus? The church? Individual believers? What do readers of this text stand to gain?

Scripture Passage: Read Revelation 4:5–8, 5:1–14

Scripture Passage: Ezekiel 11:16–20

> Therefore say, "Thus says the Lord GOD, 'Though I had removed them far away among the nations and though I had scattered them among the countries, yet I was a sanctuary for them a little while in the countries where they had gone.'" Therefore say, "Thus says the Lord GOD, 'I will gather you from the peoples and assemble you out of the countries among which you have been scattered, and I will give you the land of Israel.'" When they come there, they will remove all its detestable things and all its abominations from it. And I will give them one heart, and put a new spirit within them. And I will take the heart of stone out of their flesh and give them a heart of flesh, that they may walk in My statutes and keep My ordinances and do them. Then they will be My people, and I shall be their God.

A LITTLE DEEPER...

1. List the symbols you find in these passages along with their meanings, if you know them.

_____

_____

_____

2. Review the timeline addressed in the previous session. To which "week" does Ezekiel's prophecy refer?

_____

_____

_____

3. What exactly has Christ purchased with His blood?

_____

_____

_____

4. What has He made us, the saints, to be, and what is our purpose as described in that same verse (10)?

_____

_____

_____

SESSION TWENTY-TWO

Revelation 4:5–8; 5:1–14

> ***Remember the Golden Rule:*** *When the plain sense of Scripture makes common sense, we seek no other sense.*

Video Twenty-Two

Topical overview: Review of what we've learned so far. Beginning to unpack the vision of Revelation 5.

Learning goals: Expand understanding of the character of both God the Father and Jesus. Recognize the connection between both Leviticus 26 and Ezekiel 10 to Revelation. Deepen knowledge of symbolism.

CORE QUESTIONS

Before watching video twenty-two, read Revelation 4:5–8; 5:1–14. Use the two-column graphic organizer to help you organize your thoughts. Discuss your observations as a group.

As you watch the video, complete the following section. For many, reading the questions before watching the video will aid their understanding of the video content.

Overview

1. What do we find in Leviticus 26?

_____

_____

Revelation

2. Why does the Tribulation happen?

_____
_____
_____

3. What does God have for His actions?

_____
_____
_____

God is in no way capricious; He keeps His promises and finishes what He starts.

4. What is the accurate biblical term for what is popularly known as the rapture?

_____
_____
_____

5. What event ends the age of the Gentiles?

_____
_____
_____

6. What topic is described in Revelation 6–18?

_____
_____
_____

Revelation 4:5–8

1. What sort of creatures surround the throne in this passage?

_____

REVELATION 4:5–8; 5:1–14

2. What are the three classes of angelic beings?

3. What is the purpose of cherubim?

4. What do we learn about the glory of God in Ezekiel 10, right before Nebuchadnezzar attacks?

5. How is Ezekiel 10 connected to Revelation 5?

Revelation 5:1–14

1. Where does the focus shift from this point on in Revelation, and how is He pictured here?

REVELATION

2. What is Father God holding?

_____

_____

_____

3. What is the significance of the scroll having writing on both on the inside and the outside?

_____

_____

_____

DISCUSSION QUESTIONS

1. For everyone's benefit, review the timeline. If anyone in your group has any confusion about the things on this timeline, take some time to help them understand.

_____

_____

_____

2. Ezekiel 10 serves as a sort of preamble for Revelation 5. What is a preamble? How does it affect you to know that God has known the entirety of Scripture since before even a single word was penned? How does it affect you to know the old and new testaments we have today are not just inter*related* but also inter*dependent*?

_____

_____

_____

3. Before this lesson, what did you know or believe about angels? Has this lesson affected your beliefs about them in any way? Why or why not?

_____

_____

_____

REVELATION 4:5–8; 5:1–14

4. Pastor Armstrong points out in this lesson that God is in no way capricious. What did you learn about who He is and how He acts in this lesson? (If *capricious* is a new word for you, it's a synonym for unpredictable that has a connotation of lack of care.)

___

5. Reread Revelation 5:1–7. The Hero of the story enters the scene in verse 6. Who is He, how is He described, and how did you feel when He showed up?

___

6. What did you learn about who Jesus is in this lesson?

___

7. In the space below, record your takeaway from Revelation 4:5–5:14 and any questions you have that remain unanswered.

___

DIGGING DEEPER (OPTIONAL)

Should you choose to dig deeper, complete the following Digging Deeper section. Each meeting will open with discussion of what you've learned and observed in Scripture, and this section will prepare you for that discussion.

In a two-column graphic organizer, record what you observe in each passage and the questions you have about it. Things to look for: Who is speaking? To whom is he speaking? What does he say about God? Jesus? The church? Individual believers? What do readers of this text stand to gain?

Revelation

Scripture Passage: Read Revelation 5:8–14

Scripture Passage: Ezekiel 11:16–20

Therefore say, "Thus says the Lord GOD, 'Though I had removed them far away among the nations and though I had scattered them among the countries, yet I was a sanctuary for them a little while in the countries where they had gone.'" Therefore say, "Thus says the Lord GOD, 'I will gather you from the peoples and assemble you out of the countries among which you have been scattered, and I will give you the land of Israel.'" When they come there, they will remove all its detestable things and all its abominations from it. And I will give them one heart, and put a new spirit within them. And I will take the heart of stone out of their flesh and give them a heart of flesh, that they may walk in My statutes and keep My ordinances and do them. Then they will be My people, and I shall be their God.

Scripture Passage: John 16:33

These things I have spoken to you, so that in Me you may have peace. In the world you have tribulation, but take courage; I have overcome the world.

Scripture Passage: 1 John 2:14

I have written to you, fathers, because you know Him who has been from the beginning. I have written to you, young men, because you are strong, and the word of God abides in you, and you have overcome the evil one.

Scripture Passage: Hebrews 2:14–15

Therefore, since the children share in flesh and blood, He Himself likewise also partook of the same, that through death He might render powerless him who had the power of death, that is, the devil, and might free those who through fear of death were subject to slavery all their lives.

Scripture Passage: Acts 10:42

And He ordered us to preach to the people, and solemnly to testify that this is the One who has been appointed by God as Judge of the living and the dead.

REVELATION 4:5–8; 5:1–14

Scripture Passage: Isaiah 2:12–22

For the LORD of hosts will have a day of reckoning against everyone who is proud and lofty and against everyone who is lifted up, that he may be abased. And it will be against all the cedars of Lebanon that are lofty and lifted up, against all the oaks of Bashan, against all the lofty mountains, against all the hills that are lifted up, against every high tower, against every fortified wall, against all the ships of Tarshish and against all the beautiful craft. The pride of man will be humbled and the loftiness of men will be abased; and the LORD alone will be exalted in that day, but the idols will completely vanish. Men will go into caves of the rocks and into holes of the ground before the terror of the LORD and the splendor of His majesty, when He arises to make the earth tremble. In that day men will cast away to the moles and the bats their idols of silver and their idols of gold, which they made for themselves to worship, in order to go into the caverns of the rocks and the clefts of the cliffs before the terror of the LORD and the splendor of His majesty, when He arises to make the earth tremble. Stop regarding man, whose breath of life is in his nostrils; for why should he be esteemed?

A LITTLE DEEPER...

1. In Ezekiel 11:16–20, we read something we see repeated in Scripture: God will replace hearts of stone with hearts of flesh. How have you heard this teaching applied? Now that you read it in context, what is God promising?

_____

_____

_____

2. Many times, when verses are used out of context, they're used to make theologically incorrect claims. In the case of hearts of stone replaced by hearts of flesh, do you think the associated popular teaching is theologically correct or incorrect? Explain your answer.

_____

_____

_____

3. Romans 8:37 teaches us that in Christ we are more than conquerors. We are more than overcomers. Review the passages included here about overcoming. What exactly have we overcome, and how have we been able to do so?

_____

4. In Isaiah 2, we read that God will humble the proud in spectacular fashion. When you consider this passage in conjunction with what we read in Revelation 5, what is the sin of pride? Why are humans so prone to commit sins of pride? And why will God not allow our pride to go unpunished?

SESSION TWENTY-THREE

Revelation 5:1–14

> ***Remember the Golden Rule:*** *When the plain sense of Scripture makes common sense, we seek no other sense.*

Video Twenty-Three

Topical overview: Additional unpacking of John's vision in Revelation 5. Beginning to build background for Revelation 6.

Learning goals: Recognize Jesus and His authority as Judge of the whole earth. Understand the roles of those present in the throne room.

CORE QUESTIONS

Before watching video twenty-three, read Revelation 5:1–14. Use the two-column graphic organizer to help you organize your thoughts. Discuss your observations as a group.

As you watch the video, complete the following section. For many, reading the questions before watching the video will aid their understanding of the video content.

1. What is the purpose of John's description of a land deed?

_____

_____

_____

Revelation

2. Who had the authority to break seals on a land deed?

3. What are the qualifications for being a mediator between God and man in the case of this land deed agreement?

4. What specifically qualifies Jesus to act as mediator and judge?

5. How does John convey Jesus and His authority to rule on earth?

6. How has Jesus made Himself worthy to judge the world?

7. What role do the prayers of the saints play in God's throne room?

8. What is the role of a priest, and how are we priests?

9. Why can chapter six be frustrating?

10. What is the significance of the quoted portion of Isaiah 2? Who is the audience for the events of Revelation 6?

DISCUSSION QUESTIONS

1. What did you learn about who Jesus is in this session? Who God is? Who we are?

2. Review the significance of the "book" in God's hands being a land deed. How do we know this is a land deed? What is the deed to? Who are the parties involved? Why does He give it to Jesus? Why seven seals?

Revelation

3. Discuss what it means for believers to be a "kingdom of priests." What does that look like practically?

_____

_____

_____

4. The next session will continue building background information for understanding Revelation 6. We'll be reading passages from all over Scripture. Have you been surprised by the interconnectedness of Scripture as a whole with Revelation? Why or why not?

_____

_____

_____

5. In the space below, record your takeaway from Revelation 5 and any questions you have that remain unanswered.

_____

_____

_____

DIGGING DEEPER (OPTIONAL)

Should you choose to dig deeper, complete the following Digging Deeper section. Each meeting will open with discussion of what you've learned and observed in Scripture, and this section will prepare you for that discussion.

In a two-column graphic organizer, record what you observe in each passage and the questions you have about it. Things to look for: Who is speaking? To whom is he speaking? What does he say about God? Jesus? The church? Individual believers? What do readers of this text stand to gain?

Scripture Passage: Jeremiah 30:4–9

> Now these are the words which the LORD spoke concerning Israel and concerning Judah: "For thus says the LORD, 'I have heard a sound of terror, of dread, and there is no peace. Ask now, and see if a male can give birth. Why do I see every man with his hands on his loins, as a woman

REVELATION 5:1–14

in childbirth? And why have all faces turned pale? Alas! for that day is great, there is none like it; and it is the time of Jacob's distress, but he will be saved from it. It shall come about on that day,' declares the LORD of hosts, 'that I will break his yoke from off their neck and will tear off their bonds; and strangers will no longer make them their slaves. But they shall serve the LORD their God and David their king, whom I will raise up for them.'"

Scripture Passage: Deuteronomy 29:10–15; 30:1–8

You stand today, all of you, before the LORD your God: your chiefs, your tribes, your elders and your officers, even all the men of Israel, your little ones, your wives, and the alien who is within your camps, from the one who chops your wood to the one who draws your water, that you may enter into the covenant with the LORD your God, and into His oath which the LORD your God is making with you today, in order that He may establish you today as His people and that He may be your God, just as He spoke to you and as He swore to your fathers, to Abraham, Isaac, and Jacob. Now not with you alone am I making this covenant and this oath, but both with those who stand here with us today in the presence of the LORD our God and with those who are not with us here today. ...

So it shall be when all of these things have come upon you, the blessing and the curse which I have set before you, and you call them to mind in all nations where the LORD your God has banished you, and you return to the LORD your God and obey Him with all your heart and soul according to all that I command you today, you and your sons, then the LORD your God will restore you from captivity, and have compassion on you, and will gather you again from all the peoples where the LORD your God has scattered you. If your outcasts are at the ends of the earth, from there the LORD your God will gather you, and from there He will bring you back. The LORD your God will bring you into the land which your fathers possessed, and you shall possess it; and He will prosper you and multiply you more than your fathers. Moreover the LORD your God will circumcise your heart and the heart of your descendants, to love the LORD your God with all your heart and with all your soul, so that you may live. The LORD your God will inflict all these curses on your enemies and on those who hate you, who persecuted you. And you shall again obey the LORD, and observe all His commandments which I command you today.

Scripture Passage: Leviticus 26:1–4, 14–18, 40–46

You shall not make for yourselves idols, nor shall you set up for yourselves an image or a sacred pillar, nor shall you place a figured stone in your land to bow down to it; for I am the LORD your God. You shall keep My sabbaths and reverence My sanctuary; I am the LORD. If you walk in My statutes and keep My commandments so as to carry them out, then I shall give you rains in their season, so that the land will yield its produce and the trees of the field will bear their fruit. ...

But if you do not obey Me and do not carry out all these commandments, if, instead, you reject My statutes, and if your soul abhors My ordinances so as not to carry out all My commandments, and so break My covenant, I, in turn, will do this to you: I will appoint over you a sudden terror, consumption and fever that will waste away the eyes and cause the soul to pine away; also, you will sow your seed uselessly, for your enemies will eat it up. I will set My face against you so that you will be struck down before your enemies; and those who hate you will rule over you, and you will flee when no one is pursuing you. If also after these things you do not obey Me, then I will punish you seven times more for your sins. ...

If they confess their iniquity and the iniquity of their forefathers, in their unfaithfulness which they committed against Me, and also in their acting with hostility against Me—I also was acting with hostility against them, to bring them into the land of their enemies—or if their uncircumcised heart becomes humbled so that they then make amends for their iniquity, then I will remember My covenant with Jacob, and I will remember also My covenant with Isaac, and My covenant with Abraham as well, and I will remember the land. For the land will be abandoned by them, and will make up for its sabbaths while it is made desolate without them. They, meanwhile, will be making amends for their iniquity, because they rejected My ordinances and their soul abhorred My statutes. Yet in spite of this, when they are in the land of their enemies, I will not reject them, nor will I so abhor them as to destroy them, breaking My covenant with them; for I am the LORD their God. But I will remember for them the covenant with their ancestors, whom I brought out of the land of Egypt in the sight of the nations, that I might be their God. I am the LORD. These are the statutes and ordinances and laws which the LORD established between Himself and the sons of Israel through Moses at Mount Sinai.

Scripture Passage: Galatians 3:10–14, 19–24

For as many as are of the works of the Law are under a curse; for it is written, "CURSED IS EVERYONE WHO DOES NOT ABIDE BY ALL THINGS WRITTEN IN THE BOOK OF THE LAW, TO PERFORM THEM." Now that no one is justified by the Law before God is evident; for, "THE RIGHTEOUS MAN SHALL LIVE BY FAITH." However, the Law is not of faith; on the contrary, "HE WHO PRACTICES THEM SHALL LIVE BY THEM." Christ redeemed us from the curse of the Law, having become a curse for us—for it is written, "CURSED IS EVERYONE WHO HANGS ON A TREE"—in order that in Christ Jesus the blessing of Abraham might come to the Gentiles, so that we would receive the promise of the Spirit through faith. …

Why the Law then? It was added because of transgressions, having been ordained through angels by the agency of a mediator, until the seed would come to whom the promise had been made. Now a mediator is not for one party only; whereas God is only one. Is the Law then contrary to the promises of God? May it never be! For if a law had been given which was able to impart life, then righteousness would indeed have been based on law. But the Scripture has shut up everyone under sin, so that the promise by faith in Jesus Christ might be given to those who believe. But before faith came, we were kept in custody under the law, being shut up to the faith which was later to be revealed. Therefore the Law has become our tutor to lead us to Christ, so that we may be justified by faith.

Scripture Passage: Romans 11:25–27

For I do not want you, brethren, to be uninformed of this mystery—so that you will not be wise in your own estimation—that a partial hardening has happened to Israel until the fullness of the Gentiles has come in; and so all Israel will be saved; just as it is written, "THE DELIVERER WILL COME FROM ZION, HE WILL REMOVE UNGODLINESS FROM JACOB. THIS IS MY COVENANT WITH THEM, WHEN I TAKE AWAY THEIR SINS."

REVELATION 5:1–14

A LITTLE DEEPER...

1. Explain the balance between faith and the Law as you understand it. Use Scripture to support your answer.

_____

_____

_____

2. Spend some time reading about the Jewish Diaspora. Jewishvirtuallibrary.org is an excellent resource. You'll also find several reliable resources (.org and .edu are generally better) in a quick internet search. Compare what you learned about the historical movement of the Jewish people to what God has promised in Leviticus and Deuteronomy. What do you observe?

_____

_____

_____

3. In Matthew 5:17–18, Jesus says, "Do not think that I came to abolish the Law or the Prophets; I did not come to abolish but to fulfill. For truly I say to you, until heaven and earth pass away, not the smallest letter or stroke shall pass from the Law until all is accomplished." Given what we've learned up to this point, what do you think Jesus means when He says He's come to fulfill rather than abolish the Law?

_____

_____

_____

SESSION TWENTY-FOUR

Covenants and Consequences

> ***Remember the Golden Rule:*** *When the plain sense of Scripture makes common sense, we seek no other sense.*

Video Twenty-Four

Topical overview: National covenants and national consequences.
Learning goals: Explore the balance between faith and the Law when it comes to Jews and their covenant relationship with God.

Core Questions

Before watching video twenty-four, review the Digging Deeper Scripture passages from Session Twenty-Three. Use the two-column graphic organizer to help you organize your thoughts. Discuss your observations as a group.

As you watch the video, complete the following section. For many, reading the questions before watching the video will aid their understanding of the video content.

1. Who is the focus of the Tribulation, despite its affecting the whole world and rightly so?

_____

_____

_____

2. What pattern do we see emerging from these Old Testament passages?

___

3. How will God preserve a portion of Israel without breaking the Law?

___

Israel's covenant with God is national, collective, multigenerational, and comprehensive. Every Jew present that day in Deuteronomy and every Jew born since is bound to abide by the terms of the Law.

4. What do the blessings of obedience outlined in Leviticus 26 mirror?

___

5. What does it mean for the covenant to be national in nature?

___

It's obvious the nation couldn't uphold every bit of the Law, but they still agreed to it.

6. From what point of view do we need to understand the events of the Tribulation?

___

7. How do Jews escape the penalties of the Law encompassed in the Tribulation?

8. How does Jesus's first coming, effectively for the Gentiles, avoid being an abandonment of His people, the Jews?

DISCUSSION QUESTIONS

1. Do you struggle to believe that God keeps His promises? Why or why not?

2. Before this session, how familiar were you with the promises God afforded His people? Are you surprised by anything you've learned in this session?

3. What is the balance between faith and the Law? For Gentiles? For Israel?

4. Have you struggled with God's administering consequences for sin? How does it affect you to know that despite the Law being clearly unachievable in its entirety, Israel still agreed as a nation to uphold it?

_____

_____

_____

5. In this session, Pastor Armstrong discussed that God's covenant is all-or-nothing. How is this consistent with what you know of God's character? Where else in Scripture do we find evidence of this?

_____

_____

_____

6. In the space below, record your takeaway from Session Twenty-Four and any questions you have that remain unanswered.

_____

_____

_____

DIGGING DEEPER (OPTIONAL)

Should you choose to dig deeper, complete the following Digging Deeper section. Each meeting will open with discussion of what you've learned and observed in Scripture, and this section will prepare you for that discussion.

In a two-column graphic organizer, record what you observe in each passage and the questions you have about it. Things to look for: Who is speaking? To whom is he speaking? What does he say about God? Jesus? The church? Individual believers? What do readers of this text stand to gain?

Scripture Passage: Matthew 24:1–8

Jesus came out from the temple and was going away when His disciples came up to point out the temple buildings to Him. And He said to them, "Do you not see all these things? Truly I say to you, not one stone here will be left upon another, which will not be torn down." As He was sitting on the Mount of Olives, the disciples came to Him privately, saying, "Tell us, when will these things happen, and what will be the sign of Your coming, and of the end of the age?" And Jesus answered and said to them, "See to it that no one misleads you. For many will come in My name, saying, 'I am the Christ,' and will mislead many. You will be hearing of wars and rumors of wars. See that you are not frightened, for those things must take place, but that is not yet the end. For nation will rise against nation, and kingdom against kingdom, and in various places there will be famines and earthquakes. But all these things are merely the beginning of birth pangs."

Scripture Passage: Luke 21:7–9

They questioned Him, saying, "Teacher, when therefore will these things happen? And what will be the sign when these things are about to take place?" And He said, "See to it that you are not misled; for many will come in My name, saying, 'I am He,' and, 'The time is near.' Do not go after them. When you hear of wars and disturbances, do not be terrified; for these things must take place first, but the end does not follow immediately."

A LITTLE DEEPER...

1. In these passages, we read the teaching of Jesus Himself about the end times. What are the signs He describes here?

_____

_____

_____

2. Christ compares these signs to birth pains. When you consider the signs He gives throughout history, why might have Christ have used the analogy of birth pains to describe the coming of the end?

_____

_____

_____

3. What teaching, if any, have you heard to the effect that "this is the end" or that we are presently enduring the Tribulation? Given the words of Jesus above, what should

the response of the faithful be to such teaching?

_____

_____

_____

SESSION TWENTY-FIVE

Signs of the End of the Age Part One

Remember the Golden Rule: When the plain sense of Scripture makes common sense, we seek no other sense.

Video Twenty-Five

Topical overview: Signs of the end of the age.
Learning goals: Recognize the justification for this particular interpretation of the Olivet discourse. Prepare background knowledge for the study of Revelation 6.

CORE QUESTIONS

Before watching video twenty-five, read Matthew 24:1–8 and Luke 21:7–9. Use the two-column graphic organizer to help you organize your thoughts. Discuss your observations as a group.

As you watch the video, complete the following section. For many, reading the questions before watching the video will aid their understanding of the video content.

1. What is the purpose of the Tribulation?

_____

_____

_____

2. What is the event is always imminent, that no one knows the day or the hour?

_____

3. How do we know the rapture occurs prior to the Tribulation? Why is the church exempt?

4. The end of the church age is unknowable. The beginning of the Tribulation is knowable and signaled by the establishment of a covenant on earth. Are there signs of the coming of the end of the age?

5. What did the disciples mean when they asked Jesus for the time of His coming?

6. What two features do scholars who misinterpret these passages look over?

7. What are we *not* to look for?

8. How can we be certain we will not miss Jesus's second coming?

9. When the disciples asked about the end of the age, what specific period of time are they asking about?

DISCUSSION QUESTIONS

1. Compare some of what you've heard about the end times to what you learned in this session. When you apply the filter of "birth pangs"—increasing severity and frequency over time but same sort of cyclical pains—what do you notice about modern end times teaching?

2. In general, the Bible is very intentional about describing things in terms both of what they are but also of what they are *not*. Jesus holds to this pattern in His teaching on the end times. What are *not* signs of the end times, and how do people often misinterpret them?

3. Titus 2:11–13 teaches us, "For the grace of God has appeared, bringing salvation to all men, instructing us to deny ungodliness and worldly desires and to live sensibly, righteously and godly in the present age, looking for the blessed hope and the appearing of the glory of our great God and Savior, Christ Jesus." We wait on Jesus and watch for signs of His coming. What does that look like for us practically? How are we supposed

SIGNS OF THE END OF THE AGE PART ONE

to live in light of what we're learning?

_____

_____

_____

4. In the space below, record your takeaway from Session Twenty-Five and any questions you have that remain unanswered.

_____

_____

_____

DIGGING DEEPER (OPTIONAL)

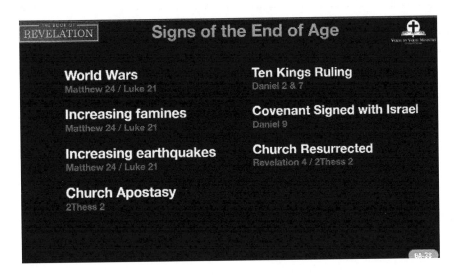

Should you choose to dig deeper, complete the following Digging Deeper section. Each meeting will open with discussion of what you've learned and observed in Scripture, and this section will prepare you for that discussion.

In a two-column graphic organizer, record what you observe in each passage and the questions you have about it. Things to look for: Who is speaking? To whom is he speaking? What does he say about God? Jesus? The church? Individual believers? What do readers of this text stand to gain?

Read the passages on the image provided above (Matthew 24, Luke 21, 2 Thessalonians 2, Daniel 2 and 7, Daniel 9, and Revelation 4. Pay specific attention to any details these passages give about their respective signs. Use the graphic organizer to help organize your thoughts.

A LITTLE DEEPER...

1. Every generation has thought their generation to be worse than the one before it. When you look at these signs as outlined in Scripture through the lens of "birth pangs" compared to what you know of the world, what do you find?

_____

_____

_____

2. How does knowing that this present time in history falls near (from God's perspective) the end of the age of Gentiles make you feel? How are we to live in light of this knowledge? Use Scripture to support your answer.

_____

_____

_____

SESSION TWENTY-SIX

Signs of the End of the Age Part Two

Remember the Golden Rule: When the plain sense of Scripture makes common sense, we seek no other sense.

Video Twenty-Six

Topical overview: Signs of the end of the age.
Learning goals: Assimilate historical fact as it relates to signs of the end.

CORE QUESTIONS

Before watching video twenty-six, review Matthew 24:1–8, Like 21:7–9, and the Scripture passages from Digging Deeper in Session Twenty-Five. Use the two-column graphic organizer to help you organize your thoughts. Discuss your observations as a group.

As you watch the video, complete the following section. For many, reading the questions before watching the video will aid their understanding of the video content.

1. How is "nation against nation" different from "wars and rumors of wars?"

___

2. What makes a sign-worthy famine?

___

3. The final sign is earthquakes. Summarize what you learned about the trends of earthquakes.

4. What new sign do we learn of in Ezekiel 20?

5. What sign do we learn of in Malachi 4?

6. What is a critical element of the beginning of the Tribulation?

We are somewhere in the transitional period between the age of the Gentiles and the beginning of the Tribulation. The church can be removed at any point in the indefinite future, and from then on, things will likely move quickly.

DISCUSSION QUESTIONS

1. Review the nine signs of the times. Prior to this session, were you aware of the global trends mentioned?

_____
_____
_____

2. When considering the two (relatively) natural phenomena that serve as signs of the end times (earthquakes and famine) consider all the factors involved in these events. What causes earthquakes? What causes famine? When you consider the precipitating factors of these signs, what do you learn about the God who controls it all?

_____
_____
_____

3. Consider the role technology plays in the creation and intensification of the three signs of the times. What Old Testament principle do we see clearly at work here (Genesis 50:20)? As humankind advances, led primarily by unbelievers, we hurtle headlong toward fulfilling the truth laid out in God's word.

_____
_____
_____

4. Review Elijah's exit from this world in 2 Kings 2. We learn his return is a sign of the end in Malachi 4. Where in the New Testament do we learn that this expectation is already established among the Jewish people by the first century? Use Scripture to support your answer.

_____
_____
_____

5. A critical element of Daniel's seventieth seven is a return of the Jewish people (as a whole) to orthodox Old Testament-style worship. Part of Isaiah's return will be to call the Jewish people back to orthodoxy. What do you know of modern Judaism?

_____

_____

_____

6. In the space below, record your takeaway from Session Twenty-Six and any questions you have that remain unanswered.

_____

_____

_____

Digging Deeper (Optional)

Should you choose to dig deeper, complete the following Digging Deeper section. Each meeting will open with discussion of what you've learned and observed in Scripture, and this section will prepare you for that discussion.

In a two-column graphic organizer, record what you observe in each passage and the questions you have about it. Things to look for: Who is speaking? To whom is he speaking? What does he say about God? Jesus? The church? Individual believers? What do readers of this text stand to gain?

Scripture Passage: Read Revelation 6: 1–4

Scripture Passage: Daniel 9:26–27

Then after the sixty-two weeks the Messiah will be cut off and have nothing, and the people of the prince who is to come will destroy the city and the sanctuary. And its end will come with a flood; even to the end there will be war; desolations are determined. And he will make a firm covenant with the many for one week, but in the middle of the week he will put a stop to sacrifice and grain offering; and on the wing of abominations will come one who makes desolate, even until a complete destruction, one that is decreed, is poured out on the one who makes desolate.

Scripture Passage: 1 John 2:22, 4:3

Who is the liar but the one who denies that Jesus is the Christ? This is the antichrist, the one who denies the Father and the Son. ...

And every spirit that does not confess Jesus is not from God; this is the spirit of the antichrist, of which you have heard that it is coming, and now it is already in the world.

Scripture Passage: 2 John 7

For many deceivers have gone out into the world, those who do not acknowledge Jesus Christ as coming in the flesh. This is the deceiver and the antichrist.

Scripture Passage: 2 Thessalonians 2:3–9

Let no one in any way deceive you, for it will not come unless the apostasy comes first, and the man of lawlessness is revealed, the son of destruction, who opposes and exalts himself above every so-called god or object of worship, so that he takes his seat in the temple of God, displaying himself as being God. Do you not remember that while I was still with you, I was telling you these things? And you know what restrains him now, so that in his time he will be revealed. For the mystery of lawlessness is already at work; only he who now restrains will do so until he is taken out of the way. Then that lawless one will be revealed whom the Lord will slay with the breath of His mouth and bring to an end by the appearance of His coming; that is, the one whose coming is in accord with the activity of Satan, with all power and signs and false wonders.

A LITTLE DEEPER...

1. We've read the word *desolate* many times in conjunction with the physical land of Israel. What is the definition of *desolate*, and how do you see this word as being applicable to what has occurred in the physical land of Israel throughout history?

_____

_____

_____

2. What is the difference between the spirit of the antichrist (the mystery of lawlessness) and the Antichrist (the man of lawlessness)? What restrains the man of lawlessness, and how do we see the spirit of lawlessness at work in the world?

_____

REVELATION

_____

_____

3. In these passages, what details do we learn about the time of Tribulation (look for specific events and general social conditions)? List them below.

_____

_____

_____

SESSION TWENTY-SEVEN

Revelation 6:1–4

> ***Remember the Golden Rule:*** *When the plain sense of Scripture makes common sense, we seek no other sense.*

Video Twenty-Seven

Topical overview: First seal judgment: the white horse and its rider. Second seal judgment: the red horse and its rider.

Learning goals: Identify the rider of the first horse and the rider of the second horse. Understand the symbolism of the details in the first two seal judgments. Recognize the roles of Christ and of the Antichrist in the first two judgments.

CORE QUESTIONS

Before watching video twenty-seven, read Revelation 6:1–4. Use the two-column graphic organizer to help you organize your thoughts. Discuss your observations as a group.

As you watch the video, complete the following section. For many, reading the questions before watching the video will aid their understanding of the video content.

Revelation 6:1–2

1. How can the Tribulation be broken down into sections?

_____

_____

Revelation

2. What is the popular term for what happens with the first four seals?

_____

_____

_____

3. In the first seal—the white horse—who is the unnamed rider (Daniel 9:27)?

_____

_____

_____

4. Summarize the symbolism surrounding the white horse and its rider.

_____

_____

_____

5. What do we know about the Antichrist?

_____

_____

_____

6. What restrains Satan and therefore the Antichrist?

_____

_____

_____

Revelation 6:3–4

1. The second seal- the red horse- who is the rider, and what does the horse represent?

_____

_____

_____

2. Despite the havoc the Antichrist will bring, who is in control?

DISCUSSION QUESTIONS

1. In this session, we're introduced to the concept of antichrists, the *spirit* of the antichrist, and *the* Antichrist. Discuss what each of these things mean and review the scriptures used to explain the difference (See Digging Deeper in Session Twenty-Six).

2. Before this session, what did you know of the Antichrist, and how has this session affected your understanding?

3. How does the Holy Spirit restrain Satan and his Antichrist? What is the role God gives each of us as individual believers in this grand design? How does realizing our role in this greater story affect you?

4. Review what you've learned about who the Antichrist will be and what he will do. What is your reaction to the knowledge that while we may hypothesize this man's identity, we will never see him in his role as the Antichrist?

6. As you begin to unpack what exactly the apocalypse entails and learn of those who have roles to play in it, how do you feel at this moment, at the precipice of truly diving in? Take some time as a group to speak truth into these feelings. Use Scripture to encourage one another.

7. In the space below, record your takeaway from Revelation 6:1–4 and any questions you have that remain unanswered.

DIGGING DEEPER (OPTIONAL)

Should you choose to dig deeper, complete the following Digging Deeper section. Each meeting will open with discussion of what you've learned and observed in Scripture, and this section will prepare you for that discussion.

In a two-column graphic organizer, record what you observe in each passage and the questions you have about it. Things to look for: Who is speaking? To whom is he speaking? What does he say about God? Jesus? The church? Individual believers? What do readers of this text stand to gain?

Scripture Passage: Read Revelation 6:5–8

A LITTLE DEEPER...

1. In popular understanding, the four horsemen of the apocalypse are considered to be 4 separate entities, regardless of whether they represent literal or figurative men. Pastor Armstrong has presented the interpretation that the horseman is actually a single man- the Antichrist- and his succession of horses represent the progression of his career. The first two stages of his power indicated a rise to power by brokering peace in the world and then subsequently starting World War III. What will he accomplish in these

latter two stages of his career?

___

2. Is this interpretation of a single, literal rider on a succession of figurative horses new to you? What is your response?

___

3. Do a little research—how much is a denarius, and what meaning is associated with the symbol of scales? Use Scripture to support your answer where possible.

___

SESSION TWENTY-EIGHT

Revelation 6:5–8

> ***Remember the Golden Rule:*** *When the plain sense of Scripture makes common sense, we seek no other sense.*

Video Twenty-Eight

Topical overview: Third and fourth seal judgments.
Learning goals: Understand the cumulative impact of the first four seal judgments.

CORE QUESTIONS

Before watching video twenty-eight, read Revelation 6:5–8. Use the two-column graphic organizer to help you organize your thoughts. Discuss your observations as a group.

As you watch the video, complete the following section. For many, reading the questions before watching the video will aid their understanding of the video content.

Overview

1. What is the purpose for studying Revelation?

_____

_____

_____

Revelation 6:5–6

1. What is the symbolism associated with a black horse and scales?

2. Summarize what you've learned about the denarius and its value.

3. While the Antichrist acts in the world for these things to occur, who is the driving force behind all of these occurrences?

4. What is a possible significance of the exclusion of wine and oil from the inflation?

Revelation 6:7–8

1. How does this horse and rider depiction break the pattern, and what is the significance?

2. What is the significance of the ashen horse?

3. What are the deaths mentioned in verse 8 a culmination of?

Discussion Questions

1. Think about who will remain to live through the Tribulation. The end result of the first four seals is the death of a full 25% of those people. Pastor Armstrong pointed out that despite God being the driving force behind this judgment, He is still good, and He is still working for good through the turmoil. How can this be true?

2. Remember what Pastor Armstrong discussed at the beginning of this session: the church will not be present for these events, so why endeavor to understand them?

3. Spend the rest of the time with your group in prayer. These first four seal judgments present a sober picture of what the world will be like in the absence of the church and the Holy Spirit. Pray that Jesus would grow His church. While such growth hastens this end, pray for more souls to escape such trouble. Pray for the souls who will endure this trouble that they will realize what they missed and choose Jesus before it's too late. Pray for specific people you know need Him. Pray for believers at work among the nations. Pray for your own heart and repent of sin. Pray for all believers to stand firm as the days grow increasingly evil. Pray particularly for brothers and sisters enduring active

persecution. God listens to the prayers of His people; those very prayers are the incense in His throne room. Offer the weight of what we've learned to the Lord and allow Him to guide you forward in peace.

4. In the space below, record your takeaway from Revelation 6:5–8 and any questions you have that remain unanswered.

DIGGING DEEPER (OPTIONAL)

Should you choose to dig deeper, complete the following Digging Deeper section. Each meeting will open with discussion of what you've learned and observed in Scripture, and this section will prepare you for that discussion.

In a two-column graphic organizer, record what you observe in each passage and the questions you have about it. Things to look for: Who is speaking? To whom is he speaking? What does he say about God? Jesus? The church? Individual believers? What do readers of this text stand to gain?

Scripture Passage: Read Revelation 6:9–17

Scripture Passage: Daniel 7:24–27

> As for the ten horns, out of this kingdom ten kings will arise; and another will arise after them, and he will be different from the previous ones and will subdue three kings. He will speak out against the Most High and wear down the saints of the Highest One, and he will intend to make alterations in times and in law; and they will be given into his hand for a time, times, and half a time. But the court will sit for judgment, and his dominion will be taken away, annihilated and destroyed forever. Then the sovereignty, the dominion and the greatness of all the kingdoms under the whole heaven will be given to the people of the saints of the Highest One; His kingdom will be an everlasting kingdom, and all the dominions will serve and obey Him.

A Little Deeper...

1. Compare the fifth and sixth seal judgments to the first–fourth seal judgments. How are they similar? How are they different?

_____

_____

_____

2. In the discussion of the fifth seal, we learn that the number of martyrs isn't yet complete. What is a martyr, and why is it significant that there will be more in the Tribulation? How does this realization impact you?

_____

_____

_____

3. At this point, what is your understanding of the sixth seal judgment? What will happen on the earth?

_____

_____

_____

SESSION TWENTY-NINE

Revelation 6:9–17

> ***Remember the Golden Rule:*** *When the plain sense of Scripture makes common sense, we seek no other sense.*

Video Twenty-Nine

Topical overview: Fifth and sixth seal judgments.
Learning goals: Recognize the impact of the fifth and sixth seal judgments. Differentiate between those whose deaths are represented in the fourth and fifth seal judgments. Understand the relationship between the first six seal judgments as they appear chronologically.

CORE QUESTIONS

Before watching video twenty-nine, read Revelation 6:9–17. Use the two-column graphic organizer to help you organize your thoughts. Discuss your observations as a group.

As you watch the video, complete the following section. For many, reading the questions before watching the video will aid their understanding of the video content.

1. Historically, who served as a birth pang to the Antichrist?

_____

_____

_____

2. How does seal five break the pattern?

3. Why is it significant that the saints in Revelation 6:9 are disembodied souls?

4. Why isn't John invited to "look" in the discussion of the fifth seal?

5. What is the significance of the dead from the fourth seal going to Hades?

6. Where do the dead from the fifth seal end up?

7. What do the dead in both the fourth and fifth seals have in common?

8. What does the sixth seal represent, and how does the sixth seal represent a shift in

the nature of the judgments on earth?

9. Summarize what you've learned of the physical calamities in the sixth seal judgment.

10. What happens among people as a result of supernatural judgment?

DISCUSSION QUESTIONS

1. The sixth seal represents cataclysmic natural events of supernatural proportions. These events lead those enduring them to acknowledge the wrath of both God the Father and Jesus the Lamb. What might it take for people to reach the same conclusion today as a result of natural phenomena?

2. Where do you hypothesize the saints represented in the fifth seal came from?

3. Review the physical calamities of the sixth seal judgment. What will happen to the earth? Remember, God destroyed the physical earth once via flood. Why did He do it?

REVELATION

How are the events in the sixth seal similar and/or different than the judgment we see in Genesis 6?

_____

_____

_____

4. Review Session Twenty-Nine. How do seals five and six differ from seals one through four?

_____

_____

_____

5. In the space below, record your takeaway from Revelation 6:9–17 and any questions you have that remain unanswered.

_____

_____

_____

DIGGING DEEPER (OPTIONAL)

Should you choose to dig deeper, complete the following Digging Deeper section. Each meeting will open with discussion of what you've learned and observed in Scripture, and this section will prepare you for that discussion.

In a two-column graphic organizer, record what you observe in each passage and the questions you have about it. Things to look for: Who is speaking? To whom is he speaking? What does he say about God? Jesus? The church? Individual believers? What do readers of this text stand to gain?

Scripture Passage: Read Revelation 7:1–17

REVELATION 6:9–17

Scripture Passage: 2 Corinthians 1:21–22

Now He who establishes us with you in Christ and anointed us is God, who also sealed us and gave us the Spirit in our hearts as a pledge.

Scripture Passage: Matthew 24:9–14

Then they will deliver you to tribulation, and will kill you, and you will be hated by all nations because of My name. At that time many will fall away and will betray one another and hate one another. Many false prophets will arise and will mislead many. Because lawlessness is increased, most people's love will grow cold. But the one who endures to the end, he will be saved. This gospel of the kingdom shall be preached in the whole world as a testimony to all the nations, and then the end will come.

A LITTLE DEEPER...

1. The editor's heading preceding Revelation 7 is "An Interlude." What is an interlude? And how does the content of Revelation 7 serve as an interlude between Revelation 6 and 8?

_____

_____

_____

2. What does 2 Corinthians teach about the sealing of the believer? And what is the significance of the bondservants in Revelation 7 being sealed in the same way?

_____

_____

_____

3. What are the angels in Revelation 7 doing? Considering what you've learned about seal judgments one through six, where on these timelines might you place the interlude of Revelation 7?

_____

_____

4. What are your thoughts at this point on the 144,000 witnesses at this point?

SESSION THIRTY

Revelation 7:1–17

> ***Remember the Golden Rule:*** *When the plain sense of Scripture makes common sense, we seek no other sense.*

Video Thirty

Topical overview: The 144,000 witnesses and the multitude.

Learning goals: Identify the 144,000 witnesses, the "great multitude," and the significance of each. Understand the role of persecution in the Tribulation. Recognize how Revelation 7 fits within the seal judgments.

CORE QUESTIONS

Before watching video thirty, read Revelation 7:1–17. Use the two-column graphic organizer to help you organize your thoughts. Discuss your observations as a group.

As you watch the video, complete the following section. For many, reading the questions before watching the video will aid their understanding of the video content.

1. Is the book of Revelation organized chronologically?

_____
_____
_____

2. How does John indicate overlapping content?

_____

3. How do we know the events of chapter 7 precede the events of chapter 6?

4. What is the significance of the detail that the Lord stopped the wind and therefore the natural water source?

5. What is the significance of the term *bondservant* in the New Testament?

6. What is the significance of sealing?

7. Who are the 144,000 witnesses?

8. Which tribe is missing from among the 144,000 and why?

REVELATION 7:1–17

9. What do we learn about the 144,000 from Revelation 14?

10. What is the significance of 12?

11. Is this number of 144,000 symbolic?

12. What is the purpose of the 144,000 witnesses?

13. There's a cause-and-effect relationship between the salvation of the 144,000 and the multitude of every tribe, tongue, and nation. What is it?

14. Where do these saints in heaven come from?

- Matthew 24:14 is connected to this image in Revelation 7.
- Revelation 6 and 7 occurred *concurrently*.

15. How do the judgments all fit together?

DISCUSSION QUESTIONS

1. Prior to this session, what had you heard about the 144,000 witnesses?

2. Review what you've learned about who the 144,000 witnesses will be and what they will do.

3. Do you see any symmetry between the way God made His name known in the Old Testament and the way He does so here in Revelation 7? If so, what do you observe?

4. In this session, we also learned that faith in Christ will be both a death sentence and a blessing in the Tribulation. How is this true?

_____
_____
_____

5. We live in a world where persecution, even to the point of martyrdom, happens, but it's not necessarily widespread. Even still, we live with the same tension that faith in Christ is both a death sentence and the ultimate blessing. How so? Use Scripture to support your answer.

_____
_____
_____

6. Spend some of your group time tonight in prayer for the persecuted church. Their suffering is but a foretaste of what's to come in the Tribulation, but that doesn't make it any less. Pray that our brothers and sisters who suffer for their faith will be able to stand strong until the end and that God will guide the peace of their hearts as they serve Him with boldness in treacherous times.

_____
_____
_____

7. In the space below, record your takeaway from Revelation 7 and any questions you have that remain unanswered.

_____
_____
_____

DIGGING DEEPER (OPTIONAL)

Should you choose to dig deeper, complete the following Digging Deeper section. Each meeting will open with discussion of what you've learned and observed in Scripture, and this section will prepare you for that discussion.

Revelation

In a two-column graphic organizer, record what you observe in each passage and the questions you have about it. Things to look for: Who is speaking? To whom is he speaking? What does he say about God? Jesus? The church? Individual believers? What do readers of this text stand to gain?

Scripture Passage: Read Revelation 8:1–7

Scripture Passage: Daniel 12:1

Now at that time Michael, the great prince who stands guard over the sons of your people, will arise. And there will be a time of distress such as never occurred since there was a nation until that time; and at that time your people, everyone who is found written in the book, will be rescued.

Scripture Passage: Exodus 9:23–24

Moses stretched out his staff toward the sky, and the LORD sent thunder and hail, and fire ran down to the earth. And the LORD rained hail on the land of Egypt. So there was hail, and fire flashing continually in the midst of the hail, very severe, such as had not been in all the land of Egypt since it became a nation.

A LITTLE DEEPER...

1. What patterns or themes do you notice in the verses above?

_____
_____
_____

2. Who again are the saints under the altar, and what is the significance of their prayers being added to the censer the angel throws to the earth?

_____
_____
_____

3. What did Daniel foretell for the Jews of Israel in 12:1?

_____

4. How might the trumpet judgments follow the pattern of the plagues in Egypt in Exodus?

5. For future reference, write out the plagues God sends to set His people free in Exodus.

SESSION THIRTY-ONE

Revelation 8:1–7

> ***Remember the Golden Rule:*** *When the plain sense of Scripture makes common sense, we seek no other sense.*

Video Thirty-One

Topical overview: Interrelationship between seal and trumpet judgments. First trumpet judgment.

Learning goals: Identify the pattern or relationship (typology) between the plagues of Exodus and the trumpet judgments of Revelation 8–9. Recognize the evidence of God's mercy amidst the judgment of Tribulation.

CORE QUESTIONS

Before watching video thirty-one, read Revelation 8:1–7. Use the two-column graphic organizer to help you organize your thoughts. Discuss your observations as a group.

As you watch the video, complete the following section. For many, reading the questions before watching the video will aid their understanding of the video content.

Overview

The big picture view of Revelation Chapters 1–7 is that God is accomplishing both *mercy* and *judgment* simultaneously.

1. Why might chapter 7 be placed at this point in Revelation?

2. What is the opening of the seventh seal?

Revelation 8:1–4

1. What is the significance of the moment of silence in heaven?

2. Why is the length of the pause vague?

3. Trumpet judgments one through three affect what?

4. Trumpet judgments four through six, the woe judgments, affect what?

Revelation

5. What is the symbolism associated with a trumpet?

6. At what point of the Tribulation will the seal and trumpet judgments play out?

Revelation 8:5–7

1. How does God warn the world that the trumpet judgments are coming?

2. What is the first trumpet judgment?

3. What do the judgments of Revelation loosely resemble?

REVELATION 8:1–7

DISCUSSION QUESTIONS

1. In the sessions leading up to this point, we've repeatedly read of God providing warnings to people. He is not a God who is silent by any means. What sort of warnings do we see from God in our time, and how are they similar and/or different from the ways He's given warnings in the past and will give warnings in the future?

_____
_____
_____

2. Where do you see the theme of God's mercy throughout the book of Revelation? As we continue our study, how can we maintain our awareness that God is both merciful and just? As we explain the truths we find here in Revelation, how can we clearly convey God's mercy and justice amid the complete upheaval of Tribulation?

_____
_____
_____

3. Review the timeline once again of when each judgment happens in the context of the seven-year period of Tribulation. What do you notice about the progression of judgments we've learned of so far? Is there a pattern? If so, what is it?

_____
_____
_____

4. In the space below, record your takeaway from Revelation 8:1–7 and any questions you have that remain unanswered.

_____
_____
_____

Revelation

Digging Deeper (Optional)

Should you choose to dig deeper, complete the following Digging Deeper section. Each meeting will open with discussion of what you've learned and observed in Scripture, and this section will prepare you for that discussion.

In a two-column graphic organizer, record what you observe in each passage and the questions you have about it. Things to look for: Who is speaking? To whom is he speaking? What does he say about God? Jesus? The church? Individual believers? What do readers of this text stand to gain?

Scripture Passage: Read Revelation 8:8–13; 9:1–6

A Little Deeper...

1. Review the plagues you summarized for Digging Deeper in Session Thirty. How do the trumpet judgments here line up with the plagues of Exodus?

_____

_____

_____

2. Each of the trumpet judgments affecting the physical earth do so in three different ways to one third of the earth. As Pastor Armstrong has mentioned, both patterns and specifics are cause for closer attention. Do some research. What might the significance of three and one-third be? Use Scripture to support your answer if possible.

_____

_____

_____

3. Notice the pause in judgment represented by the eagle flying in "midheaven." What does God take time to do, yet again?

_____

_____

_____

4. Consider the implications of the first three trumpet judgments. What is the state of the earth by the time that eagle takes its flight in 8:13?

_____

_____

_____

SESSION THIRTY-TWO

Revelation 8:8–13; 9:1–6

> ***Remember the Golden Rule:*** *When the plain sense of Scripture makes common sense, we seek no other sense.*

Video Thirty-Two

Topical overview: Third and fourth trumpet judgments.
Learning goals: Recognize God's plan for the world in the judgments on the physical land/ sea.

CORE QUESTIONS

Before watching video thirty-two, read Revelation 8:8–13; 9:1–6. Use the two-column graphic organizer to help you organize your thoughts. Discuss your observations as a group.

As you watch the video, complete the following section. For many, reading the questions before watching the video will aid their understanding of the video content.

Revelation 8:8–9

1. What meaning should we apply to the idea that one-third of the earth is destroyed?

_____

_____

_____

2. What does the fact that John doesn't quite have the words to describe what he sees hit the water in Revelation 8:8 indicate?

3. How do we know this particular passage is literal?

4. Why is God cutting off patches of the globe?

5. What does Pastor Armstrong interpret to be that first chunk of land and water to be affected by the first and second trumpet judgments?

Revelation 8:10–11

1. What would the best interpretation of this "falling star" named Wormwood be?

2. Who sends Wormwood, and what is his purpose?

3. What does Wormword accomplish?

Revelation 8:12

1. How do we interpret this reduction of light by one-third?

2. What is the result of this particular judgment in a physical sense?

3. What's the overall theme of these judgments in their effects on the earth?

Revelation 8:13

1. What does the term *mid-heaven* signify?

2. So there's an eagle flying in outer space speaking a message. What is the figurative significance of this aspect of the vision?

Discussion Questions

1. There is an interesting interplay in this session between John's vision of the trumpet judgments and our modern understanding of science. What do you observe about the relationship between these two things, and what is your response to this interpretive principle (applying modern science to understand figurative Scripture)?

2. The trumpet judgments involve making the majority of the earth uninhabitable by various means. Reflect on your knowledge of how people have moved throughout history. Is this forced migration consistent with the character of God we see displayed throughout Scripture and history at large? Why or why not? Use Scripture to support your answer where possible. What does this teach you about the nature of God and how He works within the world?

3. Review the discussion of Wormwood in Revelation 8:10–11. Here we see even the demons working within God's larger plan. Does this comfort or alarm you? Why? As a group, explore what these two verses in particular teach us about who God is and how He works.

4. Review the discussion about the Hebrew understanding of "heavens." Ensure that all in the group grasp this Hebrew convention and its effect on John's expression of His vision. Can anyone recollect other places in Scripture where this same convention is used? If your group has time, consider exploring some of these passages to understand the Hebrew convention of numbered heavens.

_____

_____

_____

5. In the space below, record your takeaway from Revelation 8:8–13, 9:1–6 and any questions you have that remain unanswered.

_____

_____

_____

DIGGING DEEPER (OPTIONAL)

Should you choose to dig deeper, complete the following Digging Deeper section. Each meeting will open with discussion of what you've learned and observed in Scripture, and this section will prepare you for that discussion.

In a two-column graphic organizer, record what you observe in each passage and the questions you have about it. Things to look for: Who is speaking? To whom is he speaking? What does he say about God? Jesus? The church? Individual believers? What do readers of this text stand to gain?

Scripture Passage: Read Revelation 9:1–12

Scripture Passage: Job 33:26

Then he will pray to God, and He will accept him, that he may see His face with joy, and He may restore His righteousness to man.

REVELATION 8:1–7

Scripture Passage: 2 Peter 2:4–5, 9

For if God did not spare angels when they sinned, but cast them into hell and committed them to pits of darkness, reserved for judgment; and did not spare the ancient world, but preserved Noah, a preacher of righteousness, with seven others, when He brought a flood upon the world of the ungodly. ...

Then the Lord knows how to rescue the godly from temptation, and to keep the unrighteous under punishment for the day of judgment.

Scripture Passage: Luke 8:30–31, 12:4–5

And Jesus asked him, "What is your name?" And he said, "Legion"; for many demons had entered him. They were imploring Him not to command them to go away into the abyss. ...

"I say to you, My friends, do not be afraid of those who kill the body and after that have no more that they can do. But I will warn you whom to fear: fear the One who, after He has killed, has authority to cast into hell; yes, I tell you, fear Him!"

A LITTLE DEEPER...

1. What do you notice in these passages that supports the interpretation of fallen stars in Revelation 9 as demons sent to do God's bidding?

_____

_____

_____

2. Research the torment a scorpion inflicts on a man? What happens? Is there a range of afflictions depending on the species of scorpion? If so, focus your search to species common to the Middle East and Mediterranean. What sort of pain do the scorpions that live there inflict?

_____

_____

_____

3. Notice the limitations of the afflictions God authorizes in this fifth trumpet judgment. How is this judgment prefigured by a plague of Exodus, and what do both the limitations and the commission tell you about the God who authorizes them?

4. Research the significance of the names Abaddon and Apollyon. What do they signify?

5. Consider the physical description of the locusts. If you are so inclined, attempt to illustrate what the text describes. If not, attempt to find an accurate depiction online. Bring the image(s) to your next group meeting to share if time allows.

SESSION THIRTY-THREE

Revelation 9:1–12

> ***Remember the Golden Rule:*** *When the plain sense of Scripture makes common sense, we seek no other sense.*

Video Thirty-Three

Topical overview: Fifth trumpet judgment.
Learning goals: Process the purely supernatural nature of this judgment. Expand understanding of *sheol.*

CORE QUESTIONS

Before watching video thirty-three, read Revelation 9:1–12. Use the two-column graphic organizer to help you organize your thoughts. Discuss your observations as a group.

As you watch the video, complete the following section. For many, reading the questions before watching the video will aid their understanding of the video content.

Revelation 9:1–6

1. What entity executes the fifth trumpet judgment?

_____

_____

_____

Revelation

2. To what is Abaddon given the key?

3. Summarize what you learn about the three sections of sheol.

4. What are some significant guidelines about the commission of the demons in this judgment?

5. What is the significance of the sealed in this judgment and who does it include?

6. Summarize the torment these demons will cause.

Revelation 9:7–11

1. How do we know these "locusts" are supernatural rather than natural?

2. Why is this passage often misinterpreted?

3. So what do we know to be true of these locusts?

4. How does God reveal His grace in this judgment?

5. What is the symbolic significance of the number five?

Discussion Questions

1. For a time in this session, Pastor Armstrong explains the need some feel to attach a known quantity to the supernatural things described in Revelation as in the example of Apache helicopters being the means by which the fifth trumpet judgment is accomplished. Sometimes, we must accept Scripture as truth, even (especially) when it's bizarre, and just rest in faith that some of it is beyond our understanding. Do you struggle with this need to attach known quantities to the supernatural elements of Scripture? Why or why not? Use this time to build each other up in faith. Scripture is real and true, even when it's bizarre and beyond our complete understanding.

2. The fifth trumpet judgment is literally a glimpse of hell on earth. By God's grace and Christ's blood, as sealed believers, this description of judgment is the closest we will ever come to experiencing such ourselves. How does this knowledge affect your witness? Spend some time praying for the unbelievers in your lives that they may escape such judgment by way of repentance.

3. Review what you've learned about *sheol.* Who is there at this present moment? What is it like? Where is it? Who is present at the moment of Revelation 9? Have you previously learned about the Hebrew concepts of Abraham's bosom and sheol? If so, share what you'd learned previously and how that knowledge is enriched by what you learned in this session.

4. If anyone in your group completed the artistic portion of Digging Deeper from Session Thirty-Two, take some time to enjoy their depictions of the "locusts" of Revelation 9.

5. In the space below, record your takeaway from Revelation 9:1–12 and any questions you have that remain unanswered.

REVELATION 9:1–12

DIGGING DEEPER (OPTIONAL)

Should you choose to dig deeper, complete the following Digging Deeper section. Each meeting will open with discussion of what you've learned and observed in Scripture, and this section will prepare you for that discussion.

In a two-column graphic organizer, record what you observe in each passage and the questions you have about it. Things to look for: Who is speaking? To whom is he speaking? What does he say about God? Jesus? The church? Individual believers? What do readers of this text stand to gain?

Scripture Passage: Read Revelation 9:13–19

Scripture Passage: Joel 2:1–4

> Blow a trumpet in Zion, and sound an alarm on My holy mountain! Let all the inhabitants of the land tremble, for the day of the LORD is coming; surely it is near, a day of darkness and gloom, a day of clouds and thick darkness. As the dawn is spread over the mountains, so there is a great and mighty people; there has never been anything like it, nor will there be again after it to the years of many generations. A fire consumes before them and behind them a flame burns. The land is like the garden of Eden before them but a desolate wilderness behind them, and nothing at all escapes them. Their appearance is like the appearance of horses; and like war horses, so they run.

A LITTLE DEEPER...

1. When you read these two passages together, how do they enrich your understanding of each passage on its own? What is your response to the realization that God might show the same vision of the end to two men separated by thousands of years, inspire their writing about what they were shown, to the benefit of Gentiles who come thousands of years behind them?

_____

_____

_____

2. Do some research. What is the significance of the River Euphrates? Where is it, and how might this physical location play a role in this sixth trumpet judgment?

_____

_____

Revelation

3. Make a prediction: at this point, do you feel this judgment's description is more literal or more symbolic? How might this destruction play out within the world?

4. An army of 200 million destroys another one-third of the world's population. Do some research. About how many people physically reside in the Middle Eastern region? Imagine a world physically limited to this location whose inhabitants have survived the horrendous events of the judgments up to this point (seals and trumpets). How would you describe it?

SESSION THIRTY-FOUR

Revelation 9:13–19

> ***Remember the Golden Rule:*** *When the plain sense of Scripture makes common sense, we seek no other sense.*

Video Thirty-Four

Topical overview: Sixth trumpet judgment.

Learning goals: Acquire criteria for discerning the accuracy of prophetic interpretation by modern readers. Begin unpacking the destruction outlined in the sixth trumpet judgment.

CORE QUESTIONS

Before watching video thirty-four, read Revelation 9:13–19. Use the two-column graphic organizer to help you organize your thoughts. Discuss your observations as a group.

As you watch the video, complete the following section. For many, reading the questions before watching the video will aid their understanding of the video content.

Overview

1. What is the fifth trumpet judgment?

_____

_____

_____

REVELATION

Revelation 9:13–19

The woe judgments are sequential and do not overlap.

1. Who is the chief actor in the events of this woe, and how does this affect the interpretation of this passage?

2. What do we know about the bound angels released in verse 14?

3. What interpretive principle does the numbered horsemen remind us of?

4. Summarize what we can learn about the horsemen?

5. About what does Joel 2 prophesy?

6. What do the demon army do to the land?

7. Describe the Eden connection to the sixth trumpet judgment.

DISCUSSION QUESTIONS

1. Again, we have a judgment accomplished by demonic forces at God's direction. What does this teach us about God?

2. How does the prophecy of Joel 2 enrich our understanding of the sixth trumpet judgment of Revelation 9?

3. Again, we have an often-misinterpreted passage by those who attempt to apply symbolism where there is none. John clearly describes some sort of supernatural horse chimera, and Joel leaves it as *like* a horse. These passages are a clear example of Pastor Armstrong's rule of thumb about when to seek out symbolism in Scripture. How would you describe his interpretive rule, and do you feel comfortable applying it in your own independent Scripture reading? Why or why not?

4. Review the physical destruction of the physical world by judgment up through the sixth trumpet. What has become uninhabitable (desolate) and how? Remember God's purpose: shrinking the inhabitable portion of the world down to just the Middle East. How must this army have accomplished its task of destruction given its starting point at the Euphrates River? Get out a world map if necessary to help you visualize.

_____

_____

_____

5. In the space below, record your takeaway from Revelation 9:13–19 and any questions you have that remain unanswered.

_____

_____

_____

DIGGING DEEPER (OPTIONAL)

Should you choose to dig deeper, complete the following Digging Deeper section. Each meeting will open with discussion of what you've learned and observed in Scripture, and this section will prepare you for that discussion.

In a two-column graphic organizer, record what you observe in each passage and the questions you have about it. Things to look for: Who is speaking? To whom is he speaking? What does he say about God? Jesus? The church? Individual believers? What do readers of this text stand to gain?

Scripture Passage: Joel 2:5–11

> *With a noise as of chariots they leap on the tops of the mountains, like the crackling of a flame of fire consuming the stubble, like a mighty people arranged for battle. Before them the people are in anguish; all faces turn pale. They run like mighty men, they climb the wall like soldiers; and they each march in line, nor do they deviate from their paths. They do not crowd each other, they march everyone in their path; when they burst through the defenses, they do not break ranks. They rush on the city, they run on the wall; they climb into the houses, they enter through the windows like a thief. Before them the earth quakes, the heavens tremble, the sun and the moon grow dark and the stars lose their brightness. The LORD utters His voice before His army; surely His camp is very great, for strong is the one who carries out His word. The day of the LORD is indeed great and very awesome, and who can endure it?*

REVELATION 9:13–19

Scripture Passage: Read Revelation 9:20–21, 10:1–7

Scripture Passage: Romans 2:4

Or do you think lightly of the riches of His kindness and tolerance and patience, not knowing that the kindness of God leads you to repentance?

A Little Deeper…

1. The passage from Joel 2 further describes the behavior of the demon army from the sixth trumpet judgment. Read Joel's words closely. How would you describe this army and their actions?

_____

_____

_____

2. Consider the import of John's brief statement in Revelation 9:20–21. Who is left alive at this point? In combination with what we learn of God in Romans 2:4, why might John have included this statement here, just before we begin to learn of the last stages of judgment, the bowl judgments?

_____

_____

_____

3. Considering this portion of history is a literal seven years, and considering what those who have survived up until this point have experienced, what can we assume about their character?

_____

_____

_____

4. Notice who's missing on the earth as of Revelation 9:20–21. What group of people have been exterminated between the fifth and seventh trumpet judgments, and to what two causes can we attribute their physical demise?

_____

_____

_____

5. Revelation 10 offers a bit of a break from mayhem and destruction. Considering the brief overview we've seen of the Tribulation timeline, why might John have been instructed to seal up the last set of judgments at this point?

_____

_____

_____

SESSION THIRTY-FIVE

Revelation 9:20–10:7

> ***Remember the Golden Rule:*** *When the plain sense of Scripture makes common sense, we seek no other sense.*

Video Thirty-Five

Topical overview: Behavior of the demon army of the sixth trumpet judgment. Introduction to mid-Tribulation.

Learning goals: Assimilate what has happened to the people of earth and the physical earth in the first half (three and a half years) of Tribulation.

CORE QUESTIONS

Before watching video thirty-five, read Revelation 9:20–10:7. Use the two-column graphic organizer to help you organize your thoughts. Discuss your observations as a group.

As you watch the video, complete the following section. For many, reading the questions before watching the video will aid their understanding of the video content.

Overview

1. What is the latter half of Joel's prophecy confirmation of?

_____

_____

_____

2. What is the significance of one-third of the population dying?

3. For the unbeliever, what is the death of those they know and love?

Revelation 9:20–21

1. Is the Lord using this suffering to bring more to faith?

2. How many of those who survived this sixth judgment are faithful?

3. What does this judgment reveal about the nature of calamity in relationship to salvation?

4. What is faith based in?

5. Summarize what has happened in the first three and a half years of Tribulation.

6. How do we know the events of mid-Tribulation are so important?

7. In the sense of how time passes, how do we understand the events contained in Revelation 10–15?

Revelation 10:1–7

1. How do we know this angel is good and not fallen?

2. How do we determine the identity of this particular angel, and what passage of Scripture does it allude to?

Discussion Questions

1. Discuss all the heavenly and supernatural actors we've learned about in the events of Tribulation so far. Does this fit with what you've heard or known about end times events prior to this study? Why or why not? How does this understanding of events compare to popular descriptions of the end times (whether religious in nature or otherwise)?

_____

_____

_____

2. Address any questions about the timing of events in the first half of Tribulation and those of mid-Tribulation as discussed in this session.

_____

_____

_____

3. At the conclusion of the sixth trumpet judgment, who is left on earth, and do they have hope of salvation and repentance? Given what you know about the events to come, why is this detail significant, and what does it teach us about God?

_____

_____

_____

4. In the space below, record your takeaway from Revelation 9:20–10:7 and any questions you have that remain unanswered.

_____

_____

_____

Digging Deeper (Optional)

Should you choose to dig deeper, complete the following Digging Deeper section.

Each meeting will open with discussion of what you've learned and observed in Scripture, and this section will prepare you for that discussion.

In a two-column graphic organizer, record what you observe in each passage and the questions you have about it. Things to look for: Who is speaking? To whom is he speaking? What does he say about God? Jesus? The church? Individual believers? What do readers of this text stand to gain?

Scripture Passage: Daniel 12:1–11

"Now at that time Michael, the great prince who stands guard over the sons of your people, will arise. And there will be a time of distress such as never occurred since there was a nation until that time; and at that time your people, everyone who is found written in the book, will be rescued. Many of those who sleep in the dust of the ground will awake, these to everlasting life, but the others to disgrace and everlasting contempt. Those who have insight will shine brightly like the brightness of the expanse of heaven, and those who lead the many to righteousness, like the stars forever and ever. But as for you, Daniel, conceal these words and seal up the book until the end of time; many will go back and forth, and knowledge will increase." Then I, Daniel, looked and behold, two others were standing, one on this bank of the river and the other on that bank of the river. And one said to the man dressed in linen, who was above the waters of the river, "How long will it be until the end of these wonders?" I heard the man dressed in linen, who was above the waters of the river, as he raised his right hand and his left toward heaven, and swore by Him who lives forever that it would be for a time, times, and half a time; and as soon as they finish shattering the power of the holy people, all these events will be completed. As for me, I heard but could not understand; so I said, "My lord, what will be the outcome of these events?" He said, "Go your way, Daniel, for these words are concealed and sealed up until the end time. Many will be purged, purified and refined, but the wicked will act wickedly; and none of the wicked will understand, but those who have insight will understand. From the time that the regular sacrifice is abolished and the abomination of desolation is set up, there will be 1,290 days."

Scripture Passage: Matthew 24:21

For then there will be a great tribulation, such as has not occurred since the beginning of the world until now, nor ever will.

Scripture Passage: Read Revelation 10:8–11

A Little Deeper...

1. This passage in Revelation is not the only time in which someone in the Bible is told to eat words or books. What is the significance of such instruction? What does the passage in Daniel 12 indicate is contained in the book? What is the significance of it tasting good on the way in and making his stomach upset once it settles?

_____

_____

_____

2. The passage in Daniel seems to indicate that righteous Jews will be rescued at this point and then the "power" of the "holy people" will be "shattered." Who might the holy people be, what might their power be, and what would it mean for this power to be shattered?

_____

_____

_____

SESSION THIRTY-SIX

Revelation 10:8–11

Remember the Golden Rule: When the plain sense of Scripture makes common sense, we seek no other sense.

Video Thirty-Six

Topical overview: Precipitating events to those marking the midpoint of Tribulation.

Learning goals: Understand the purpose and structure of the seven years of Tribulation. Explore the connection between Daniel 12 and Revelation 10.

CORE QUESTIONS

Before watching video thirty-six, read Daniel 12 and Revelation 10:8–11. Use the two-column graphic organizer to help you organize your thoughts. Discuss your observations as a group.

As you watch the video, complete the following section. For many, reading the questions before watching the video will aid their understanding of the video content.

Revelation 10 is intended to make a clear connection to Daniel 12 by those who've read and studied the Bible.

Daniel 12:1–9

1. What is the context for Daniel 12?

_____

_____

REVELATION

2. Who arises at the midpoint of Tribulation?

3. How do we know the second half of Tribulation will be worse than the first?

4. Who was the first and only (for a long time) to know what happens in the second half of the Tribulation?

5. When will Daniel's sealed prophecy be revealed?

Revelation 10:8–11

1. What is the little scroll the angel gives John?

2. When will the events of the little scroll take place?

_____

_____

_____

3. What is the significance of John eating the scroll, its taste, and how it sits in his stomach?

_____

_____

_____

As much as we struggle with the concept of judgment, we don't struggle with faithfulness. But in prophecy, those things go hand in hand.

4. What defines the midpoint of Tribulation?

_____

_____

_____

Chapters 11–14 describe the moment that covenant is broken and the effects of that single event.

DISCUSSION QUESTIONS

1. As the teaching points out in this session, there's no reason to assume John didn't physically eat the little scroll as this vision describes. Where else in Scripture do we find similar instructions to "eat" words and books? In those cases, what is the figurative meaning of this instruction to eat, and how does this enrich our understanding of John's physical experience in Revelation 10?

_____

_____

_____

REVELATION

2. In terms of plot and narrative structure, the midpoint of Tribulation might also be described as the climax of this apocalyptic narrative, the moment everything changes as the story moves on to its resolution. Take what we've learned up to this point of study and create a plot triangle as a group in the space below. Use the various timelines from the study to help you complete this task. [Helpful definitions: *exposition:* setting, background information, conflict—in this case, Revelation 1–3. *Inciting incident:* the specific event that kicks things off—in this case, the rapture. *Rising action:* events occurring after the inciting incident building toward the climax—in this case, chapters 4–10, the seal and trumpet judgments. *Climax:* the moment in which everything changes, in this case, mid-Tribulation—chapters 11–14. *Falling action:* events leading to the resolution; everything falls apart, or everything falls into place—in this case, chapters 15–22. *Resolution:* the conflict is resolved, and things wrap up to an end—in this case, Jesus wins and establishes His kingdom.]

_____

_____

_____

3. God reveals the end times events to Daniel, a faithful prophet in exile in Babylon. Daniel records them and leaves them in care of the archangel Michael who then delivers the events to John, a faithful disciple also in exile in the beginning of the last days, to reveal to the church to prepare them for the end. Discuss the similarities and differences in the callings of Daniel and John and explore the connection God created between the two men across centuries of time.

_____

_____

_____

4. In the space below, record your takeaway from Revelation 10:8–11 and any questions you have that remain unanswered.

_____

_____

_____

REVELATION 10:8–11

DIGGING DEEPER (OPTIONAL)

Should you choose to dig deeper, complete the following Digging Deeper section. Each meeting will open with discussion of what you've learned and observed in Scripture, and this section will prepare you for that discussion.

In a two-column graphic organizer, record what you observe in each passage and the questions you have about it. Things to look for: Who is speaking? To whom is he speaking? What does he say about God? Jesus? The church? Individual believers? What do readers of this text stand to gain?

Scripture Passage: Read Revelation 10:11–11:6

Scripture Passage: Daniel 12:7

> I heard the man dressed in linen, who was above the waters of the river, as he raised his right hand and his left toward heaven, and swore by Him who lives forever that it would be for a time, times, and half a time; and as soon as they finish shattering the power of the holy people, all these events will be completed.

Scripture Passage: Luke 21:24

> And they will fall by the edge of the sword, and will be led captive into all the nations; and Jerusalem will be trampled under foot by the Gentiles until the times of the Gentiles are fulfilled.

A LITTLE DEEPER…

1. What do we learn about the second half of Tribulation from these verses? What is happening in Jerusalem? Who is there, and what are they doing?

_____

_____

_____

2. What signals the end of the times of the Gentiles according to these verses? As we've discussed in previous sessions, what happens after the end of the times of the Gentiles?

_____

_____

SESSION THIRTY-SEVEN

Revelation 10:11–11:6

> ***Remember the Golden Rule:*** *When the plain sense of Scripture makes common sense, we seek no other sense.*

Video Thirty-Seven

Topical overview: Mid-Tribulation timeline and the two witnesses.
Learning goals: Discuss the interconnectivity of Scripture. Draw conclusions about the conditions in the physical land of Israel at mid-Tribulation.

CORE QUESTIONS

Before watching video thirty-seven, read Revelation 10:11–11:6. Use the two-column graphic organizer to help you organize your thoughts. Discuss your observations as a group.

As you watch the video, complete the following section. For many, reading the questions before watching the video will aid their understanding of the video content.

Overview

1. Who is the main character of Revelation 11–14?

_____

_____

_____

2. How do these mid-Tribulation chapters indicate that they refer to this midpoint?

3. Why does God have Daniel write the scroll that John is given to reveal?

4. In the sense of a timeline, how would we plot the mid-Tribulation events of Revelation 11–14?

Revelation 10:11–11:2

1. What do we know about the inhabitable portion of the world and its inhabitants?

2. What do we learn at the outset of chapter 11?

3. What are the three points of the instructions to not measure the Court of the Gentiles?

4. What's the significance of these things being true?

Revelation 11:3–6

1. Which two characters do we meet in this passage?

Discussion Questions

1. How does God make it clear that Revelation and Daniel are connected? How does this guide our interpretation of each individual book?

2. What three things do we learn from God's instructions to John in Revelation 10:11–11:2? As you review those things, discuss the effects of these three things on the people alive at this time.

REVELATION 10:11–11:6

3. The events of Revelation 11–14 happen relatively simultaneously at the midpoint of Daniel's seventieth seven, the three-and-a-half-year point. Which three characters will have roles of prominence in these events? What have you heard about these three prior to this study? What do we know about these three characters from what we've studied so far?

4. In the space below, record your takeaway from Revelation 10:11–11:6 and any questions you have that remain unanswered.

DIGGING DEEPER (OPTIONAL)

Should you choose to dig deeper, complete the following Digging Deeper section. Each meeting will open with discussion of what you've learned and observed in Scripture, and this section will prepare you for that discussion.

In a two-column graphic organizer, record what you observe in each passage and the questions you have about it. Things to look for: Who is speaking? To whom is he speaking? What does he say about God? Jesus? The church? Individual believers? What do readers of this text stand to gain?

Scripture Passage: Read Revelation 11:3–6.

Scripture Passage: Deuteronomy 19:15

A single witness shall not rise up against a man on account of any iniquity or any sin which he has committed; on the evidence of two or three witnesses a matter shall be confirmed.

Scripture Passage: Zechariah 4:1–14

Then the angel who was speaking with me returned and roused me, as a man who is awakened from his sleep. He said to me, "What do you see?" And I said, "I see, and behold, a lampstand all of gold with its bowl on the top of it, and its seven lamps on it with seven spouts belonging to each of the lamps which are on the top of it; also two olive trees by it, one on the right side of the bowl and the other on its left side." Then I said to the angel who was speaking with me saying, "What are these, my lord?" So the angel who was speaking with me answered and said to me, "Do you not know what these are?" And I said, "No, my lord." Then he said to me, "This is the word of the LORD to Zerubbabel saying, 'Not by might nor by power, but by My Spirit,' says the LORD of hosts. 'What are you, O great mountain? Before Zerubbabel you will become a plain; and he will bring forth the top stone with shouts of "Grace, grace to it!"'" Also the word of the LORD came to me, saying, "The hands of Zerubbabel have laid the foundation of this house, and his hands will finish it. Then you will know that the LORD of hosts has sent me to you. For who has despised the day of small things? But these seven will be glad when they see the plumb line in the hand of Zerubbabel—these are the eyes of the LORD which range to and fro throughout the earth." Then I said to him, "What are these two olive trees on the right of the lampstand and on its left?" And I answered the second time and said to him, "What are the two olive branches which are beside the two golden pipes, which empty the golden oil from themselves?" So he answered me, saying, "Do you not know what these are?" And I said, "No, my lord." Then he said, "These are the two anointed ones who are standing by the Lord of the whole earth."

A LITTLE DEEPER...

1. These passages illustrate some truths of Scripture that we've seen on multiple occasions: Scripture interprets itself, and God operates by His own principles, as we see here with the statute about having two or more witnesses being necessary to prove veracity. God could have called any number of witnesses to the temple during Tribulation, but He calls two. What does this teach you about who God is and how He works? What does this teach you about Scripture?

_____

_____

_____

2. Do some background research. Who is Zerubbabel, and why is he mentioned by Zechariah here?

_____

_____

_____

3. What do you make of the symbolism of the lampstand in this vision? The olive trees?

_____

_____

SESSION THIRTY-EIGHT

Revelation 11:3–6

Remember the Golden Rule: When the plain sense of Scripture makes common sense, we seek no other sense.

Video Thirty-Eight

Topical overview: Interpret Zechariah 4. Discuss the two witnesses.
Learning goals: Unpack the Scripture surrounding the two witnesses.

CORE QUESTIONS

Before watching video thirty-eight, read Revelation 11:3–6. Use the two-column graphic organizer to help you organize your thoughts. Discuss your observations as a group.

As you watch the video, complete the following section. For many, reading the questions before watching the video will aid their understanding of the video content.

1. What two things does John intentionally connect?

_____

_____

_____

2. What part of our Tribulation timeline describes the ministry of the two witnesses?

_____

3. What is the purpose of these two witnesses' ministry?

4. How are these witnesses described?

5. Who are these witnesses?

6. What do the oil and lampstand represent in Zechariah's vision?

7. What is the role of Zerubbabel in the vision?

8. Who are the two olive trees representing?

9. Why are the witnesses hated so much that they need supernatural self-defense?

10. What might these witnesses be preaching?

11. What is the role of these two witnesses in the overall story of Revelation?

DISCUSSION QUESTIONS

1. Have you heard of these two witnesses before? If so, share what you've heard. Compare these things to the truth of Scripture from this session. Do they hit or miss the mark?

2. In this session, Pastor Armstrong mentioned several wild interpretations of this passage in Revelation. How did Pastor Armstrong arrive at the interpretation he taught? What can we learn from this that we can apply to the interpretation of the whole of Scripture?

REVELATION

_____

_____

3. Review the role of the two witnesses in the overall story of Tribulation. God is very intentional in His calling and equipping of these two witnesses to carry out His purposes through their ministry. What does this teach you about who God is and how He works?

_____

_____

_____

4. Consider the balance between the power of the Holy Spirit and human actors as represented by the two olive trees and the lampstand in Zechariah 4. How do you see this principle at work in Scripture as a whole? How do you see consistency in the ways in which God accomplishes His will?

_____

_____

_____

5. In the space below, record your takeaway from Revelation 11:3–6 and any questions you have that remain unanswered.

_____

_____

_____

DIGGING DEEPER (OPTIONAL)

Should you choose to dig deeper, complete the following Digging Deeper section. Each meeting will open with discussion of what you've learned and observed in Scripture, and this section will prepare you for that discussion.

In a two-column graphic organizer, record what you observe in each passage and the questions you have about it. Things to look for: Who is speaking? To whom is he speaking? What does he say about God? Jesus? The church? Individual believers? What do readers of this text stand to gain?

REVELATION 11:3–6

Scripture Passage: Read Revelation 11:7–19

A LITTLE DEEPER...

1. What happens to the two witnesses, and how does it affect the others who remain on earth?

_____
_____
_____

2. How do the others on earth respond to their deaths? What does this tell you about the hearts of people in this day?

_____
_____
_____

3. The seventh trumpet is blown (remember, this seventh trumpet encompasses all seven bowl judgments we will read about after the mid-Tribulation section of Revelation). What happens?

_____
_____
_____

SESSION THIRTY-NINE

Revelation 11:7–19

> ***Remember the Golden Rule:*** *When the plain sense of Scripture makes common sense, we seek no other sense.*

Video Thirty-Nine

Topical overview: The two witnesses and their end.
Learning goals: Understand the ministry, purpose, and function of the two witnesses, and how their death reflects these aspects of their role.

Core Questions

Before watching video thirty-nine, read Revelation 11:7–19. Use the two-column graphic organizer to help you organize your thoughts. Discuss your observations as a group.

As you watch the video, complete the following section. For many, reading the questions before watching the video will aid their understanding of the video content.

Revelation 11:7–10

1. Summarize what we learn about the two witnesses in this section.

_____

_____

_____

2. What is the significance of the reference to Egypt and Sodom?

3. At this mid-Tribulation point, how would Jerusalem be described?

4. How does the world react to the witnesses' deaths?

5. What is the role of the "beast" in all this?

6. How are the two witnesses connected to the temple in this period?

Revelation 11:11–14

1. What happens to the two witnesses after three and a half days, and what is the significance of these events?

Revelation

2. Are the witnesses operating in the first or second half of the Tribulation?

_____
_____
_____

Note: Pastor Armstrong is emphasizing this point because it's directly addressing a popular interpretive misconception.

We know that there will be three woe judgments and then the Tribulation will come to an end.

Revelation 11:15–19

1. What does the seventh trumpet represent?

_____
_____
_____

2. Why might the saints in heaven be so excited about God's kingdom on earth?

_____
_____
_____

3. How does this section fit on our Tribulation timeline?

_____
_____
_____

Discussion Questions

1. In this lesson, we learn that Jerusalem has become like Sodom and Egypt, both depraved and idolatrous. Considering that for the first three and a half years of the Tribulation, the temple is restored and is in operation, how might this be?

_____

2. Can you imagine the whole world hating two men so much that they'd celebrate over their corpses for three whole days? What does it say about the people who remain on the earth at this time?

3. Discuss the ministry, purpose, and function of the two witnesses. What did God ordain for them and why? Can you think of other times in the Bible God has appointed people for such dramatic representation of Himself? Who comes to mind?

4. Some of the teaching alludes to a truth of modern society: we are very concerned with the timing of things, especially when it comes to the future. Pastor Armstrong has discussed several misguided interpretations of end times events and their timing. This concern extends beyond the Christian worldview and the Book of Revelation, too (y2k, the Mayan calendar, Nostradamus, horoscopes, palm reading, etc.). Why might it be that such a fascination with the "end" seems common to humanity? How does the world act on this fascination? How does God expect His people to act on this fascination?

5. In the space below, record your takeaway from Revelation 11:7–19 and any questions you have that remain unanswered.

Digging Deeper (Optional)

Should you choose to dig deeper, complete the following Digging Deeper section. Each meeting will open with discussion of what you've learned and observed in Scripture, and this section will prepare you for that discussion.

In a two-column graphic organizer, record what you observe in each passage and the questions you have about it. Things to look for: Who is speaking? To whom is he speaking? What does he say about God? Jesus? The church? Individual believers? What do readers of this text stand to gain?

Scripture Passage: Read Revelation 12:1–5

Scripture Passage: Psalm 2:7–9

I will surely tell of the decree of the LORD: He said to Me, "You are My Son, today I have begotten You. Ask of Me, and I will surely give the nations as Your inheritance, and the very ends of the earth as Your possession. You shall break them with a rod of iron, You shall shatter them like earthenware."

Scripture Passage: Genesis 37:5–10

Then Joseph had a dream, and when he told it to his brothers, they hated him even more. He said to them, "Please listen to this dream which I have had; for behold, we were binding sheaves in the field, and lo, my sheaf rose up and also stood erect; and behold, your sheaves gathered around and bowed down to my sheaf." Then his brothers said to him, "Are you actually going to reign over us? Or are you really going to rule over us?" So they hated him even more for his dreams and for his words. Now he had still another dream, and related it to his brothers, and said, "Lo, I have had still another dream; and behold, the sun and the moon and eleven stars were bowing down to me." He related it to his father and to his brothers; and his father rebuked him and said to him, "What is this dream that you have had? Shall I and your mother and your brothers actually come to bow ourselves down before you to the ground?"

Scripture Passage: Jeremiah 3:8

And I saw that for all the adulteries of faithless Israel, I had sent her away and given her a writ of divorce, yet her treacherous sister Judah did not fear; but she went and was a harlot also.

A Little Deeper...

1. Look up the word *sign* in the dictionary. Which definition applies to John's use of the word *sign* in Revelation 12? Can you think of other (real world, practical) examples of using the word *sign* in the same way?

_____

_____

_____

2. List out all the signs and symbols discussed in the quoted passages and write their meanings *as explained in these passages* next to them.

_____

_____

_____

SESSION FORTY

Revelation 12:1–5

> ***Remember the Golden Rule:*** *When the plain sense of Scripture makes common sense, we seek no other sense.*

Video Forty

Topical overview: What signs are and how to interpret them.
Learning goals: Identify the woman, child, and dragon in Revelation 12.

CORE QUESTIONS

Before watching video forty, read Revelation 12:1–5. Use the two-column graphic organizer to help you organize your thoughts. Discuss your observations as a group.

As you watch the video, complete the following section. For many, reading the questions before watching the video will aid their understanding of the video content.

Overview

1. What narrative function do the two witnesses serve in the storyline of the Tribulation?

___

2. What are the events of mid-Tribulation?

___

Revelation 12:1–5

1. How do we approach interpreting signs in Scripture?

2. What mistake do Bible students often make?

3. What are the two signs that open chapter 12, and how do we know they are in fact signs?

4. What do we learn about the son in verse 5?

5. What do we learn about the woman?

REVELATION

The first sign is the woman, Israel, giving birth to, or producing, the Messiah, Jesus.

6. Who is the red dragon, and what does he do?

___

DISCUSSION QUESTIONS

1. So far, what we've learned of the signs in chapter 12 is that they represent the metanarrative, or big picture view, of Scripture. What function might this vision of signs serve when positioned at the midpoint of Tribulation?

___

2. Review what signs are and how they're intended to be interpreted. Based on what we've seen so far in this study of Revelation, what would you say signs have in common with symbols, and how are they different?

___

3. Pastor Armstrong's example of misinterpreting the woman in Revelation 12 as Mary, mother of Jesus, clearly illustrates how interpretation divorced from context can lead to issues. This particular example illustrates how misinterpretation of even one portion can misdirect interpretation of the whole. How have you seen this principle to be true in other places of Scripture? What does the phrase "the whole counsel of Scripture" mean to you, and how can you practically apply the concept of consulting "the whole counsel of Scripture" to your life?

___

REVELATION 12:1–5

4. In the space below, record your takeaway from Revelation 12:1–5 and any questions you have that remain unanswered.

___

___

___

DIGGING DEEPER (OPTIONAL)

Should you choose to dig deeper, complete the following Digging Deeper section. Each meeting will open with discussion of what you've learned and observed in Scripture, and this section will prepare you for that discussion.

In a two-column graphic organizer, record what you observe in each passage and the questions you have about it. Things to look for: Who is speaking? To whom is he speaking? What does he say about God? Jesus? The church? Individual believers? What do readers of this text stand to gain?

Scripture Passage: Read Revelation 12:6–12

Scripture Passage: Daniel 7:7–8, 23–25

After this I kept looking in the night visions, and behold, a fourth beast, dreadful and terrifying and extremely strong; and it had large iron teeth. It devoured and crushed and trampled down the remainder with its feet; and it was different from all the beasts that were before it, and it had ten horns. While I was contemplating the horns, behold, another horn, a little one, came up among them, and three of the first horns were pulled out by the roots before it; and behold, this horn possessed eyes like the eyes of a man and a mouth uttering great boasts. ...

Thus he said: "The fourth beast will be a fourth kingdom on the earth, which will be different from all the other kingdoms and will devour the whole earth and tread it down and crush it. As for the ten horns, out of this kingdom ten kings will arise; and another will arise after them, and he will be different from the previous ones and will subdue three kings. He will speak out against the Most High and wear down the saints of the Highest One, and he will intend to make alterations in times and in law; and they will be given into his hand for a time, times, and half a time."

Scripture Passage: 2 Corinthians 4:3

And even if our gospel is veiled, it is veiled to those who are perishing.

Scripture Passage: Genesis 3:15

And I will put enmity between you and the woman, and between your seed and her seed; he shall bruise you on the head, and you shall bruise him on the heel.

Scripture Passage: Job 1:6–7

Now there was a day when the sons of God came to present themselves before the LORD, and Satan also came among them. The LORD said to Satan, "From where do you come?" Then Satan answered the LORD and said, "From roaming about on the earth and walking around on it."

A LITTLE DEEPER...

1. What time cues do you notice in the quoted passages, and what significance do those times have in our Tribulation timeline?

_____
_____
_____

2. What do you learn about the nature and activity of Satan from these passages?

_____
_____
_____

3. Remember: Where will we be when all of this is happening? What are we doing? What are we waiting for?

_____
_____
_____

4. Notice God hides the woman (Israel, the remnant) away for this final portion of the vision. The church and the Old Testament saints are in heaven, and the remnant is hidden away in the "wilderness." Who remains on earth at this point? What do these specific details teach you about who God is? About whom we are?

SESSION FORTY-ONE

Revelation 12:6–12

> ***Remember the Golden Rule:*** *When the plain sense of Scripture makes common sense, we seek no other sense.*

Video Forty-One

Topical overview: The war in heaven and the mid-Tribulation.
Learning goals: Understand the implications of the war in heaven for Satan, for the earth, and for those who believe in Christ.

CORE QUESTIONS

Before watching video forty-one, read Revelation 12:6–12. Use the two-column graphic organizer to help you organize your thoughts. Discuss your observations as a group.

As you watch the video, complete the following section. For many, reading the questions before watching the video will aid their understanding of the video content.

Overview

1. Summarize the big picture view of Scripture's story as explained in the beginning of video 41.

_____

_____

_____

2. What do the signs and symbols of this passage teach us about Satan?

3. Where is the symbol of ten horns explained?

4. What does Daniel's fourth beast represent?

Revelation 12 *Expands* on Daniel 7

1. What is the governing structure of the world at the midpoint of Tribulation?

2. Genesis 3:15 is the *protoevangelion*. What does this mean?

3. Satan is *not* omniscient, so he couldn't possibly know who the Messiah would be. So how did he approach his mission to thwart the Messiah and world redemption?

Revelation

_____

_____

Revelation 12:1–5 is the shortest overview of the whole Bible there is. It's the background for what comes next.

Revelation 12:6–12

1. What is the significance of 1,260 days?

_____

_____

_____

2. What happens to the nation of Israel at mid-Tribulation?

_____

_____

_____

3. Here we read about the heart of the mid-Tribulation moment. What is it?

_____

_____

_____

4. What does the passage in Job teach us about sin?

_____

_____

_____

5. Where is the only other place Satan could go after being barred from heaven?

_____

_____

6. What effect does this permanent banishment from heaven have on Satan?

DISCUSSION QUESTIONS

1. Reread Revelation 12:1–5. How is this the shortest story (summary) of the Bible you can possibly find?

2. What purpose does this vision of signs serve in the overall narrative of Revelation in general and chapter 12 in particular?

3. Review Pastor Armstrong's description of Satan's work throughout history. Have you ever thought of history from this perspective before? In retrospect, we can see the fingerprints of Satan just as clearly as we can the fingerprints of God. How do you see the same to be true of your own life?

4. Have you ever wondered why Satan tries so hard when the Bible clearly says Jesus wins? In light of Pastor Armstrong's teaching in this session, why do you think Satan tries (is trying) so hard to thwart God's plan? Did this teaching affect your estimation of Satan? If so, how?

5. Notice what happens to Israel in Revelation 12:6. Remember, where are the followers of Jesus and Old Testament saints at this point? What does this teach you about who God is, how He works, and who we are?

_____

_____

_____

6. In the space below, record your takeaway from Revelation 12:6–12 and any questions you have that remain unanswered.

_____

_____

_____

DIGGING DEEPER (OPTIONAL)

Should you choose to dig deeper, complete the following Digging Deeper section. Each meeting will open with discussion of what you've learned and observed in Scripture, and this section will prepare you for that discussion.

In a two-column graphic organizer, record what you observe in each passage and the questions you have about it. Things to look for: Who is speaking? To whom is he speaking? What does he say about God? Jesus? The church? Individual believers? What do readers of this text stand to gain?

Scripture Passage: Read Revelation 12:13–17

Scripture Passage: Exodus 19:3–4

> *Moses went up to God, and the LORD called to him from the mountain, saying, "Thus you shall say to the house of Jacob and tell the sons of Israel: 'You yourselves have seen what I did to the Egyptians, and how I bore you on eagles' wings, and brought you to Myself.'"*

Scripture Passage: Matthew 24:15–21

Therefore when you see the ABOMINATION OF DESOLATION which was spoken of through Daniel the prophet, standing in the holy place (let the reader understand), then those who are in Judea must flee to the mountains. Whoever is on the housetop must not go down to get the things out that are in his house. Whoever is in the field must not turn back to get his cloak. But woe to those who are pregnant and to those who are nursing babies in those days! But pray that your flight will not be in the winter, or on a Sabbath. For then there will be a great tribulation, such as has not occurred since the beginning of the world until now, nor ever will.

Scripture Passage: Isaiah 43:1, 13–17

But now, thus says the LORD, your Creator, O Jacob, and He who formed you, O Israel, "Do not fear, for I have redeemed you; I have called you by name; you are Mine!" ...

"Even from eternity I am He, and there is none who can deliver out of My hand; I act and who can reverse it?" Thus says the LORD your Redeemer, the Holy One of Israel, "For your sake I have sent to Babylon, and will bring them all down as fugitives, even the Chaldeans, into the ships in which they rejoice. I am the LORD, your Holy One, the Creator of Israel, your King." Thus says the LORD, who makes a way through the sea and a path through the mighty waters, who brings forth the chariot and the horse, the army and the mighty one (they will lie down together and not rise again; they have been quenched and extinguished like a wick).

Scripture Passage: Micah 2:10–13

Arise and go, for this is no place of rest because of the uncleanness that brings on destruction, a painful destruction. If a man walking after wind and falsehood had told lies and said, "I will speak out to you concerning wine and liquor," he would be spokesman to this people. I will surely assemble all of you, Jacob, I will surely gather the remnant of Israel. I will put them together like sheep in the fold; like a flock in the midst of its pasture they will be noisy with men. The breaker goes up before them; they break out, pass through the gate and go out by it. So their king goes on before them, and the LORD at their head.

A LITTLE DEEPER…

1. A clear theme among these passages is that of *rescue* combined with multiple references to the first Passover and the initial flight from Egypt. Refresh your memory of this story by reading Exodus 12–14, paying special attention to the manner in which the Israelites were to eat their Passover meal and to the theme of rescue throughout these chapters. Take note of your observations in the space below.

Revelation

2. There is a clear parallel between the first exodus and this last exodus. What connections do you notice?

3. The same God who rescued the Israelites in Exodus and who will rescue them from the Great Tribulation is the same God who rescues you and me from the schemes and snares of Satan. Do you have a story of God's rescue in your life? Share it in the space below.

SESSION FORTY-TWO

Revelation 12:13–17

> ***Remember the Golden Rule:*** *When the plain sense of Scripture makes common sense, we seek no other sense.*

Video Forty-Two

Topical overview: The remnant.

Learning goals: Identify who and who isn't included among the remnant. Hypothesize the location of the remnant's protection in the wilderness. Explore how and why Satan will act from the mid-Tribulation time until the end.

CORE QUESTIONS

Before watching video forty-two, read Revelation 12:13–17. Use the two-column graphic organizer to help you organize your thoughts. Discuss your observations as a group.

As you watch the video, complete the following section. For many, reading the questions before watching the video will aid their understanding of the video content.

Overview

1. Summarize Satan's response to his banishment from God's throne room.

_____

_____

_____

2. Why does God choose to banish Satan at this point?

3. Who is the target of Satan's aggression at this point, and how does he respond?

Revelation 12:13–17

1. Why does God rescue Israel?

2. What does the symbol of being borne on eagles' wings indicate?

3. Where does Israel go, who is included, and how do we know this?

4. Why is the second half of the Tribulation called the "Great Tribulation?"

5. Since Satan can't attack the preserved remnant, who does he attack?

6. Does Satan martyr *all* of the unbelieving Jews and believing Gentiles?

DISCUSSION QUESTIONS

1. Did this lesson challenge your understanding of the character (personality, nature) of God and/or Satan? If so, how? If not, why not?

2. God keeps His promises. How do we see this to be true in this lesson? What does God promise Israel? What does God promise you?

3. Review Pastor Armstrong's logic behind identifying the remnant's wilderness refuge as Petra. What do you know of Petra and the land around it? Has anyone in your group been there? If so, give them an opportunity to share with the group what it is like.

4. Think back through Satan's actions as described in this lesson. Do you see a pattern or theme, a driving characteristic motivating his actions? If so, what do you notice? Which scriptures support your observation of this trait?

_____

_____

_____

5. In the space below, record your takeaway from Revelation 12:13–17 and any questions you have that remain unanswered.

_____

_____

_____

DIGGING DEEPER (OPTIONAL)

Should you choose to dig deeper, complete the following Digging Deeper section. Each meeting will open with discussion of what you've learned and observed in Scripture, and this section will prepare you for that discussion.

In a two-column graphic organizer, record what you observe in each passage and the questions you have about it. Things to look for: Who is speaking? To whom is he speaking? What does he say about God? Jesus? The church? Individual believers? What do readers of this text stand to gain?

Scripture Passage: Read Revelation 13:1–2

Scripture Passage: Isaiah 37:31–32

> *The surviving remnant of the house of Judah will again take root downward and bear fruit upward. For out of Jerusalem will go forth a remnant and out of Mount Zion survivors. The zeal of the LORD of hosts will perform this.*

Scripture Passage: Romans 11:1–5

> *I say then, God has not rejected His people, has He? May it never be! For I too am an Israelite, a descendant of Abraham, of the tribe of Benjamin. God has not rejected His people whom He*

REVELATION 12:13–17

foreknew. Or do you not know what the Scripture says in the passage about Elijah, how he pleads with God against Israel? "Lord, THEY HAVE KILLED YOUR PROPHETS, THEY HAVE TORN DOWN YOUR ALTARS, AND I ALONE AM LEFT, AND THEY ARE SEEKING MY LIFE." But what is the divine response to him? "I HAVE KEPT for Myself SEVEN THOUSAND MEN WHO HAVE NOT BOWED THE KNEE TO BAAL." In the same way then, there has also come to be at the present time a remnant according to God's gracious choice.

Scripture Passage: Daniel 7:1–3

In the first year of Belshazzar king of Babylon Daniel saw a dream and visions in his mind as he lay on his bed; then he wrote the dream down and related the following summary of it. Daniel said, "I was looking in my vision by night, and behold, the four winds of heaven were stirring up the great sea. And four great beasts were coming up from the sea, different from one another."

A LITTLE DEEPER...

1. Look up and record the definition for the word *zeal*. The part of Isaiah 34 that says, "The zeal of the LORD of Hosts will do this," is a common refrain in the Old Testament. What would it mean for God to be zealous? What is He zealous about? How will His zeal accomplish the preservation of the remnant?

_____

_____

_____

2. Illustrate (or find an illustration of) the beast of Revelation 13. Considering what you've learned in this study so far, what does the beast of Revelation 13 bring to mind?

_____

_____

_____

3. Consider the role of water in Genesis (creation, the flood) and the ministry of Jesus (walking on water, calming the storm). Consider the difference in how larger bodies of water like seas are portrayed in the Bible as compared to moving fresh water (rivers and streams... consider the imagery in Psalms in particular). Do you see any patterns? What might water symbolize in the Bible? Is there a tension in the symbolism? If so, what is it? What is the significance of the Revelation 12 dragon calling the Revelation 13 beast up out of the sea? Notice the same imagery appears in Daniel 7. What's the

REVELATION

connection?

_____
_____
_____

SESSION FORTY-THREE

Revelation 13:1–2

> ***Remember the Golden Rule:*** *When the plain sense of Scripture makes common sense, we seek no other sense.*

Video Forty-Three

Topical overview: The rise of the Antichrist and who he persecutes.
Learning goals: Identify how Satan's methods change after he's barred from heaven.

CORE QUESTIONS

Before watching video forty-three, read Revelation 13:1–2. Use the two-column graphic organizer to help you organize your thoughts. Discuss your observations as a group.

As you watch the video, complete the following section. For many, reading the questions before watching the video will aid their understanding of the video content.

Overview

1. What is Satan's mission as described in Revelation 12:17?

___
___
___

2. Who comprise the remnant?

3. Why does the remnant represent a minority within the Jewish people?

4. So who comprise the persecuted of Tribulation?

Revelation 13:1–2

1. What does the repetitive use of symbols indicate to the discerning reader?

The story of chapter 13 centers on how Satan's methods change dramatically after being barred from heaven.

2. Who becomes Satan's primary agent on earth, and how has he been portrayed up to this point?

3. What does the rising of a beast from water indicate, and how do we know this to be true?

Discussion Questions

1. Have you ever thought of the symbols and story of Revelation as being a continuation of earlier Scripture? How does recognizing the relationship between disparate portions of Scripture affect your understanding of individual portions of Scripture? Is this a new or old idea for you? If it's a new concept, how has your view of Scripture changed?

2. Discuss everything we've learned about the Antichrist so far. Who is he? How does he come to power? What is he like? How has he been described?

3. Who comprise the persecuted during the Tribulation during this point, and how does their persecution occur?

4. Persecution is an age-old tactic of Satan to thwart God's plan. How does is this technique an effective pursuit of Satan's goals? Consider the effect persecution has had on the church historically. How will the persecution of the Great Tribulation differ from persecution of previous eras?

_____

_____

5. In the space below, record your takeaway from Revelation 13:1–2 and any questions you have that remain unanswered.

_____

_____

_____

DIGGING DEEPER (OPTIONAL)

Should you choose to dig deeper, complete the following Digging Deeper section. Each meeting will open with discussion of what you've learned and observed in Scripture, and this section will prepare you for that discussion.

In a two-column graphic organizer, record what you observe in each passage and the questions you have about it. Things to look for: Who is speaking? To whom is he speaking? What does he say about God? Jesus? The church? Individual believers? What do readers of this text stand to gain?

Scripture Passage: Read Revelation 13:1–4

Scripture Passage: Daniel 7:3–8, 23–27

And four great beasts were coming up from the sea, different from one another. The first was like a lion and had the wings of an eagle. I kept looking until its wings were plucked, and it was lifted up from the ground and made to stand on two feet like a man; a human mind also was given to it. And behold, another beast, a second one, resembling a bear. And it was raised up on one side, and three ribs were in its mouth between its teeth; and thus they said to it, "Arise, devour much meat!" After this I kept looking, and behold, another one, like a leopard, which had on its back four wings of a bird; the beast also had four heads, and dominion was given to it. After this I kept looking in the night visions, and behold, a fourth beast, dreadful and terrifying and extremely strong; and it had large iron teeth. It devoured and crushed and trampled down the remainder with its feet; and it was different from all the beasts that were before it, and it had ten horns. While I was contemplating the horns, behold, another horn, a little one, came up among them, and three of the first horns were pulled out by the roots before it; and behold, this horn possessed eyes like the eyes of a man and a mouth uttering great boasts. …

Thus he said: "The fourth beast will be a fourth kingdom on the earth, which will be different from all the other kingdoms and will devour the whole earth and tread it down and crush it. As for the ten horns, out of this kingdom ten kings will arise; and another will arise after them, and he will be different from the previous ones and will subdue three kings. He will speak out against the

REVELATION 13:1–2

Most High and wear down the saints of the Highest One, and he will intend to make alterations in times and in law; and they will be given into his hand for a time, times, and half a time. But the court will sit for judgment, and his dominion will be taken away, annihilated and destroyed forever. Then the sovereignty, the dominion and the greatness of all the kingdoms under the whole heaven will be given to the people of the saints of the Highest One; His kingdom will be an everlasting kingdom, and all the dominions will serve and obey Him."

Scripture Passage: 2 Thessalonians 2:8–9

Then that lawless one will be revealed whom the Lord will slay with the breath of His mouth and bring to an end by the appearance of His coming; that is, the one whose coming is in accord with the activity of Satan, with all power and signs and false wonders.

A LITTLE DEEPER…

1. What similarities do you notice between the beasts of Daniel 7 and Revelation 13? What differences?

_____

_____

_____

2. What will the Antichrist accomplish in his time in power? What will be his end?

_____

_____

_____

3. Notice the description we are given here of Christ's coming kingdom. What will it be like? Who will be in it? Consider who you'd like to see in this coming kingdom. Pray for their salvation and their faith. Pray that they'll join you there when the time comes.

_____

_____

_____

SESSION FORTY-FOUR

Revelation 13:3–4

> ***Remember the Golden Rule:*** *When the plain sense of Scripture makes common sense, we seek no other sense.*

Video Forty-Four

Topical overview: The beast of Revelation 13.
Learning goals: Connect Revelation 13 and Daniel 7. Gain a basic understanding of what the Antichrist will do.

CORE QUESTIONS

Before watching video forty-four, read Revelation 13:3–4. Use the two-column graphic organizer to help you organize your thoughts. Discuss your observations as a group.

As you watch the video, complete the following section. For many, reading the questions before watching the video will aid their understanding of the video content.

Overview

1. How is the beast of Daniel 7 similar to the beast of Revelation 13?

_____
_____
_____

2. The Revelation 13 beast combines elements of the four beasts of Daniel 7. How is this significant?

3. The beast of Revelation 13 coincides with what element of Daniel's vision in Daniel 7?

4. Which historical figure prefigures the Antichrist?

5. Whose power does the Antichrist possess?

6. How might the beast acquire such power?

7. Where are the symbols of the heads, horns, crowns, and blasphemous names explained?

Revelation 13:3–4

1. Who is the slain head representative of, and when will we learn more?

2. What happens to the slain head—the Antichrist?

3. How does the Antichrist resurrect?

4. What's the result of his resurrection?

False faith comes from signs and wonders alone. True faith comes from God alone. Satan, acting as God's pawn, creates his own opportunity to be king of the world.

Discussion Questions

1. Remember: what is the purpose or function of the age of Gentiles? What is the purpose of the seven years of Tribulation? Why is it significant that the Antichrist is the climactic Gentile leader, the last of the age?

2. Between this lesson and the previous one, there's been much discussion of faith and belief. Has your understanding of these two concepts been affected by these lessons? If so, how?

3. This lesson mentioned the idea of typology. What does it mean for a historical figure to *prefigure* a present/ future figure? What can we learn about the Antichrist from the typological relationship between Nebuchadnezzar and the Antichrist?

4. Remember: Satan is not omniscient. He may know much, but he cannot know all. How does it make you feel to hear Satan described as God's *pawn*?

5. In the space below, record your takeaway from Revelation 13:3–4 and any questions you have that remain unanswered.

Digging Deeper (Optional)

Should you choose to dig deeper, complete the following Digging Deeper section. Each meeting will open with discussion of what you've learned and observed in

Scripture, and this section will prepare you for that discussion.

In a two-column graphic organizer, record what you observe in each passage and the questions you have about it. Things to look for: Who is speaking? To whom is he speaking? What does he say about God? Jesus? The church? Individual believers? What do readers of this text stand to gain?

Scripture Passage: Read Revelation 13:5–18

Scripture Passage: 2 Thessalonians 2:3–4

Let no one in any way deceive you, for it will not come unless the apostasy comes first, and the man of lawlessness is revealed, the son of destruction, who opposes and exalts himself above every so-called god or object of worship, so that he takes his seat in the temple of God, displaying himself as being God.

Scripture Passage: Daniel 9:27, 11:36–39, 12:11

And he will make a firm covenant with the many for one week, but in the middle of the week he will put a stop to sacrifice and grain offering; and on the wing of abominations will come one who makes desolate, even until a complete destruction, one that is decreed, is poured out on the one who makes desolate. …

Then the king will do as he pleases, and he will exalt and magnify himself above every god and will speak monstrous things against the God of gods; and he will prosper until the indignation is finished, for that which is decreed will be done. He will show no regard for the gods of his fathers or for the desire of women, nor will he show regard for any other god; for he will magnify himself above them all. But instead he will honor a god of fortresses, a god whom his fathers did not know; he will honor him with gold, silver, costly stones and treasures. He will take action against the strongest of fortresses with the help of a foreign god; he will give great honor to those who acknowledge him and will cause them to rule over the many, and will parcel out land for a price. …

From the time that the regular sacrifice is abolished and the abomination of desolation is set up, there will be 1,290 days.

Scripture Passage: Matthew 24:15–16

Therefore when you see the abomination of desolation which was spoken of through Daniel the prophet, standing in the holy place (let the reader understand), then those who are in Judea must flee to the mountains.

Scripture Passage: Isaiah 28:14–15, 18

Therefore, hear the word of the LORD, O scoffers, who rule this people who are in Jerusalem, because you have said, "We have made a covenant with death, and with Sheol we have made a pact. The overwhelming scourge will not reach us when it passes by, for we have made falsehood our refuge and we have concealed ourselves with deception." ...

Your covenant with death will be canceled, and your pact with Sheol will not stand; when the overwhelming scourge passes through, then you become its trampling place.

A LITTLE DEEPER...

1. In these passages, what do you learn about the Antichrist?

2. A new figure appears, commonly known as the False Prophet. What do you learn of this character from these passages? Why might this character be referred to as a prophet? If the Antichrist is the opposite of Christ, of whom might the False Prophet be the opposite? Remember, Satan wants to be God. He wants what God has, and he's doing his best to recreate God's power and glory his own way.

3. How is the rise of these two figures to power connected to the remnant?

4. Consider what these passages tell us of those who are not secured with the remnant. What are these people like? What will they experience at the hands of the Antichrist?

SESSION FORTY-FIVE

Revelation 13:5–18

> ***Remember the Golden Rule:*** *When the plain sense of Scripture makes common sense, we seek no other sense.*

Video Forty-Five

Topical overview: The Antichrist and the False Prophet.
Learning goals: Explore the roles and character of those involved in mid-Tribulation events.

CORE QUESTIONS

Before watching video forty-five, read Revelation 13:5–18. Use the two-column graphic organizer to help you organize your thoughts. Discuss your observations as a group.

As you watch the video, complete the following section. For many, reading the questions before watching the video will aid their understanding of the video content.

Overview

1. Explain the role and actions of the Antichrist.

_____

_____

_____

Revelation 13:5–10

1. What do the Antichrist's words and actions accomplish?

_____
_____
_____

2. Who helps the Antichrist wage war against unbelieving Jews and Gentile believers?

_____
_____
_____

3. If someone chooses to worship the Antichrist, is it possible at that point for them to ever be saved?

_____
_____
_____

4. In terms of faith, what's significant of this mid-Tribulation moment?

_____
_____
_____

5. Will there be any rebellion or resistance against the Antichrist?

_____
_____
_____

Revelation 13:11–14

1. What is the symbolic significance of this second dragon-lamb beast?

_____

2. What is significant of the False Prophet's limited power?

Revelation 13:15–18

1. What's significant about the False Prophet's image of the Antichrist?

2. What is the abomination of desolation from Daniel 12?

3. What does the Antichrist require of his followers to counterfeit God?

4. What is the significance of the number 666?

5. Can you "back into" the number of someone's name?

6. So, what is the purpose of this information?

Everything Satan does is a distortion of truth, a counterfeit.

DISCUSSION QUESTIONS

1. Much of this lesson explored the idea that Satan is a counterfeiter, a liar. We see clearly how the events of the mid-Tribulation moment set up a clear counterfeit religious structure. How do we see Satan working to create counterfeits in our environments today?

2. Discuss the word *desolate*. What exactly does it mean? (If you need to, look it up.) In the context of Scripture, how is this word used?

3. "It was given to him..." is a refrain in Revelation 13. What does this phrase tell us about God's role in these events of Tribulation? Remember, God does not change. If this is true of God at the end, the same is true of Him today. What can we learn about how God works in our lives today from how He acts in Tribulation?

4. At this point in history, the midpoint of Tribulation, God finally makes His last call for people to come to faith. There are no more chances after this. Considering all that comes before and all that comes after, what does this reveal about God's character? Use Scripture to support your answer.

5. Review the limitations of the False Prophet's power. Compare this to the power of the two witnesses in the first half of the Tribulation and to that of Old Testament prophets. Discuss where their power comes from and what we can learn about the entities that provide it.

6. Review the nature and implications of the "mark of the beast." Discuss common misconceptions of the mark, and apply the truth of Scripture to these misconceptions.

7. In the space below, record your takeaway from Revelation 13:5–18 and any questions you have that remain unanswered.

DIGGING DEEPER (OPTIONAL)

Should you choose to dig deeper, complete the following Digging Deeper section.

REVELATION 13:5–18

Each meeting will open with discussion of what you've learned and observed in Scripture, and this section will prepare you for that discussion.

In a two-column graphic organizer, record what you observe in each passage and the questions you have about it. Things to look for: Who is speaking? To whom is he speaking? What does he say about God? Jesus? The church? Individual believers? What do readers of this text stand to gain?

Scripture Passage: Read Revelation 14:1–5

Scripture Passage: Revelation 5:9; 13:8

And they sang a new song, saying, "Worthy are You to take the book and to break its seals; for You were slain, and purchased for God with Your blood men from every tribe and tongue and people and nation." ...

All who dwell on the earth will worship him, everyone whose name has not been written from the foundation of the world in the book of life of the Lamb who has been slain.

Scripture Passage: Romans 11:26

And so all Israel will be saved; just as it is written, "THE DELIVERER WILL COME FROM ZION, HE WILL REMOVE UNGODLINESS FROM JACOB."

Scripture Passage: Hebrews 12:22

But you have come to Mount Zion and to the city of the living God, the heavenly Jerusalem, and to myriads of angels.

A LITTLE DEEPER...

1. Altogether, these scriptures paint a picture of martyrdom and salvation for whom exactly?

_____
_____
_____

2. Whose names are written in the Lamb's Book of Life?

_____

_____

_____

3. The Lamb's Book of Life has been written, complete and sealed, since the foundation of the world. Spend some time praying God's will be done in the lives of those you know. Pray that they would seek Him and find Him.

_____

_____

_____

SESSION FORTY-SIX

Revelation 14:1–5

> ***Remember the Golden Rule:*** *When the plain sense of Scripture makes common sense, we seek no other sense.*

Video Forty-Six

Topical overview: Review of mid-Tribulation moment. Introduction to 144,000.
Learning goals: Understand the macro-view of how heavenly interactions affect life on earth. Identify the figurative significance of Mount Zion in multiple settings.

CORE QUESTIONS

Before watching video forty-six, read Revelation 14:1–5. Use the two-column graphic organizer to help you organize your thoughts. Discuss your observations as a group.

As you watch the video, complete the following section. For many, reading the questions before watching the video will aid their understanding of the video content.

Overview

1. What is the trigger event for mid-Tribulation events?

_____

_____

_____

REVELATION

2. About how long is the mid-Tribulation "moment?"

_____
_____
_____

3. At the close of this mid-Tribulation moment, what is the primary human dilemma?

_____
_____
_____

4. Describe the fourth group of persecuted in the Tribulation: who are they, and when will they be killed?

_____
_____
_____

Revelation 14:1

In present-day Jerusalem, a wall runs between Mt. Gerazim and Mt. Zion. Zion is a bit shorter and the southernmost of the two.

1. What is the significance of Jesus standing on Mt. Zion at mid-Tribulation alongside the 144,000 Jewish martyred evangelists?

_____
_____
_____

Revelation 14:2–5

1. Where are the 144,000 and what are they doing?

_____
_____

2. So what is the symbolic significance of Zion?

3. What does "purchased" mean in this context?

DISCUSSION QUESTIONS

1. How do heavenly events affect earthly events?

2. Review the groups of the persecuted during the Tribulation and their collective fates.

3. Review the various contextual uses for the term *Zion*. With this term in particular, why is understanding the context in which it's used so significant?

Revelation

4. Describe the use of transactional language in Revelation 14. Why is it used? What is the significance of this imagery?

_____

_____

_____

5. In the space below, record your takeaway from Revelation 14:1–5 and any questions you have that remain unanswered.

_____

_____

_____

DIGGING DEEPER (OPTIONAL)

Should you choose to dig deeper, complete the following Digging Deeper section. Each meeting will open with discussion of what you've learned and observed in Scripture, and this section will prepare you for that discussion.

In a two-column graphic organizer, record what you observe in each passage and the questions you have about it. Things to look for: Who is speaking? To whom is he speaking? What does he say about God? Jesus? The church? Individual believers? What do readers of this text stand to gain?

Scripture Passage: Read Revelation 14:6–11; 7:2–3; 12:10–11; 13:10

Scripture Passage: Matthew 24:12–14

> *Because lawlessness is increased, most people's love will grow cold. But the one who endures to the end, he will be saved. This gospel of the kingdom shall be preached in the whole world as a testimony to all the nations, and then the end will come.*

A LITTLE DEEPER...

1. When considered as a whole, to what element of God's character do these scriptures point?

_____

2. What do these scriptures reveal about how believers should respond to persecution? Explore this topic in the Bible, particularly as Jesus addresses it in the Sermon on the Mount. How are believers instructed to respond to persecution? What does this look like in your current context?

SESSION FORTY-SEVEN

Revelation 14:6–11

> ***Remember the Golden Rule:*** *When the plain sense of Scripture makes common sense, we seek no other sense.*

Video Forty-Seven

Topical overview: The 144,000 and the mark of the beast. Eternal fates and hell.

Learning goals: Explore the role of evangelism before, during, and after the mid-Tribulation moment. Understand the concept of firstfruits and how it can apply to things other than fruit. Acknowledge Revelation's teaching on hell.

CORE QUESTIONS

Before watching video forty-seven, read Revelation 14:6–11. Use the two-column graphic organizer to help you organize your thoughts. Discuss your observations as a group.

As you watch the video, complete the following section. For many, reading the questions before watching the video will aid their understanding of the video content.

Overview

1. Who were these 144,000 witnesses?

_____

_____

_____

2. What is the concept of firstfruits outside of the agrarian context?

3. So why are the 144,000 the first and the best, and what is their reward?

4. The 144,000 and the land of Israel were preserved or sealed from judgment in Revelation 7. What happened and why?

The opportunity to be saved by the grace of God has come to an end at this point. The undecided are forced to decide. There's no one left to evangelize.

Revelation 14:6–7

1. What does this heavenly messenger preach?

This is the final presentation of the gospel to anyone on earth. This is the last chance before Christ returns.

2. How is this angelic declaration a fulfillment of Matthew 24:14?

Revelation 14:8–11

1. What is the message of the second angel?

2. What is the significance of Babylon in this context?

3. What's the message of the third angel?

4. What does this passage teach of hell?

5. Why are the people who take the mark doomed to suffer forever?

Discussion Questions

1. What sets the 144,000 apart, and how is their martyrdom an extra measure of grace?

2. What is the one gospel that has been the same from the beginning and will be the same to the end?

3. How does much missionary teaching take elements of Revelation out of context? How does this affect your understanding of the Great Commission and its role in the life of the individual believer and in the life of the church as a whole?

4. How can we understand God's decision to close off the opportunity for salvation at this mid-Tribulation moment. What is your reaction to this truth and why?

5. In the space below, record your takeaway from Revelation 14:6–11 and any questions you have that remain unanswered.

DIGGING DEEPER (OPTIONAL)

Should you choose to dig deeper, complete the following Digging Deeper section.

Revelation

Each meeting will open with discussion of what you've learned and observed in Scripture, and this section will prepare you for that discussion.

In a two-column graphic organizer, record what you observe in each passage and the questions you have about it. Things to look for: Who is speaking? To whom is he speaking? What does he say about God? Jesus? The church? Individual believers? What do readers of this text stand to gain?

Scripture Passage: Read Revelation 14:12–20; 19:12; 20:4

Scripture Passage: Matthew 24:31

And He will send forth His angels with A GREAT TRUMPET AND THEY WILL GATHER TOGETHER His elect from the four winds, from one end of the sky to the other.

Scripture Passage: 2 Peter 2:1–3

But false prophets also arose among the people, just as there will also be false teachers among you, who will secretly introduce destructive heresies, even denying the Master who bought them, bringing swift destruction upon themselves. Many will follow their sensuality, and because of them the way of the truth will be maligned; and in their greed they will exploit you with false words; their judgment from long ago is not idle, and their destruction is not asleep.

Scripture Passage: Daniel 7:24–25

As for the ten horns, out of this kingdom ten kings will arise; and another will arise after them, and he will be different from the previous ones and will subdue three kings. He will speak out against the Most High and wear down the saints of the Highest One, and he will intend to make alterations in times and in law; and they will be given into his hand for a time, times, and half a time.

A LITTLE DEEPER...

1. Based on the Scripture collected here, what do you believe Daniel means when he writes "He will speak out against the Most High and wear down the saints of the Highest One, and he will intend to make alterations in times and in law; and they will be given into his hand for a time, times, and half a time?"

_____

_____

2. Consider the imagery from the Revelation 14 passage. Who or what is completing the harvest according to God's command? Who or what is represented by the crop being harvested? What does this harvest look like from an earthly perspective?

SESSION FORTY-EIGHT

Revelation 14:12–20

> ***Remember the Golden Rule:*** *When the plain sense of Scripture makes common sense, we seek no other sense.*

Video Forty-Eight

Topical overview: Martyrdom during the Tribulation. The coming judgment.
Learning goals: Explore martyrdom, hope, and perseverance as represented in Revelation.

CORE QUESTIONS

Before watching video forty-eight, read Revelation 14:12–20. Use the two-column graphic organizer to help you organize your thoughts. Discuss your observations as a group.

As you watch the video, complete the following section. For many, reading the questions before watching the video will aid their understanding of the video content.

Overview

1. What is Pastor Armstrong's response to those who would say there is no eternal punishment or hell?

_____
_____
_____

Revelation 14:12–13

1. Who is the speaker in verse 12, and what is its purpose?

_____

_____

_____

2. Why is martyrdom a blessing in the Tribulation?

_____

_____

_____

3. What is the hope of the Christian?

_____

_____

_____

4. What is the perseverance of a saint?

_____

_____

_____

5. What reward do these martyrs earn?

_____

_____

_____

Revelation 14:14–16

1. Who is the people depicted in these verses?

_____

2. How does this section connect to the mid-Tribulation moment?

Revelation 14:17–20

1. What is the significance of the reaping symbology here?

2. How does verse 20 fit into the overall timeline of Tribulation?

3. Since the numbers here are so specific, what sort of literal reality might it represent?

4. What is a simple summary of the latter half of the Tribulation?

REVELATION 14:12–20

DISCUSSION QUESTIONS

1. In the space below, record your takeaway from Revelation 14:12–20 and any questions you have that remain unanswered.

_____

_____

_____

2. Have you ever considered that hell will be physically visible from Christ's earthly kingdom?

_____

_____

_____

3. What do you believe about hell? What does the Bible teach about hell?

_____

_____

_____

4. What is the "hope" of the believer? What does it look like to maintain this hope in today's world?

_____

_____

_____

5. Prior to this study, what did you know and believe about angels? What have you learned?

_____

_____

_____

6. In this section, we see a vivid picture of God's wrath poured out on the unbeliever. What is your response to this? As you consider your response, consider what your

Revelation

response reveals about your own heart. How are we as believers supposed to interact with, think about, and feel about unbelievers in today's world? What is different between our circumstances today and those of the people alive in the Tribulation?

_____

_____

_____

DIGGING DEEPER (OPTIONAL)

Should you choose to dig deeper, complete the following Digging Deeper section. Each meeting will open with discussion of what you've learned and observed in Scripture, and this section will prepare you for that discussion.

In a two-column graphic organizer, record what you observe in each passage and the questions you have about it. Things to look for: Who is speaking? To whom is he speaking? What does he say about God? Jesus? The church? Individual believers? What do readers of this text stand to gain?

Scripture Passage: Read Revelation 15:1–4

Scripture Passage: Exodus 15:9–18

The enemy said, "I will pursue, I will overtake, I will divide the spoil; my desire shall be gratified against them; I will draw out my sword, my hand will destroy them." You blew with Your wind, the sea covered them; they sank like lead in the mighty waters. Who is like You among the gods, O LORD? Who is like You, majestic in holiness, awesome in praises, working wonders? You stretched out Your right hand, the earth swallowed them. In Your lovingkindness You have led the people whom You have redeemed; in Your strength You have guided them to Your holy habitation. The peoples have heard, they tremble; anguish has gripped the inhabitants of Philistia. Then the chiefs of Edom were dismayed; the leaders of Moab, trembling grips them; all the inhabitants of Canaan have melted away. Terror and dread fall upon them; by the greatness of Your arm they are motionless as stone; until Your people pass over, O LORD, until the people pass over whom You have purchased. You will bring them and plant them in the mountain of Your inheritance, the place, O LORD, which You have made for Your dwelling, the sanctuary, O Lord, which Your hands have established. "The LORD shall reign forever and ever.

Scripture Passage: Deuteronomy 32:5–7, 17–18, 35–37, 41

They have acted corruptly toward Him, they are not His children, because of their defect; but are a perverse and crooked generation. Do you thus repay the LORD, O foolish and unwise people? Is not He your Father who has bought you? He has made you and established you. Remember the days of old, consider the years of all generations. Ask your father, and he will inform you, your elders, and they will tell you. ...

They sacrificed to demons who were not God, to gods whom they have not known, new gods who came lately, whom your fathers did not dread. You neglected the Rock who begot you, and forgot the God who gave you birth. ...

Vengeance is Mine, and retribution, in due time their foot will slip; for the day of their calamity is near, and the impending things are hastening upon them. For the LORD will vindicate His people, and will have compassion on His servants, when He sees that their strength is gone, and there is none remaining, bond or free. And He will say, "Where are their gods, the rock in which they sought refuge?" ...

"If I sharpen My flashing sword, and My hand takes hold on justice, I will render vengeance on My adversaries, and I will repay those who hate Me."

Scripture Passage: Isaiah 48:8–12

You have not heard, you have not known. Even from long ago your ear has not been open, because I knew that you would deal very treacherously; and you have been called a rebel from birth. For the sake of My name I delay My wrath, and for My praise I restrain it for you, in order not to cut you off. Behold, I have refined you, but not as silver; I have tested you in the furnace of affliction. For My own sake, for My own sake, I will act; for how can My name be profaned? And My glory I will not give to another. Listen to Me, O Jacob, even Israel whom I called; I am He, I am the first, I am also the last.

Scripture Passage: Zechariah 13:7–9

"Awake, O sword, against My Shepherd, and against the man, My Associate," declares the LORD of hosts. "Strike the Shepherd that the sheep may be scattered; and I will turn My hand against the little ones. It will come about in all the land," declares the LORD, "that two parts in it will be cut off and perish; but the third will be left in it. And I will bring the third part through the fire, refine them as silver is refined, and test them as gold is tested. They will call on My name, and I will answer them; I will say, 'They are My people,' and they will say, 'The LORD is my God.'"

Scripture Passage: Daniel 9:24

Seventy weeks have been decreed for your people and your holy city, to finish the transgression, to make an end of sin, to make atonement for iniquity, to bring in everlasting righteousness, to seal up vision and prophecy and to anoint the most holy place.

A Little Deeper...

1. What has Israel done, and how does God respond. What does this reveal about the character of the God we worship?

_____

_____

_____

2. What is the purpose of Israel's suffering as revealed in these passages? What is the purpose of our suffering? Use Scripture to support your answer.

_____

_____

_____

SESSION FORTY-NINE

Revelation 15:1–4

> ***Remember the Golden Rule:*** *When the plain sense of Scripture makes common sense, we seek no other sense.*

Video Forty-Nine

Topical overview: Introducing the Great Tribulation.
Learning goals: Identify the connection between Revelation 15 and Daniel 9:24; Understand the purpose of the coming bowl judgments.

CORE QUESTIONS

Before watching video forty-nine, read Revelation 15:1–4. Use the two-column graphic organizer to help you organize your thoughts. Discuss your observations as a group.

As you watch the video, complete the following section. For many, reading the questions before watching the video will aid their understanding of the video content.

Overview

1. Why is the second half of the Tribulation relatively unaddressed in the Bible?

_____

_____

_____

Revelation 15:1–4

1. All of Revelation 15 represents what sort of symbolic significance?

2. According to Daniel, what are the outcomes of this final set of judgments?

3. Who are these final judgments for?

4. What are God's intentions for these judgments?

5. Who stands on the glassy, fiery sea, and what is their victory?

6. What sort of eternal perspective should every believer maintain?

7. What is the purpose of singing the song of the Lamb?

8. What is the purpose of singing the song of Moses?

DISCUSSION QUESTIONS

1. In this session and those previous, what have you learned about God's judgment? What does God's judgment reveal about His character?

2. What does being disciplined by the Lord look like? Do we today receive the same warnings of the nature of discipline? Support your answer with Scripture.

3. What is the victory of the believer? How do we live in such a way that the same might be said of us?

4. In the space below, record your takeaway from Revelation 15:1–4 and any questions

REVELATION

you have that remain unanswered.

_____

_____

_____

DIGGING DEEPER (OPTIONAL)

Should you choose to dig deeper, complete the following Digging Deeper section. Each meeting will open with discussion of what you've learned and observed in Scripture, and this section will prepare you for that discussion.

In a two-column graphic organizer, record what you observe in each passage and the questions you have about it. Things to look for: Who is speaking? To whom is he speaking? What does he say about God? Jesus? The church? Individual believers? What do readers of this text stand to gain?

Scripture Passage: Revelation 15:5–8, 16:1–11

Scripture Passage: Romans 2:5–6

But because of your stubbornness and unrepentant heart you are storing up wrath for yourself in the day of wrath and revelation of the righteous judgment of God, WHO WILL RENDER TO EACH PERSON ACCORDING TO HIS DEEDS.

Scripture Passage: Ezekiel 43:5–9

And the Spirit lifted me up and brought me into the inner court; and behold, the glory of the LORD filled the house. Then I heard one speaking to me from the house, while a man was standing beside me. He said to me, "Son of man, this is the place of My throne and the place of the soles of My feet, where I will dwell among the sons of Israel forever. And the house of Israel will not again defile My holy name, neither they nor their kings, by their harlotry and by the corpses of their kings when they die, by setting their threshold by My threshold and their door post beside My door post, with only the wall between Me and them. And they have defiled My holy name by their abominations which they have committed. So I have consumed them in My anger. Now let them put away their harlotry and the corpses of their kings far from Me; and I will dwell among them forever."

REVELATION 15:1–4

Scripture Passage: Hebrews 9:23–24

Therefore it was necessary for the copies of the things in the heavens to be cleansed with these, but the heavenly things themselves with better sacrifices than these. For Christ did not enter a holy place made with hands, a mere copy of the true one, but into heaven itself, now to appear in the presence of God for us.

A LITTLE DEEPER...

1. What does wrath mean, and what do these passages teach us about God's wrath? What is your reaction when you read of God's wrath?

___

2. Hebrews 9 refers to a difficult truth: the judgment and destruction described in Revelation is *necessary*. Why?

___

3. Summarize the bowl judgments. What will happen to whom? Why?

___

SESSION FIFTY

Revelation 15:5–16:6

> ***Remember the Golden Rule:*** *When the plain sense of Scripture makes common sense, we seek no other sense.*

Video Fifty

Topical overview: The first three bowl judgments.
Learning goals: Understand the meaning of the tabernacle and the bowls. Recognize the significance of the first three bowl judgments.

CORE QUESTIONS

Before watching video fifty, read Revelation 15:5–16:6. Use the two-column graphic organizer to help you organize your thoughts. Discuss your observations as a group.

As you watch the video, complete the following section. For many, reading the questions before watching the video will aid their understanding of the video content.

Overview

1. How are the songs of Revelation 15 a sign, and what do they signify?

_____

_____

_____

2. What is the purpose of these songs, and how do we know?

Revelation 15:5–8

1. How do we know there is a physical tabernacle in heaven?

2. How does the Bible often describe God's wrath?

3. What's the significance of God's wrath being contained in a bowl rather than a cup?

4. What is the significance of entrance to the heavenly tabernacle being inaccessible?

Revelation 16:1–11

1. What do we need to know about Revelation 16–22 before we begin studying it?

2. What pattern exists among the bowl judgments?

3. What significance can be attributed to "loathsome" sores?

4. What greater significance attaches to the sea and fresh water turning to blood?

Discussion Questions

1. God consistently patterns His earthly creation after heavenly realities. In this session, we learn of the heavenly tabernacle. What other examples of this patterning of earthly things after heavenly counterparts do we find in Scripture? Why might God choose to create and communicate in this manner?

2. Discuss the concept of wrath. Why is God justified in His wrath? How is it characterized? What is your personal response to the concept or wrath, and why?

3. Notice the judgments described here are discerning and precise. What does this reveal about God's character, and how can we extend this element of God's character to our present circumstances?

4. In the space below, record your takeaway from Revelation 15:5–16:6 and any questions you have that remain unanswered.

DIGGING DEEPER (OPTIONAL)

Should you choose to dig deeper, complete the following Digging Deeper section. Each meeting will open with discussion of what you've learned and observed in Scripture, and this section will prepare you for that discussion.

In a two-column graphic organizer, record what you observe in each passage and the questions you have about it. Things to look for: Who is speaking? To whom is he speaking? What does he say about God? Jesus? The church? Individual believers? What do readers of this text stand to gain?

Scripture Passage: Read Revelation 16:7–16

A LITTLE DEEPER...

1. Consider the symbolic and literal significance of the bowl judgments. Throughout Scripture, what symbolic weight do blood and water carry? What is the symbolic significance of water becoming blood? What are the literal, physical impacts of this change?

2. Consider the symbolic and literal significance of darkness as presented in Scripture. What do the symbols of light and dark represent?

3. What pattern do these bowl judgments follow? Of what is God giving those on earth a foretaste, and what is their reaction?

SESSION FIFTY-ONE

Revelation 16:7–16

> ***Remember the Golden Rule:*** *When the plain sense of Scripture makes common sense, we seek no other sense.*

Video Fifty-One

Topical overview: The fourth through sixth bowl judgments.
Learning goals: Explore the relative information and contributing factors to the War of Armageddon.

CORE QUESTIONS

Before watching video fifty-one, read Revelation 16:7–16. Use the two-column graphic organizer to help you organize your thoughts. Discuss your observations as a group.

As you watch the video, complete the following section. For many, reading the questions before watching the video will aid their understanding of the video content.

Revelation 15:7–11

1. How does darkness create pain?

_____
_____
_____

2. As a whole, what are these bowl judgments a pattern of?

3. What does an evil, unrepentant heart do?

An unbeliever's sin nature is eternal, and so their rebellion will remain eternal without God's intervention to change their nature. This eternal sin nature necessitates eternal punishment.

4. What is the significance of the direct parallels between the bowl judgments and those of the Exodus?

5. How do these first five bowls fit into the larger picture of the Great Tribulation?

How do the latter two bowl judgments set themselves apart from the previous five?

6. Summarize what you've learned about the War of Armageddon.

Revelation 16:12–16

1. What does the sixth bowl accomplish?

2. What does removing all water from earth facilitate?

The first five bowl judgments create urgency and incentive. The sixth creates opportunity.

3. Will those left on earth recognize that Christ's return and their judgment is imminent?

DISCUSSION QUESTIONS

1. An unbeliever's sin nature is eternal, and so their rebellion will remain eternal without God's intervention to change their nature. This eternal sin nature necessitates eternal punishment. Do you struggle with the concept of eternity? The concept that there is quite literally no hope of regeneration or salvation outside of Christ, and there will come a time where God will withhold the opportunity to choose reformation? Why or why not? How should we live in response to the truth that both punishment and reward from God are eternal? To the truth that there will come a day when God no longer will allow for reconciliation to Himself?

REVELATION

2. Those who experience these bowl judgments will have permanently hardened hearts to the truth. God is the one who both hardens and softens hearts. Consider the example of Pharaoh in Exodus and Saul (Paul) in Acts. How does this truth about the nature of God impact you on a personal level?

3. Again, we see an example of God using judgment to shape history and the events of earth to His will. We know from Scripture He does the same with blessing. How have you seen this to be true in your life lately?

4. In the space below, record your takeaway from Revelation 16:7–16 and any questions you have that remain unanswered.

DIGGING DEEPER (OPTIONAL)

Should you choose to dig deeper, complete the following Digging Deeper section. Each meeting will open with discussion of what you've learned and observed in Scripture, and this section will prepare you for that discussion.

In a two-column graphic organizer, record what you observe in each passage and the questions you have about it. Things to look for: Who is speaking? To whom is he speaking? What does he say about God? Jesus? The church? Individual believers? What do readers of this text stand to gain?

REVELATION 16:7–16

Scripture Passage: Read Revelation 11:8; 15:1; 16:17–21; 18:21

Scripture Passage: Jeremiah 51:24

"But I will repay Babylon and all the inhabitants of Chaldea for all their evil that they have done in Zion before your eyes," declares the LORD.

Scripture Passage: Genesis 2:10–14

Now a river flowed out of Eden to water the garden; and from there it divided and became four rivers. The name of the first is Pishon; it flows around the whole land of Havilah, where there is gold. The gold of that land is good; the bdellium and the onyx stone are there. The name of the second river is Gihon; it flows around the whole land of Cush. The name of the third river is Tigris; it flows east of Assyria. And the fourth river is the Euphrates.

Scripture Passage: John 3:36; 19:30

"He who believes in the Son has eternal life; but he who does not obey the Son will not see life, but the wrath of God abides on him." ...

Therefore, when Jesus had received the sour wine, He said, "It is finished!" And He bowed His head and gave up His spirit.

A LITTLE DEEPER...

1. What might it mean for the wrath of God to be "finished?"

_____

_____

_____

2. Do some research on the ancient city of Babylon and its influence throughout history relative to its present-day location. Summarize your findings in the space below.

_____

_____

_____

3. Why might God's wrath seem to have a geographical focus on Babylon? Use Scripture to support your answer.

_____

_____

_____

SESSION FIFTY-TWO

Revelation 16:17–21

> *Remember the Golden Rule:* When the plain sense of Scripture makes common sense, we seek no other sense.

Video Fifty-Two

Topical overview: Idolatry, Babylon, and Armageddon.
Learning goals: Understand the role of Babylon in the larger story of the Bible. Explore the connection between idolatry, Babylon, and Armageddon.

CORE QUESTIONS

Before watching video fifty-two, read Revelation 16:17–21. Use the two-column graphic organizer to help you organize your thoughts. Discuss your observations as a group.

As you watch the video, complete the following section. For many, reading the questions before watching the video will aid their understanding of the video content.

Overview

1. Where does the Antichrist amass his forces and why?

_____

_____

_____

Revelation 16:17–21

1. What is the impact of the earthquake of the seventh bowl judgment?

2. In the big picture of God's judgment, what is the role of this last bowl judgment?

3. What sort of hailstorm accompanies the earthquake?

4. Somehow people still survive. What is their response to these disasters?

5. What is the purpose of this last bowl judgment?

6. What is the "great city" of verse 17?

7. What are the two major themes of the Bible?

_____

_____

_____

8. Why does Babylon get so much attention in this section of Revelation?

_____

_____

_____

9. What is idolatry?

_____

_____

_____

Discussion Questions

1. What is the significance of the Jezreel Valley, both strategically and scripturally? Take time as a group to locate this area on a map to further enrich your discussion.

_____

_____

_____

2. What is the significance of Babylon in the literal sense? In the figurative and prophetic sense? This section of Revelation is an excellent example of layered meaning. Reread Revelation 16:17–21. Discuss both the literal and figurative import of the city of Babylon in this passage.

_____

_____

_____

3. What does the Bible teach about idolatry? What is it? What does it look like in this

current era? How and why are humans in possession of hearts continually prone to idolatry, and what is the role of the Holy Spirit in safeguarding our hearts against it?

_____

_____

_____

4. In the space below, record your takeaway from Revelation 16:17–21 and any questions you have that remain unanswered.

_____

_____

_____

Digging Deeper (Optional)

Should you choose to dig deeper, complete the following Digging Deeper section. Each meeting will open with discussion of what you've learned and observed in Scripture, and this section will prepare you for that discussion.

In a two-column graphic organizer, record what you observe in each passage and the questions you have about it. Things to look for: Who is speaking? To whom is he speaking? What does he say about God? Jesus? The church? Individual believers? What do readers of this text stand to gain?

Scripture Passage: Read Revelation 13:1–2; 17:1–18

Scripture Passage: 2 Corinthians 4:3–4

And even if our gospel is veiled, it is veiled to those who are perishing, in whose case the god of this world has blinded the minds of the unbelieving so that they might not see the light of the gospel of the glory of Christ, who is the image of God.

Scripture Passage: Daniel 11:36–38

Then the king will do as he pleases, and he will exalt and magnify himself above every god and will speak monstrous things against the God of gods; and he will prosper until the indignation is finished, for that which is decreed will be done. He will show no regard for the gods of his fathers or for the desire of women, nor will he show regard for any other god; for he will magnify himself above them all. But instead he will honor a god of fortresses, a god whom his fathers did not know; he will honor him with gold, silver, costly stones and treasures.

A LITTLE DEEPER...

1. Why is imagery of harlotry so closely tied to idolatry? What is God trying to teach us about Himself and ourselves through this association?

_____

_____

_____

2. Unpack the symbolism layered throughout Revelation 17. Record your thoughts in the space below.

_____

_____

_____

3. Spend some time thinking over the last part of Revelation 17. What can this passage teach us about the nature of sin and idolatry?

_____

_____

_____

4. Reflect on what 2 Corinthians teaches about a "veiled" gospel. Does this fit in with how you understand God and His Holy Spirit to work in the world? How so? If not, spend some time in prayer reconciling your beliefs with the truth of Scripture.

_____

_____

_____

SESSION FIFTY-THREE

Revelation 17:1–8

> ***Remember the Golden Rule:*** *When the plain sense of Scripture makes common sense, we seek no other sense.*

Video Fifty-Three

Topical overview: Physical and spiritual Babylon; the harlot.
Learning goals: Comprehend the literal and symbolic significance of Babylon and the harlot.

CORE QUESTIONS

Before watching video fifty-three, read Revelation 17:1–8. Use the two-column graphic organizer to help you organize your thoughts. Discuss your observations as a group.

As you watch the video, complete the following section. For many, reading the questions before watching the video will aid their understanding of the video content.

Overview

1. When you hear the word *Babylon*, what should you think?

_____

_____

_____

2. Summarize what you've learned about false religions as they relate to Babylon.

3. Symbolically, what is the direct opposite of Babylon?

4. Symbolically, what are East and West?

At this point in Tribulation, the *figurative* becomes *literal*.

5. What must happen to physical and symbolic Babylon in order for Christ's rule and reign on earth to be as it should?

6. What do Revelation 17 and 18 describe?

Revelation 17:1–8

1. What does the harlot of Revelation 17 symbolize?

2. How does the symbolism of world leaders with the harlot of Babylon play out?

3. Which beast does the harlot ride? Where have we seen this beast before, what does this image symbolize, and who is it?

DISCUSSION QUESTIONS

1. Review what you've learned about false religions from this session. Compare these things you've learned to the beliefs you held about false religions prior to this session. Have you identified any lies that you've believed? Use this opportunity to speak the truth of the gospel into your group.

2. Review the biblical, symbolic significance of east and west. Do you see these meanings convey into modern usage? If so, provide examples.

3. How are harlotry and idolatry related? What is the significance of the harlot riding the beast in Revelation 17? The harlot isn't riding the beast of Revelation 17 at this present moment in time, so what do you observe of her in the current day?

4. What's the big deal about Babylon? Why does God's judgment narrow into this physical location?

5. In the space below, record your takeaway from Revelation 17:1–8 and any questions you have that remain unanswered.

DIGGING DEEPER (OPTIONAL)

Should you choose to dig deeper, complete the following Digging Deeper section. Each meeting will open with discussion of what you've learned and observed in Scripture, and this section will prepare you for that discussion.

In a two-column graphic organizer, record what you observe in each passage and the questions you have about it. Things to look for: Who is speaking? To whom is he speaking? What does he say about God? Jesus? The church? Individual believers? What do readers of this text stand to gain?

Scripture Passage: Read Revelation 13:2; 17:9–18

Scripture Passage: Daniel 11:36–38

> *Then the king will do as he pleases, and he will exalt and magnify himself above every god and will speak monstrous things against the God of gods; and he will prosper until the indignation is finished, for that which is decreed will be done. He will show no regard for the gods of his fathers or for the desire of women, nor will he show regard for any other god; for he will magnify himself above them all. But instead he will honor a god of fortresses, a god whom his fathers did not know; he will honor him with gold, silver, costly stones and treasures.*

A Little Deeper...

1. Based on these passages, what is the outcome of idolatry? What happens to false religions?

___

2. This section of Revelation 17 unpacks symbolism from earlier in Revelation 17. Reread chapter 17 as a whole and make any notes of symbolic relationships as you understand them below.

___

3. Focus on the second to last sentence of Revelation 17: "For God has put it in their hearts to execute His purpose by having a common purpose, and by giving their kingdom to the beast, until the words of God will be fulfilled." Who is the "they" referred to here? What is the role of God in the lives of these people, and what does this tell you about God?

___

SESSION FIFTY-FOUR

Revelation 17:9–18

> ***Remember the Golden Rule:*** *When the plain sense of Scripture makes common sense, we seek no other sense.*

Video Fifty-Four

Topical overview: The end of spiritual Babylon. The beasts of Revelation 17.

Learning goals: Understand the historical significance of the beast in Revelation 17. Follow God's work and plan as He systematically shapes world events to prepare for the final showdown between Jesus and Satan.

CORE QUESTIONS

Before watching video fifty-four, read Revelation 17:9–18. Use the two-column graphic organizer to help you organize your thoughts. Discuss your observations as a group.

As you watch the video, complete the following section. For many, reading the questions before watching the video will aid their understanding of the video content.

Overview

1. At this point in Tribulation, how many false religions are left in the world?

_____

_____

_____

2. Summarize the reviews of the two beasts and their symbology.

Revelation 17:9–14

1. What does the phrase "to those who have wisdom" signify?

2. Summarize the explanation of the symbols in this passage.

Revelation 17:15–18

1. What impact does the seventh bowl judgment have on false religion?

2. How does this fit into the plan of God?

3. What remains of spiritual Babylon at the close of Revelation 17?

Discussion Questions

1. Recall the meaning of the phrase "to those who have wisdom." Do you feel this phrase applies to you? As a group, read James 1:5–8. Is the wisdom Revelation 17 speaks of attainable? How so and by whom?

2. As a group, review the topics of this session to ensure comprehension. What do the various elements of the vision of Revelation 17 symbolize?

3. As the seventh bowl judgment progresses, God uses wicked actors to accomplish His will, despite their ongoing perception of their own rebellion. In the context of Revelation 17, how does God accomplish His will? As you reflect on history up to the present, how has the same concept proven true? Discuss specific historical examples of how evil actors accomplished God's purposes.

4. How is the complete physical and spiritual destruction in line with the character of God?

5. In the space below, record your takeaway from Revelation 17:9–18 and any questions you have that remain unanswered.

_____

_____

_____

DIGGING DEEPER (OPTIONAL)

Should you choose to dig deeper, complete the following Digging Deeper section. Each meeting will open with discussion of what you've learned and observed in Scripture, and this section will prepare you for that discussion.

In a two-column graphic organizer, record what you observe in each passage and the questions you have about it. Things to look for: Who is speaking? To whom is he speaking? What does he say about God? Jesus? The church? Individual believers? What do readers of this text stand to gain?

Scripture Passage: Revelation 17:13–17, 18:1–2

Scripture Passage: Colossians 1:12–14

> ...giving thanks to the Father, who has qualified us to share in the inheritance of the saints in Light. For He rescued us from the domain of darkness, and transferred us to the kingdom of His beloved Son, in whom we have redemption, the forgiveness of sins.

A LITTLE DEEPER...

1. There are two kingdoms at work in this world. What are they, to which do you belong and why, and what evidence do you see of their existence in the world around you?

_____

_____

_____

2. What is the fate of Babylon, both physically and spiritually?

_____

_____

3. Notice Babylon is described as a prison. What does it contain? And given the events of the remainder of the seventh bowl judgment, what is the significance of its prisoners being contained at this juncture?

SESSION FIFTY-FIVE

Revelation 18:1–3

> ***Remember the Golden Rule:*** *When the plain sense of Scripture makes common sense, we seek no other sense.*

Video Fifty-Five

Topical overview: Review of Revelation 17. Background of Revelation 18.
Learning goals: Understand the function of Revelation 16–18 in the larger story of Revelation. Recollect the physical and spiritual significance of Babylon and its leaders.

CORE QUESTIONS

Before watching video fifty-five, read Revelation 18:1–3. Use the two-column graphic organizer to help you organize your thoughts. Discuss your observations as a group.

As you watch the video, complete the following section. For many, reading the questions before watching the video will aid their understanding of the video content.

Overview

1. What is a good image of the way the seventh bowl judgment plays out?

_____

_____

_____

2. What will Babylon be or become in the Tribulation?

3. At which points of history do Babylon's spiritual and physical power coincide?

4. Revelation 17 describes which phase of God's destruction of Babylon?

5. What is the effect of Satan consolidating his physical and spiritual power during Tribulation?

Revelation 18:1–3

1. What's the significance of the phrase "after these things?"

2. How does chapter 17 fit into the sequential narrative of Revelation?

DISCUSSION QUESTIONS

1. Review the evidence for the claim that Babylon is Satan's home base on earth. Have you heard this before? What is your response?

_____

_____

_____

2. What are the simultaneous physical and spiritual battles happening at this point in Revelation? Do you see the same battles happening in the world today? Why or why not.

_____

_____

_____

3. Consider those who fill the role of "adversary" throughout Scripture. As these adversaries accomplish their evil aims, how does God use their actions to further His plan? Give specific examples.

_____

_____

_____

4. In the space below, record your takeaway from Revelation 18:1–3 and any questions you have that remain unanswered.

_____

_____

_____

DIGGING DEEPER (OPTIONAL)

Should you choose to dig deeper, complete the following Digging Deeper section.

REVELATION 18:1–3

Each meeting will open with discussion of what you've learned and observed in Scripture, and this section will prepare you for that discussion.

In a two-column graphic organizer, record what you observe in each passage and the questions you have about it. Things to look for: Who is speaking? To whom is he speaking? What does he say about God? Jesus? The church? Individual believers? What do readers of this text stand to gain?

Scripture Passage: Read Revelation 18:4–8

Scripture Passage: Isaiah 13:19–22

> *And Babylon, the beauty of kingdoms, the glory of the Chaldeans' pride, will be as when God overthrew Sodom and Gomorrah. It will never be inhabited or lived in from generation to generation; nor will the Arab pitch his tent there, nor will shepherds make their flocks lie down there. But desert creatures will lie down there, and their houses will be full of owls; ostriches also will live there, and shaggy goats will frolic there. Hyenas will howl in their fortified towers and jackals in their luxurious palaces. Her fateful time also will soon come and her days will not be prolonged.*

Scripture Passage: Jeremiah 51:5–10, 35–37, 49–50

> *For neither Israel nor Judah has been forsaken by his God, the LORD of hosts, although their land is full of guilt before the Holy One of Israel. Flee from the midst of Babylon, and each of you save his life! Do not be destroyed in her punishment, for this is the LORD's time of vengeance; He is going to render recompense to her. Babylon has been a golden cup in the hand of the LORD, intoxicating all the earth. The nations have drunk of her wine; therefore the nations are going mad. Suddenly Babylon has fallen and been broken; wail over her! Bring balm for her pain; perhaps she may be healed. We applied healing to Babylon, but she was not healed; forsake her and let us each go to his own country, for her judgment has reached to heaven and towers up to the very skies. The LORD has brought about our vindication; come and let us recount in Zion the work of the LORD our God! …*

> *"May the violence done to me and to my flesh be upon Babylon," the inhabitant of Zion will say; and, "May my blood be upon the inhabitants of Chaldea," Jerusalem will say. Therefore thus says the LORD, "Behold, I am going to plead your case and exact full vengeance for you; and I will dry up her sea and make her fountain dry. Babylon will become a heap of ruins, a haunt of jackals, an object of horror and hissing, without inhabitants." …*

> *Indeed Babylon is to fall for the slain of Israel, as also for Babylon the slain of all the earth have fallen. You who have escaped the sword, depart! Do not stay! Remember the LORD from afar, and let Jerusalem come to your mind.*

Revelation

Scripture Passage: 2 Peter 2:9–10

Then the Lord knows how to rescue the godly from temptation, and to keep the unrighteous under punishment for the day of judgment, and especially those who indulge the flesh in its corrupt desires and despise authority. Daring, self-willed, they do not tremble when they revile angelic majesties.

Scripture Passage: Psalm 137:1–9

By the rivers of Babylon, there we sat down and wept, when we remembered Zion. Upon the willows in the midst of it we hung our harps. For there our captors demanded of us songs, and our tormentors mirth, saying, "Sing us one of the songs of Zion." How can we sing the LORD's song in a foreign land? If I forget you, O Jerusalem, may my right hand forget her skill. May my tongue cling to the roof of my mouth if I do not remember you, if I do not exalt Jerusalem above my chief joy. Remember, O LORD, against the sons of Edom the day of Jerusalem, who said, "Raze it, raze it to its very foundation." O daughter of Babylon, you devastated one, how blessed will be the one who repays you with the recompense with which you have repaid us. How blessed will be the one who seizes and dashes your little ones against the rock.

A LITTLE DEEPER...

1. Trace the role of Babylon throughout biblical history, specifically that of the Old Testament. What happened there? What happened because of its rulers and people? How do these events earn God's judgment?

_____

_____

_____

2. Consider the assorted animals Jeremiah says will make their home in Babylon. What do they have in common? Why might these animals reside in Babylon in judgment?

_____

_____

_____

3. Second Peter 2 points out that our omniscient and omnipotent God is able to selectively punish and reward according to individual merit. Read Matthew 13:24–30. As we continue to read and study destruction and judgment, where can we place our hope? Why?

___

___

___

SESSION FIFTY-SIX

Revelation 18:1–8

> ***Remember the Golden Rule:*** *When the plain sense of Scripture makes common sense, we seek no other sense.*

Video Fifty-Six

Topical overview: Old Testament prophecy elaborating on the destruction of Babylon. Babylon's physical destruction.

Learning goals: Understand why the fulfillment of Isaiah's and Jeremiah's prophecies remains in the future. Follow the path of Babylon's physical destruction.

CORE QUESTIONS

Before watching video fifty-six, read Revelation 18:1–8. Use the two-column graphic organizer to help you organize your thoughts. Discuss your observations as a group.

As you watch the video, complete the following section. For many, reading the questions before watching the video will aid their understanding of the video content.

Revelation 18:1–3

1. What will remain of Babylon?

_____

_____

_____

2. Why must these passages of Isaiah and Jeremiah refer to an event still yet to come?

3. Are the animal habitants of Babylon as described in Revelation 18 literal?

Revelation 18:4–8

1. Who does God give warning of impending judgment on Babylon?

2. Where has God previously given this same warning?

3. Where will those who flee Babylon go?

4. What is the purpose of this physical destruction of Babylon?

Revelation

5. What will be the two-stage destruction of physical Babylon?

_____
_____
_____

Discussion Questions

1. Even at this late stage of Tribulation, God provides warnings of what is yet to come. Why? Who are the warnings for, and what do the warnings reveal about the nature of God?

_____
_____
_____

2. Why is the utter destruction of Babylon justified, and how does God accomplish it?

_____
_____
_____

3. When you consider God's means for accomplishing Babylon's preordained destruction, what do you notice? How do you see God working in a similar manner in the world around you?

_____
_____
_____

4. In the space below, record your takeaway from Revelation 18:1–8 and any questions you have that remain unanswered.

_____
_____
_____

REVELATION 18:1–8

DIGGING DEEPER (OPTIONAL)

Should you choose to dig deeper, complete the following Digging Deeper section. Each meeting will open with discussion of what you've learned and observed in Scripture, and this section will prepare you for that discussion.

In a two-column graphic organizer, record what you observe in each passage and the questions you have about it. Things to look for: Who is speaking? To whom is he speaking? What does he say about God? Jesus? The church? Individual believers? What do readers of this text stand to gain?

Scripture Passage: Read Revelation 16:19; 17:17; 18:9–24

Scripture Passage: Isaiah 13:1–5

The oracle concerning Babylon which Isaiah the son of Amoz saw. Lift up a standard on the bare hill, raise your voice to them, wave the hand that they may enter the doors of the nobles. I have commanded My consecrated ones, I have even called My mighty warriors, My proudly exulting ones, to execute My anger. A sound of tumult on the mountains, like that of many people! A sound of the uproar of kingdoms, of nations gathered together! The LORD of hosts is mustering the army for battle. They are coming from a far country, from the farthest horizons, the LORD and His instruments of indignation, to destroy the whole land.

Scripture Passage: Jeremiah 50:1–3, 9, 41–43, 46; 51:1–4, 27–29, 31

The word which the LORD spoke concerning Babylon, the land of the Chaldeans, through Jeremiah the prophet: "Declare and proclaim among the nations. Proclaim it and lift up a standard. Do not conceal it but say, 'Babylon has been captured, Bel has been put to shame, Marduk has been shattered; her images have been put to shame, her idols have been shattered.' For a nation has come up against her out of the north; it will make her land an object of horror, and there will be no inhabitant in it. Both man and beast have wandered off, they have gone away! ...

"For behold, I am going to arouse and bring up against Babylon a horde of great nations from the land of the north, and they will draw up their battle lines against her; from there she will be taken captive. Their arrows will be like an expert warrior who does not return empty-handed." ...

"Behold, a people is coming from the north, and a great nation and many kings will be aroused from the remote parts of the earth. They seize their bow and javelin; they are cruel and have no mercy. Their voice roars like the sea; and they ride on horses, marshalled like a man for the battle against you, O daughter of Babylon. The king of Babylon has heard the report about them, and his hands hang limp; distress has gripped him, agony like a woman in childbirth." ...

At the shout, "Babylon has been seized!" the earth is shaken, and an outcry is heard among the nations. ...

REVELATION

Thus says the LORD: "Behold, I am going to arouse against Babylon and against the inhabitants of Leb-kamai the spirit of a destroyer. I will dispatch foreigners to Babylon that they may winnow her and may devastate her land; for on every side they will be opposed to her in the day of her calamity. Let not him who bends his bow bend it, nor let him rise up in his scale-armor; so do not spare her young men; devote all her army to destruction. They will fall down slain in the land of the Chaldeans, and pierced through in their streets." ...

Lift up a signal in the land, blow a trumpet among the nations! Consecrate the nations against her, summon against her the kingdoms of Ararat, Minni and Ashkenaz; appoint a marshal against her, bring up the horses like bristly locusts. Consecrate the nations against her, The kings of the Medes, their governors and all their prefects, and every land of their dominion. So the land quakes and writhes, for the purposes of the LORD against Babylon stand, to make the land of Babylon a desolation without inhabitants. ...

One courier runs to meet another, and one messenger to meet another, to tell the king of Babylon that his city has been captured from end to end.

A LITTLE DEEPER...

1. What happens to physical Babylon, and who does these things?

2. What does the angel's pronouncement effectively end in Babylon?

3. What do the merchants and traders use to describe Babylon in the Revelation passage? How might these same things symbolically describe spiritual Babylon?

4. Consider the various nations to the north Jeremiah includes in his call to arms. What do they all have in common, and why is it significant that God has consecrated them to the purpose of destroying Babylon?

___

SESSION FIFTY-SEVEN

Revelation 18:9–24

> ***Remember the Golden Rule:*** *When the plain sense of Scripture makes common sense, we seek no other sense.*

Video Fifty-Seven

Topical overview: The fall of physical Babylon.
Learning goals: Connect Old Testament prophetic details to big picture Revelation events

CORE QUESTIONS

Before watching video fifty-seven, read Revelation 18:9–24. Use the two-column graphic organizer to help you organize your thoughts. Discuss your observations as a group.

As you watch the video, complete the following section. For many, reading the questions before watching the video will aid their understanding of the video content.

1. Where do we find the details of the destruction of Babylon?

_____

_____

_____

2. What is this "spirit of the destroyer?"

_____

3. What region does "Leb-kamai" or "heart of my adversaries" reference?

4. What are the modern equivalents of the nations mentioned in Jeremiah 51?

5. Why would an army attack Babylon, the devil or Antichrist's headquarters, and what do they accomplish?

6. How long does it take for Babylon to fall, and what does this indicate?

7. How can all of the blood of prophets and saints be blamed on this one city?

8. What is the Antichrist's reaction to the fall of Babylon?

Revelation

Chapter 18 ends with the second stage of the War of Armageddon complete and stage 3 setting the stage for the Lord's return in chapter 19.

DISCUSSION QUESTIONS

1. Are military maneuvers something you grasp easily? How does your understanding (or lack thereof) of military maneuvering affect your grasp of this section of Revelation?

2. In the events of this portion of Tribulation, God is accomplishing His will by removing Satan's alternatives for action. How have you seen God work in the same manner in modern times or in your own life specifically?

3. Which modern nations comprise the Mesopotamian region of *Leb-kamai*? How do their current and historical relations with Israel reflect the meaning of the term *leb-kamai*?

4. How does God accomplish the full measure of His wrath on Babylon, and how is the focus of His judgment on this one city for martyrdom and persecution throughout history justified?

5. In the space below, record your takeaway from Revelation 18:9–24 and any questions you have that remain unanswered.

DIGGING DEEPER (OPTIONAL)

Should you choose to dig deeper, complete the following Digging Deeper section. Each meeting will open with discussion of what you've learned and observed in Scripture, and this section will prepare you for that discussion.

In a two-column graphic organizer, record what you observe in each passage and the questions you have about it. Things to look for: Who is speaking? To whom is he speaking? What does he say about God? Jesus? The church? Individual believers? What do readers of this text stand to gain?

Scripture Passage: Read Revelation 19:1–10

Scripture Passage: Ephesians 5:25–27, 32

> *Husbands, love your wives, just as Christ also loved the church and gave Himself up for her, so that He might sanctify her, having cleansed her by the washing of water with the word, that He might present to Himself the church in all her glory, having no spot or wrinkle or any such thing; but that she would be holy and blameless. ...*
>
> *This mystery is great; but I am speaking with reference to Christ and the church.*

Scripture Passage: Matthew 26:26–29

> *While they were eating, Jesus took some bread, and after a blessing, He broke it and gave it to the disciples, and said, "Take, eat; this is My body." And when He had taken a cup and given thanks, He gave it to them, saying, "Drink from it, all of you; for this is My blood of the covenant, which is poured out for many for forgiveness of sins. But I say to you, I will not drink of this fruit of the vine from now on until that day when I drink it new with you in My Father's kingdom."*

REVELATION

A LITTLE DEEPER...

1. Based on your understanding, what is the biblical definition and purpose of marriage? How are we supposed to live within the covenant of marriage?

_____
_____
_____

2. Review what you've learned about biblical era Jewish wedding customs.

_____
_____
_____

3. How does the metaphor of a marriage and wedding feast translate to the relationship of the church to Jesus?

_____
_____
_____

4. Take some time to worship God, who was and is, and who forever will be. He reigns over all and holds the world and every soul in it in the palm of His hand. He is surely and completely in control, no matter what your present circumstances might lead you to believe. He is righteous and good. He will accomplish justice for His people. And His mercy for those who worship Him endures forever.

_____
_____
_____

SESSION FIFTY-EIGHT

Revelation 19:1–10

> ***Remember the Golden Rule:*** *When the plain sense of Scripture makes common sense, we seek no other sense.*

Video Fifty-Eight

Topical overview: The heavenly worship service of Revelation 19. The marriage supper of the Lamb.

Learning goals: Understand the movement of God's Spirit throughout history. Unpack the metaphor of the wedding feast of the Lamb.

CORE QUESTIONS

Before watching video fifty-eight, read Revelation 19:1–10. Use the two-column graphic organizer to help you organize your thoughts. Discuss your observations as a group.

As you watch the video, complete the following section. For many, reading the questions before watching the video will aid their understanding of the video content.

Overview

1. What part of the Bible tells us the most about Christ's second coming?

_____

_____

_____

Revelation

Revelation 19:1–5

1. What does the phrase "after these things" indicate?

___

2. How does the fall of Babylon pave the way for Christ's return?

___

3. Where will we be when the events of Revelation 19 occur?

___

4. At this point, where is the believing church?

___

5. What is worship?

___

Revelation 19:6–10

1. Who is the bride of Christ?

___

2. What is significant about the period of the church, the bride of Christ?

3. Why does God use the metaphor of a wedding?

4. What is the connection between the Passover of Matthew 26 and the wedding feast of Revelation 19?

Discussion Questions

1. Does the metaphor of the wedding feast help you understand what God is telling us? Why or why not? Are there pieces of this metaphor you don't quite understand? Use this time as a group to ensure all fully understand ancient Jewish wedding practices and their correlation to end times events.

2. Does the heavenly worship service described in Revelation line up with what you've thought heaven will be like? Why or why not?

Revelation

_____

_____

3. How are the last supper and the wedding feast of the Lamb connected? What does this teach you about the bridegroom (Jesus)?

_____

_____

_____

4. In the space below, record your takeaway from Revelation 19:1–10 and any questions you have that remain unanswered.

_____

_____

_____

Digging Deeper (Optional)

Should you choose to dig deeper, complete the following Digging Deeper section. Each meeting will open with discussion of what you've learned and observed in Scripture, and this section will prepare you for that discussion.

In a two-column graphic organizer, record what you observe in each passage and the questions you have about it. Things to look for: Who is speaking? To whom is he speaking? What does he say about God? Jesus? The church? Individual believers? What do readers of this text stand to gain?

Scripture Passage: Read Revelation 19:6–10

Scripture Passage: 2 Corinthians 5:10

> *For we must all appear before the judgment seat of Christ, so that each one may be recompensed for his deeds in the body, according to what he has done, whether good or bad.*

Scripture Passage: Daniel 11:36–45

Then the king will do as he pleases, and he will exalt and magnify himself above every god and will speak monstrous things against the God of gods; and he will prosper until the indignation is finished, for that which is decreed will be done. He will show no regard for the gods of his fathers or for the desire of women, nor will he show regard for any other god; for he will magnify himself above them all. But instead he will honor a god of fortresses, a god whom his fathers did not know; he will honor him with gold, silver, costly stones and treasures. He will take action against the strongest of fortresses with the help of a foreign god; he will give great honor to those who acknowledge him and will cause them to rule over the many, and will parcel out land for a price. At the end time the king of the South will collide with him, and the king of the North will storm against him with chariots, with horsemen and with many ships; and he will enter countries, overflow them and pass through. He will also enter the Beautiful Land, and many countries will fall; but these will be rescued out of his hand: Edom, Moab and the foremost of the sons of Ammon. Then he will stretch out his hand against other countries, and the land of Egypt will not escape. But he will gain control over the hidden treasures of gold and silver and over all the precious things of Egypt; and Libyans and Ethiopians will follow at his heels. But rumors from the East and from the North will disturb him, and he will go forth with great wrath to destroy and annihilate many. He will pitch the tents of his royal pavilion between the seas and the beautiful Holy Mountain; yet he will come to his end, and no one will help him.

Scripture Passage: Jeremiah 49:13–16

"For I have sworn by Myself," declares the LORD, "that Bozrah will become an object of horror, a reproach, a ruin and a curse; and all its cities will become perpetual ruins." I have heard a message from the LORD, and an envoy is sent among the nations, saying, "Gather yourselves together and come against her, and rise up for battle! For behold, I have made you small among the nations, despised among men. As for the terror of you, the arrogance of your heart has deceived you, O you who live in the clefts of the rock, who occupy the height of the hill. Though you make your nest as high as an eagle's, I will bring you down from there," declares the LORD.

A LITTLE DEEPER...

1. Where else in the Bible do we read of the saints being clothed in the fine, white linen of their individual righteousness? Seek out and read the relevant passages. Collectively, we are to be the bride at the wedding feast of the Lamb. How must we prepare ourselves? Why must we prepare ourselves as would a bride for her husband?

_____

_____

_____

2. The passages in Daniel and Jeremiah describe the physical destruction of Babylon. What will happen to it, and how will God accomplish this?

___

SESSION FIFTY-NINE

Revelation 19:6–10

Remember the Golden Rule: When the plain sense of Scripture makes common sense, we seek no other sense.

Video Fifty-Nine

Topical overview: Guests and participants of the wedding feast of the Lamb. Armageddon stage three.

Learning goals: Assimilate stage three of Armageddon into your overall understanding of end times events.

Core Questions

Before watching video fifty-nine, read Revelation 19:6–10. Use the two-column graphic organizer to help you organize your thoughts. Discuss your observations as a group.
As you watch the video, complete the following section. For many, reading the questions before watching the video will aid their understanding of the video content.

1. What is the bride of Christ clothed in?

_____

_____

_____

2. Who are the guests at this wedding feast in heaven?

3. What's significant about John's interaction with his escort angel?

The author of the message, not the conduit of that message, deserves glory.

4. Summarize stage three of Armageddon.

5. In between stages two and three, where are the Antichrist's forces?

6. Who does Antichrist target with an attack at this point?

8. In the Antichrist's next move, where does he move his forces and why?

Discussion Questions

1. Do you struggle to follow the military maneuvers that make up stage three of Armageddon? If any struggle, use this time to help the group understand how the Antichrist moves his forces, and how, in doing so, he accomplishes God's will.

___

2. Do you agree that we as humans tend to glorify the messenger or the message rather than the source? Why or why not? How do you see this principle play out in the world today?

___

3. Exodus 14:14 says, "The LORD will fight for you; you need only to be still" (NIV). How does this prove true for the Jews ensconced in Bozrah? How have you seen the same to be true in your own life? What does this teach you about the God you serve?

___

4. Who is present at the marriage feast of the Lamb, and what roles do they fill? Notice who is present in spirit form and who is present in bodily form. Which will we be? When you comprehend your personal role in this end time story, what is your response to God?

___

5. In the space below, record your takeaway from Revelation 19:6–10 and any questions you have that remain unanswered.

_____

_____

_____

Digging Deeper (Optional)

Should you choose to dig deeper, complete the following Digging Deeper section. Each meeting will open with discussion of what you've learned and observed in Scripture, and this section will prepare you for that discussion.

In a two-column graphic organizer, record what you observe in each passage and the questions you have about it. Things to look for: Who is speaking? To whom is he speaking? What does he say about God? Jesus? The church? Individual believers? What do readers of this text stand to gain?

Scripture Passage: Read Revelation 19:1–10

Scripture Passage: Joel 3:9–12

Proclaim this among the nations: prepare a war; rouse the mighty men! Let all the soldiers draw near, let them come up! Beat your plowshares into swords and your pruning hooks into spears; let the weak say, "I am a mighty man." Hasten and come, all you surrounding nations, and gather yourselves there. Bring down, O Lord, Your mighty ones. Let the nations be aroused and come up to the valley of Jehoshaphat, for there I will sit to judge all the surrounding nations.

Scripture Passage: Isaiah 29:1–7 (note: *Ariel* means Jerusalem)

Woe, O Ariel, Ariel the city where David once camped! Add year to year, observe your feasts on schedule. I will bring distress to Ariel, and she will be a city of lamenting and mourning; and she will be like an Ariel to me. I will camp against you encircling you, and I will set siegeworks against you, and I will raise up battle towers against you. Then you will be brought low; from the earth you will speak, and from the dust where you are prostrate your words will come. Your voice will also be like that of a spirit from the ground, and your speech will whisper from the dust. But the multitude of your enemies will become like fine dust, and the multitude of the ruthless ones like the chaff which blows away; and it will happen instantly, suddenly. From the Lord of hosts you will be punished with thunder and earthquake and loud noise, with whirlwind and tempest and the flame of a consuming fire. And the multitude of all the nations who wage war against Ariel, even all who wage war against her and her stronghold, and who distress her, will be like a dream, a vision of the night.

REVELATION 19:6–10

Scripture Passage: Micah 4:9–12

*Now, why do you cry out loudly? Is there no king among you, or has your counselor perished, that agony has gripped you like a woman in childbirth? Writhe and labor to give birth, Daughter of Zion, like a woman in childbirth; for now you will go out of the city, dwell in the field, and go to Babylon. There you will be rescued; there the L*ORD *will redeem you from the hand of your enemies. And now many nations have been assembled against you, who say, "Let her be polluted, and let our eyes gloat over Zion." But they do not know the thoughts of the L*ORD*, and they do not understand His purpose; for He has gathered them like sheaves to the threshing floor.*

Scripture Passage: Zechariah 12:1–9, 13:7–9

*The burden of the word of the L*ORD *concerning Israel. Thus declares the L*ORD *who stretches out the heavens, lays the foundation of the earth, and forms the spirit of man within him, "Behold, I am going to make Jerusalem a cup that causes reeling to all the peoples around; and when the siege is against Jerusalem, it will also be against Judah. It will come about in that day that I will make Jerusalem a heavy stone for all the peoples; all who lift it will be severely injured. And all the nations of the earth will be gathered against it. In that day," declares the L*ORD*, "I will strike every horse with bewilderment and his rider with madness. But I will watch over the house of Judah, while I strike every horse of the peoples with blindness. Then the clans of Judah will say in their hearts, 'A strong support for us are the inhabitants of Jerusalem through the L*ORD *of hosts, their God.' In that day I will make the clans of Judah like a firepot among pieces of wood and a flaming torch among sheaves, so they will consume on the right hand and on the left all the surrounding peoples, while the inhabitants of Jerusalem again dwell on their own sites in Jerusalem. The L*ORD *also will save the tents of Judah first, so that the glory of the house of David and the glory of the inhabitants of Jerusalem will not be magnified above Judah. In that day the L*ORD *will defend the inhabitants of Jerusalem, and the one who is feeble among them in that day will be like David, and the house of David will be like God, like the angel of the L*ORD *before them. And in that day I will set about to destroy all the nations that come against Jerusalem." ...*

*"Awake, O sword, against My Shepherd, and against the man, My Associate," declares the L*ORD *of hosts. Strike the Shepherd that the sheep may be scattered; and I will turn My hand against the little ones. It will come about in all the land," declares the L*ORD*, "that two parts in it will be cut off and perish; but the third will be left in it. And I will bring the third part through the fire, refine them as silver is refined, and test them as gold is tested. They will call on My name, and I will answer them; I will say, 'They are My people,' and they will say, 'The L*ORD *is my God.'"*

Scripture Passage: 2 Kings 19:19–20, 28–35

*"Now, O L*ORD *our God, I pray, deliver us from his hand that all the kingdoms of the earth may know that You alone, O L*ORD *are God." Then Isaiah the son of Amoz sent to Hezekiah saying, "Thus says the L*ORD *the God of Israel, 'Because you have prayed to Me about Sennacherib king of Assyria, I have heard you.' This is the word that the L*ORD *has spoken against him. ...*

"Because of your raging against Me, and because your arrogance has come up to My ears,

REVELATION

therefore I will put My hook in your nose, and My bridle in your lips, and I will turn you back by the way which you came. Then this shall be the sign for you: you will eat this year what grows of itself, in the second year what springs from the same, and in the third-year sow, reap, plant vineyards, and eat their fruit. The surviving remnant of the house of Judah will again take root downward and bear fruit upward. For out of Jerusalem will go forth a remnant, and out of Mount Zion survivors. The zeal of the L<small>ORD</small> will perform this. Therefore thus says the L<small>ORD</small> concerning the king of Assyria, 'He will not come to this city or shoot an arrow there; and he will not come before it with a shield or throw up a siege ramp against it. By the way that he came, by the same he will return, and he shall not come to this city,'" declares the L<small>ORD</small>. "For I will defend this city to save it for My own sake and for My servant David's sake." Then it happened that night that the angel of the L<small>ORD</small> went out and struck 185,000 in the camp of the Assyrians; and when men rose early in the morning, behold, all of them were dead.

A LITTLE DEEPER…

1. When applied to the armies of the Antichrist, what does it mean for God to gather them "like sheaves to the threshing floor?"

_____

_____

_____

2. What will the Antichrist's armies do to Jerusalem, how will the Jews within respond, and how will the Lord act on their behalf?

_____

_____

_____

3. What does the word *zeal* mean? How will the "zeal of the Lord" accomplish His will?

_____

_____

_____

4. Remember, God often speaks in patterns as Old Testament events prefigure or lay a pattern for those to come. The passage in 2 Kings reflects real, historical events, but those same events also prefigure those of Armageddon. How so?

_____

SESSION SIXTY

Isaiah 29:1–7

> ***Remember the Golden Rule:*** *When the plain sense of Scripture makes common sense, we seek no other sense.*

Video Sixty

Topical overview: God's salvation of Jerusalem.
Learning goals: Follow the Antichrist's movements as Armageddon progresses. Recognize how the actions of the Jews affect the Lord's defense of them and Jerusalem.

Core Questions

Before watching video sixty, read Isaiah 29:1–7. Use the two-column graphic organizer to help you organize your thoughts. Discuss your observations as a group.

As you watch the video, complete the following section. For many, reading the questions before watching the video will aid their understanding of the video content.

1. What is stage three of the War of Armageddon, and what triggers these actions?

_____

_____

_____

2. How does Antichrist mount his attack of Jerusalem?

_____

3. How does God use Antichrist's military maneuvers to accomplish His will?

4. What is Ariel?

5. How do the people in Jerusalem defeat Antichrist's forces?

6. What brings the Jewish people to this point of crying out to the Lord?

7. How does the Lord supernaturally defend Jerusalem?

8. Who all does the Lord defend?

9. Which Old Testament event does this battle mirror?

10. Is there much of an actual battle in this war of Armageddon?

Discussion Questions

1. Why are we reading Old Testament passages to learn the events of Armageddon? How are these passages relevant to Revelation 19?

2. What does it mean to be "purified by fire" in the biblical sense? How will the Jews in Jerusalem at the time of Armageddon respond to their purification? How does God accomplish "purification by fire" in our lives and for what purpose?

3. What does it mean for the Lord to defend? How does He do this, both in the specific events of Armageddon and as a general principle for how He acts of the behalf of those who love Him?

4. How does the Lord accomplish the victory of Armageddon without physical engagement or battle? How does He do the same in our lives?

5. In the space below, record your takeaway from Isaiah 29:1–7 and any questions you have that remain unanswered.

DIGGING DEEPER (OPTIONAL)

Should you choose to dig deeper, complete the following Digging Deeper section. Each meeting will open with discussion of what you've learned and observed in Scripture, and this section will prepare you for that discussion.

In a two-column graphic organizer, record what you observe in each passage and the questions you have about it. Things to look for: Who is speaking? To whom is he speaking? What does he say about God? Jesus? The church? Individual believers? What do readers of this text stand to gain?

Scripture Passage: Daniel 9:24

Seventy weeks have been decreed for your people and your holy city, to finish the transgression, to make an end of sin, to make atonement for iniquity, to bring in everlasting righteousness, to seal up vision and prophecy and to anoint the most holy place.

Scripture Passage: Zechariah 13:8–9

"It will come about in all the land," declares the LORD, "that two parts in it will be cut off and perish; but the third will be left in it. And I will bring the third part through the fire, refine them as silver is

refined, and test them as gold is tested. They will call on My name, and I will answer them; I will say, 'They are My people,' and they will say, 'The LORD is my God.'"

Scripture Passage: Deuteronomy 29:14–18, 22–25

Now not with you alone am I making this covenant and this oath, but both with those who stand here with us today in the presence of the LORD our God and with those who are not with us here today (for you know how we lived in the land of Egypt, and how we came through the midst of the nations through which you passed; moreover, you have seen their abominations and their idols of wood, stone, silver, and gold, which they had with them); so that there will not be among you a man or woman, or family or tribe, whose heart turns away today from the LORD our God, to go and serve the gods of those nations; that there will not be among you a root bearing poisonous fruit and wormwood. ...

Now the generation to come, your sons who rise up after you and the foreigner who comes from a distant land, when they see the plagues of the land and the diseases with which the LORD has afflicted it, will say, "All its land is brimstone and salt, a burning waste, unsown and unproductive, and no grass grows in it, like the overthrow of Sodom and Gomorrah, Admah and Zeboiim, which the LORD overthrew in His anger and in His wrath." All the nations will say, "Why has the LORD done thus to this land? Why this great outburst of anger?" Then men will say, "Because they forsook the covenant of the LORD, the God of their fathers, which He made with them when He brought them out of the land of Egypt."

Scripture Passage: Romans 11:4–7, 11

But what is the divine response to him? "I HAVE KEPT for Myself SEVEN THOUSAND MEN WHO HAVE NOT BOWED THE KNEE TO BAAL." In the same way then, there has also come to be at the present time a remnant according to God's gracious choice. But if it is by grace, it is no longer on the basis of works, otherwise grace is no longer grace. What then? What Israel is seeking, it has not obtained, but those who were chosen obtained it, and the rest were hardened. ...

I say then, they did not stumble so as to fall, did they? May it never be! But by their transgression salvation has come to the Gentiles, to make them jealous.

Scripture Passage: Luke 13:34–35

O Jerusalem, Jerusalem, the city that kills the prophets and stones those sent to her! How often I wanted to gather your children together, just as a hen gathers her brood under her wings, and you would not have it! Behold, your house is left to you desolate; and I say to you, you will not see Me until the time comes when you say, "BLESSED IS HE WHO COMES IN THE NAME OF THE LORD!"

ISAIAH 29:1–7

A LITTLE DEEPER…

1. In the passage from Romans, we learn the purpose of God's grace moving to the Gentiles: To make Israel jealous after their hearts had wandered from Him. A refrain from the Old Testament is that Abraham and his descendants were blessed so that they in turn might bless the nations. Research this concept in the Old Testament – blessed to be a blessing. What did you learn?

_____

_____

_____

2. In God's covenant with the Jews, what was His heart for the salvation of all? What consequences did they acquire for their rebellion? What does all this mean for us, Gentiles?

_____

_____

_____

3. Zechariah prophesies that, as a nation, the hearts of Israel will finally return to the Lord. In response, we've learned that God will fight on their behalf to save Jerusalem from the Antichrist and his armies. Throughout history, how has God refined Israel by fire to reach this point? How does He use Gentiles to make Jews jealous of grace (think about during Tribulation specifically)?

_____

_____

_____

SESSION SIXTY-ONE

Stages One–Three of Armageddon

Remember the Golden Rule: When the plain sense of Scripture makes common sense, we seek no other sense.

Video Sixty-One

Topical overview: Summarize stages one through three of Armageddon. Mosaic Covenant and its consequences.

Learning goals: Explore the connection between the Mosaic Covenant of Deuteronomy and the events of Revelation. Review the events and effects of stages one through three of Armageddon.

CORE QUESTIONS

Before watching video sixty-one, read Revelation 19:1–21. Use the two-column graphic organizer to help you organize your thoughts. Discuss your observations as a group.

As you watch the video, complete the following section. For many, reading the questions before watching the video will aid their understanding of the video content.

1. Summarize stage one of Armageddon.

_____

_____

_____

2. Summarize stage two of Armageddon.

3. Summarize stage three of Armageddon.

4. What is the purpose of Tribulation?

5. How is the Mosaic Covenant connected to Tribulation?

6. How do the events of Tribulation lead the Jews to repentance?

7. Jesus set the terms for His return. What where they? What prompted His return?

REVELATION

DISCUSSION QUESTIONS

1. There is a direct cause and effect relationship between Deuteronomy and Revelation. What is it, and what does this connection teach us about history?

_____

_____

_____

2. Do you notice any patterns in the movements of Armageddon? What do these specific events tell us about God, Christ, and the Antichrist (purpose, role, character traits, etc.)?

_____

_____

_____

3. Culturally, we hear much about Christ's second coming. This session has taught us much about what Christ Himself specifically said about His own return. What are the terms Christ laid out for His return, and how does this compare with what people believe?

_____

_____

_____

4. In the space below, record your takeaway from Session Sixty-One and any questions you have that remain unanswered.

_____

_____

_____

DIGGING DEEPER (OPTIONAL)

Should you choose to dig deeper, complete the following Digging Deeper section. Each meeting will open with discussion of what you've learned and observed in Scripture, and this section will prepare you for that discussion.

In a two-column graphic organizer, record what you observe in each passage and the questions you have about it. Things to look for: Who is speaking? To whom is he speaking? What does he say about God? Jesus? The church? Individual believers? What do readers of this text stand to gain?

Scripture Passage: Leviticus 26:40–42

If they confess their iniquity and the iniquity of their forefathers, in their unfaithfulness which they committed against Me, and also in their acting with hostility against Me—I also was acting with hostility against them, to bring them into the land of their enemies—or if their uncircumcised heart becomes humbled so that they then make amends for their iniquity, then I will remember My covenant with Jacob, and I will remember also My covenant with Isaac, and My covenant with Abraham as well, and I will remember the land.

Scripture Passage: Zechariah 12:2–3, 8–10; 14:1–2

Behold, I am going to make Jerusalem a cup that causes reeling to all the peoples around; and when the siege is against Jerusalem, it will also be against Judah. It will come about in that day that I will make Jerusalem a heavy stone for all the peoples; all who lift it will be severely injured. And all the nations of the earth will be gathered against it. ...

In that day the LORD will defend the inhabitants of Jerusalem, and the one who is feeble among them in that day will be like David, and the house of David will be like God, like the angel of the LORD before them. And in that day I will set about to destroy all the nations that come against Jerusalem. I will pour out on the house of David and on the inhabitants of Jerusalem, the Spirit of grace and of supplication, so that they will look on Me whom they have pierced; and they will mourn for Him, as one mourns for an only son, and they will weep bitterly over Him like the bitter weeping over a firstborn. ...

Behold, a day is coming for the LORD when the spoil taken from you will be divided among you. For I will gather all the nations against Jerusalem to battle, and the city will be captured, the houses plundered, the women ravished and half of the city exiled, but the rest of the people will not be cut off from the city.

Scripture Passage: Luke 18:27

But He said, "The things that are impossible with people are possible with God."

Scripture Passage: Matthew 24:13–14

But the one who endures to the end, he will be saved. This gospel of the kingdom shall be preached in the whole world as a testimony to all the nations, and then the end will come.

Revelation

Scripture Passage: Romans 11:25–27

For I do not want you, brethren, to be uninformed of this mystery—so that you will not be wise in your own estimation—that a partial hardening has happened to Israel until the fullness of the Gentiles has come in; and so all Israel will be saved; just as it is written, "THE DELIVERER WILL COME FROM ZION, HE WILL REMOVE UNGODLINESS FROM JACOB. THIS IS MY COVENANT WITH THEM, WHEN I TAKE AWAY THEIR SINS."

A LITTLE DEEPER...

1. Do some research on covenants. What is a covenant? What is the Abrahamic/ Old Covenant? What is the Mosaic Covenant? How are the two related?

_____

_____

_____

2. Trace what happens to Jerusalem and why throughout these scriptures. What will happen to Jerusalem during the final stages of Tribulation?

_____

_____

_____

SESSION SIXTY-TWO

Israel's Confession and Salvation

> ***Remember the Golden Rule:*** *When the plain sense of Scripture makes common sense, we seek no other sense.*

Video Sixty-Two

Topical overview: Israel's national confession and salvation.
Learning goals: Recognize the relationship between the Abrahamic and Mosaic Covenants and the events of Tribulation.

CORE QUESTIONS

Before watching video sixty-two, review Revelation 19. Use the two-column graphic organizer to help you organize your thoughts. Discuss your observations as a group.

As you watch the video, complete the following section. For many, reading the questions before watching the video will aid their understanding of the video content.

1. What must Israel remember and confess for God to forgive and restore them according to the Abrahamic covenant?

_____
_____
_____

Revelation

The Tribulation will bring much suffering to cause Israel, as a nation, to recognize Jesus as their Messiah, and in doing so, they'll bring about His return, ending the Tribulation, just as God promised Abraham.

2. What does "all Israel" in Romans 11:26 mean?

___

3. What specifically fulfills the Old Covenant?

___

The "Old Covenant" is the Mosaic Covenant (Exodus 19–24); The Abrahamic Covenant predates this (Genesis 12). The Mosaic/ Old Covenant and its fulfillment is the mechanism by which God fulfills the Abrahamic Covenant.

4. How does Israel reach a point where every living Jew is of a mind to confess Christ simultaneously?

___

5. Describe the infiltration of Jerusalem as a part of stage three of Armageddon?

___

6. Why has Satan always made his target the nation of Israel?

___

7. How does this national moment of saving faith come about?

DISCUSSION QUESTIONS

1. Have you ever considered the historic enmity between the nation of Israel and Satan before? Consider the history of the Jews in general and Israel in particular. How is Israel's crisis of faith in Revelation 19 both similar to and different from events in Israel's history? How do you see the enmity of Satan against Israel specifically throughout history?

2. Review the Abrahamic Covenant (Genesis 12) and the Mosaic Covenant (Exodus 19–24). What are God and the nation of Israel committing to do? For what purpose, and for what result? How are the two covenants related to each other, and what does any of this have to do with us, Gentiles?

3. In the space below, record your takeaway from Session Sixty-Two and any questions you have that remain unanswered.

Digging Deeper (Optional)

Should you choose to dig deeper, complete the following Digging Deeper section. Each meeting will open with discussion of what you've learned and observed in Scripture, and this section will prepare you for that discussion.

In a two-column graphic organizer, record what you observe in each passage and the questions you have about it. Things to look for: Who is speaking? To whom is he speaking? What does he say about God? Jesus? The church? Individual believers? What do readers of this text stand to gain?

Scripture Passage: Zechariah 12:11–14

In that day there will be great mourning in Jerusalem, like the mourning of Hadadrimmon in the plain of Megiddo. The land will mourn, every family by itself; the family of the house of David by itself and their wives by themselves; the family of the house of Nathan by itself and their wives by themselves; the family of the house of Levi by itself and their wives by themselves; the family of the Shimeites by itself and their wives by themselves; all the families that remain, every family by itself and their wives by themselves.

Scripture Passage: Psalm 79:1–13

O God, the nations have invaded Your inheritance; they have defiled Your holy temple; they have laid Jerusalem in ruins. They have given the dead bodies of Your servants for food to the birds of the heavens, the flesh of Your godly ones to the beasts of the earth. They have poured out their blood like water round about Jerusalem; and there was no one to bury them. We have become a reproach to our neighbors, a scoffing and derision to those around us. How long, O LORD? Will You be angry forever? Will Your jealousy burn like fire? Pour out Your wrath upon the nations which do not know You, and upon the kingdoms which do not call upon Your name. For they have devoured Jacob and laid waste his habitation. Do not remember the iniquities of our forefathers against us; let Your compassion come quickly to meet us, for we are brought very low. Help us, O God of our salvation, for the glory of Your name; and deliver us and forgive our sins for Your name's sake. Why should the nations say, "Where is their God?" Let there be known among the nations in our sight, vengeance for the blood of Your servants which has been shed. Let the groaning of the prisoner come before You; according to the greatness of Your power preserve those who are doomed to die. And return to our neighbors sevenfold into their bosom the reproach with which they have reproached You, O Lord. So we Your people and the sheep of Your pasture will give thanks to You forever; to all generations we will tell of Your praise.

Scripture Passage: Psalm 80:15–19

Even the shoot which Your right hand has planted, and on the son whom You have strengthened for Yourself. It is burned with fire, it is cut down; they perish at the rebuke of Your countenance.

Let Your hand be upon the man of Your right hand, upon the son of man whom You made strong for Yourself. Then we shall not turn back from You; revive us, and we will call upon Your name. O LORD God of hosts, restore us; cause Your face to shine upon us, and we will be saved.

Scripture Passage: Hosea 6:1–3

Come, let us return to the LORD. For He has torn us, but He will heal us; He has wounded us, but He will bandage us. He will revive us after two days; He will raise us up on the third day, that we may live before Him. So let us know, let us press on to know the LORD. His going forth is as certain as the dawn; and He will come to us like the rain, like the spring rain watering the earth.

Scripture Passage: Read Revelation 19:11–16

Scripture Passage: Matthew 16:27; 24:29–30

For the Son of Man is going to come in the glory of His Father with His angels, and WILL THEN REPAY EVERY MAN ACCORDING TO HIS DEEDS." ...

But immediately after the Tribulation of those days THE SUN WILL BE DARKENED, AND THE MOON WILL NOT GIVE ITS LIGHT, AND THE STARS WILL FALL from the sky, and the powers of the heavens will be shaken. And then the sign of the Son of Man will appear in the sky, and then all the tribes of the earth will mourn, and they will see the SON OF MAN COMING ON THE CLOUDS OF THE SKY with power and great glory.

Scripture Passage: Zechariah 14:6–7

In that day there will be no light; the luminaries will dwindle. For it will be a unique day which is known to the LORD, neither day nor night, but it will come about that at evening time there will be light.

A LITTLE DEEPER…

1. In the passages above, what is the state of Israel/ the Jewish people?

_____

_____

_____

2. What are the roles of God the Father and Christ the son in judgment and its execution?

_____

_____

_____

3. What must Israel do to be saved?

_____

_____

_____

SESSION SIXTY-THREE

Revelation 19:11–16

> ***Remember the Golden Rule:*** *When the plain sense of Scripture makes common sense, we seek no other sense.*

Video Sixty-Three

Topical overview: Mechanics of Christ's return.
Learning goals: Understand the manner and identity in which Christ will return.

Core Questions

Before watching video sixty-three, read Revelation 19:11–16. Use the two-column graphic organizer to help you organize your thoughts. Discuss your observations as a group.

As you watch the video, complete the following section. For many, reading the questions before watching the video will aid their understanding of the video content.

Overview

1. What does Zechariah's list of kinds of Jews coming to saving faith indicate?

_____
_____
_____

REVELATION

2. What do Psalms 79–80 express?

3. How long does the siege of Jerusalem last before Christ returns because of Israel's repentance?

Revelation 19:11–16

1. In what form does Jesus appear at this point?

2. What will be Jesus' name at this point?

3. Why does it matter that Jesus is riding a white horse?

4. Why is Jesus's robe dipped in blood?

REVELATION 19:11–16

5. Who is the army in white linen behind him?

6. There's a second army present. Who are they?

7. What sort of events will directly precede Christ's physical return?

DISCUSSION QUESTIONS

1. What is the difference between how Jesus came the first time and how He will come the second time? How do first century expectations become reality in Tribulation?

2. Jesus doesn't come back alone. Who is with Him, and how does that make you feel?

3. How does the image of Jesus we see here in Revelation 19 compare to the one you hold in your mind? What steps might you take to align your mental image of Christ with the biblical image of Christ?

_____

_____

_____

4. In the space below, record your takeaway from Revelation 19:11–16 and any questions you have that remain unanswered.

_____

_____

_____

DIGGING DEEPER (OPTIONAL)

Should you choose to dig deeper, complete the following Digging Deeper section. Each meeting will open with discussion of what you've learned and observed in Scripture, and this section will prepare you for that discussion.

In a two-column graphic organizer, record what you observe in each passage and the questions you have about it. Things to look for: Who is speaking? To whom is he speaking? What does he say about God? Jesus? The church? Individual believers? What do readers of this text stand to gain?

Scripture Passage: Read Revelation 19:12–15

Scripture Passage: Romans 11:26–27

> ...and so all Israel will be saved; just as it is written, "The Deliverer will come from Zion, He will remove ungodliness from Jacob. This is My covenant with them, when I take away their sins."

Scripture Passage: Isaiah 34:1–6; 59:16–21; 60:1–2; 63:1–2

> Draw near, O nations, to hear; and listen, O peoples! Let the earth and all it contains hear, and the world and all that springs from it. For the LORD's indignation is against all the nations, and His wrath against all their armies; He has utterly destroyed them, He has given them over to slaughter. So their slain will be thrown out, and their corpses will give off their stench, and the

mountains will be drenched with their blood. And all the host of heaven will wear away, and the sky will be rolled up like a scroll; all their hosts will also wither away as a leaf withers from the vine, or as one withers from the fig tree. For My sword is satiated in heaven, behold it shall descend for judgment upon Edom and upon the people whom I have devoted to destruction. The sword of the LORD is filled with blood, it is sated with fat, with the blood of lambs and goats, with the fat of the kidneys of rams. For the LORD has a sacrifice in Bozrah and a great slaughter in the land of Edom. …

And He saw that there was no man, and was astonished that there was no one to intercede; then His own arm brought salvation to Him, and His righteousness upheld Him. He put on righteousness like a breastplate, and a helmet of salvation on His head; and He put on garments of vengeance for clothing and wrapped Himself with zeal as a mantle. According to their deeds, so He will repay, wrath to His adversaries, recompense to His enemies; to the coastlands He will make recompense. So they will fear the name of the LORD from the west and His glory from the rising of the sun, for He will come like a rushing stream which the wind of the LORD drives. "A Redeemer will come to Zion, and to those who turn from transgression in Jacob," declares the LORD. "As for Me, this is My covenant with them," says the LORD: "My Spirit which is upon you, and My words which I have put in your mouth shall not depart from your mouth, nor from the mouth of your offspring, nor from the mouth of your offspring's offspring," says the LORD, "from now and forever." …

"Arise, shine; for your light has come, and the glory of the LORD has risen upon you. For behold, darkness will cover the earth and deep darkness the peoples; but the LORD will rise upon you and His glory will appear upon you." …

Who is this who comes from Edom, with garments of glowing colors from Bozrah, this One who is majestic in His apparel, marching in the greatness of His strength? "It is I who speak in righteousness, mighty to save." Why is Your apparel red, and Your garments like the one who treads in the wine press?

Scripture Passage: Zechariah 12:10–11

I will pour out on the house of David and on the inhabitants of Jerusalem, the Spirit of grace and of supplication, so that they will look on Me whom they have pierced; and they will mourn for Him, as one mourns for an only son, and they will weep bitterly over Him like the bitter weeping over a firstborn. In that day there will be great mourning in Jerusalem, like the mourning of Hadadrimmon in the plain of Megiddo.

Scripture Passage: Genesis 45:4–8

Then Joseph said to his brothers, "Please come closer to me." And they came closer. And he said, "I am your brother Joseph, whom you sold into Egypt. Now do not be grieved or angry with yourselves, because you sold me here, for God sent me before you to preserve life. For the famine has been in the land these two years, and there are still five years in which there will be neither plowing nor harvesting. God sent me before you to preserve for you a remnant in the earth, and to keep you alive by a great deliverance. Now, therefore, it was not you who sent me here, but God; and He has made me a father to Pharaoh and lord of all his household and ruler over all the land of Egypt."

REVELATION

Scripture Passage: Micah 2:12–13

I will surely assemble all of you, Jacob, I will surely gather the remnant of Israel. I will put them together like sheep in the fold; like a flock in the midst of its pasture they will be noisy with men. The breaker goes up before them; they break out, pass through the gate and go out by it. So their king goes on before them, and the LORD at their head.

A LITTLE DEEPER...

1. What might it mean for a sword to be "satiated?"

___

2. How does Isaiah describe Christ as He returns? What sort of image does this create in your mind?

___

3. What is typology (research if needed)? How does the life of Joseph reveal truths about the life of Jesus?

___

SESSION SIXTY-FOUR

Armageddon Stage Four

Remember the Golden Rule: When the plain sense of Scripture makes common sense, we seek no other sense.

Video Sixty-Four

Topical overview: Armageddon stage four.
Learning goals: Explore the relationship between Joseph (son of Jacob) and Jesus. Recognize who accomplishes victory at Bozrah.

CORE QUESTIONS

Before watching video sixty-four, read Revelation 19:12–15. Use the two-column graphic organizer to help you organize your thoughts. Discuss your observations as a group.

As you watch the video, complete the following section. For many, reading the questions before watching the video will aid their understanding of the video content.

1. At the close of the last session, what was the state of Israel?

___

2. Summarize how Joseph's story prefigures that of Jesus.

___

Revelation

_____

_____

3. How does Jesus's initial rejection by the Jews play into God's larger plan?

_____

_____

_____

4. At the beginning of Armageddon stage four, where are the Antichrist's forces?

_____

_____

_____

5. Where does Armageddon stage four occur?

_____

_____

_____

6. What does the "satiated" sword of Isaiah 34 signify?

_____

_____

_____

7. Who does the fighting at Bozrah, and what is the result of this battle?

_____

_____

_____

Discussion Questions

1. Think about what you've known or heard about Armageddon prior to this study. As

we're beginning to see, Christ may have an army behind Him, but He's the only one fighting. And He does so swiftly and decisively. How does this understanding of Armageddon compare with your previously held ideas? What does stage 4 of Armageddon teach us about who Jesus is?

_____
_____
_____

2. Consider the relationship between Joseph's story and that of Jesus. Have you ever noticed these parallels before? What can we learn about Jesus from Joseph's example?

_____
_____
_____

3. Israel's rejection of Jesus as Messiah opened the way for all to be saved, not just Israel. Who was originally given the task of making Yahweh known to all nations? Most if not all of us are part of the "all nations" mentioned in the Abrahamic covenant. How does it feel to know that God had a plan for you specifically to be saved, even from the beginning?

_____
_____
_____

4. In the space below, record your takeaway from Session Sixty-Four and any questions you have that remain unanswered.

_____
_____
_____

DIGGING DEEPER (OPTIONAL)

Should you choose to dig deeper, complete the following Digging Deeper section. Each meeting will open with discussion of what you've learned and observed in Scripture, and this section will prepare you for that discussion.

Revelation

In a two-column graphic organizer, record what you observe in each passage and the questions you have about it. Things to look for: Who is speaking? To whom is he speaking? What does he say about God? Jesus? The church? Individual believers? What do readers of this text stand to gain?

Scripture Passage: Read Revelation 14:18–20; 19:12–15

Scripture Passage: Isaiah 63:3–6

I have trodden the wine trough alone, and from the peoples there was no man with Me. I also trod them in My anger and trampled them in My wrath; and their lifeblood is sprinkled on My garments, and I stained all My raiment. For the day of vengeance was in My heart, and My year of redemption has come. I looked, and there was no one to help, and I was astonished and there was no one to uphold; so My own arm brought salvation to Me, and My wrath upheld Me. I trod down the peoples in My anger and made them drunk in My wrath, and I poured out their lifeblood on the earth.

Scripture Passage: Luke 18:7–8

…now, will not God bring about justice for His elect who cry to Him day and night, and will He delay long over them? I tell you that He will bring about justice for them quickly. However, when the Son of Man comes, will He find faith on the earth?

Scripture Passage: Zechariah 14:1–5

Behold, a day is coming for the LORD when the spoil taken from you will be divided among you. For I will gather all the nations against Jerusalem to battle, and the city will be captured, the houses plundered, the women ravished and half of the city exiled, but the rest of the people will not be cut off from the city. Then the LORD will go forth and fight against those nations, as when He fights on a day of battle. In that day His feet will stand on the Mount of Olives, which is in front of Jerusalem on the east; and the Mount of Olives will be split in its middle from east to west by a very large valley, so that half of the mountain will move toward the north and the other half toward the south. You will flee by the valley of My mountains, for the valley of the mountains will reach to Azel; yes, you will flee just as you fled before the earthquake in the days of Uzziah king of Judah. Then the LORD, my God, will come, and all the holy ones with Him!

Scripture Passage: Habakkuk 3:3–13

God comes from Teman, and the Holy One from Mount Paran. Selah. His splendor covers the heavens, and the earth is full of His praise. His radiance is like the sunlight; He has rays flashing from His hand, and there is the hiding of His power. Before Him goes pestilence, and plague *comes after Him. He stood and surveyed the earth; He looked and startled the nations. Yes, the perpetual mountains were shattered, the ancient hills collapsed. His ways are everlasting. I saw the tents of Cushan under distress, the tent curtains of the land of Midian were trembling. Did the L*ORD *rage against the rivers, or was Your anger against the rivers, or was Your wrath against the sea, that You rode on Your horses, on Your chariots of salvation? Your bow was made bare, the rods of chastisement were sworn. Selah. You cleaved the earth with rivers. The mountains saw You and quaked; the downpour of waters swept by. The deep uttered forth its voice, it lifted high its hands. Sun and moon stood in their places; they went away at the light of Your arrows, at the radiance of Your gleaming spear. In indignation You marched through the earth; in anger You trampled the nations. You went forth for the salvation of Your people, for the salvation of Your anointed. You struck the head of the house of the evil to lay him open from thigh to neck. Selah.*

Scripture Passage: 2 Thessalonians 2:8–9

Then that lawless one will be revealed whom the Lord will slay with the breath of His mouth and bring to an end by the appearance of His coming; that is, the one whose coming is in accord with the activity of Satan, with all power and signs and false wonders.

Scripture Passage: Hebrews 1:3; 4:12

And He is the radiance of His glory and the exact representation of His nature, and upholds all things by the word of His power. When He had made purification of sins, He sat down at the right hand of the Majesty on high. …

For the word of God is living and active and sharper than any two-edged sword, and piercing as far as the division of soul and spirit, of both joints and marrow, and able to judge the thoughts and intentions of the heart.

A LITTLE DEEPER…

1. As you read through these passages, note how Jesus is described in them. Who is He? What is He like? What will He do?

_____

_____

_____

2. Do you believe that God enacts justice swiftly? That He hears the prayers of His people for deliverance? Why or why not?

_____

REVELATION

_____

_____

3. Jesus will conquer and achieve justice by the word of His mouth. Who or what is the word? Spend some time researching the word of God as described in Scripture and summarize your findings below. After a time of prayer and reflection, write a statement of what you believe to be true of the word of God.

_____

_____

_____

SESSION SIXTY-FIVE

Christ's Final Victory

> ***Remember the Golden Rule:*** *When the plain sense of Scripture makes common sense, we seek no other sense.*

Video Sixty-Five

Topical overview: Christ's final victory at Jerusalem.
Learning goals: Understand who does what to whom in the final stage of Armageddon.

CORE QUESTIONS

Before watching video sixty-five, read Revelation 19:12–15. Use the two-column graphic organizer to help you organize your thoughts. Discuss your observations as a group.

As you watch the video, complete the following section. For many, reading the questions before watching the video will aid their understanding of the video content.

1. Where does Isaiah see Jesus coming from, and why is His robe dipped in blood?

_____

_____

_____

2. Why does it matter that the Lord keeps emphasizing that He alone is fighting?

_____

REVELATION

_____

_____

3. Where does Jesus go after He conquers the attackers of Bozrah?

_____

_____

_____

4. What state does Jesus find Jerusalem in?

_____

_____

_____

5. Who accompanies Jesus as He approaches Jerusalem, and where specifically does He go?

_____

_____

_____

6. Why does Jesus stay at the mount of Olives?

_____

_____

_____

7. What does Jesus do to change the topography of Jerusalem, and what is this reminiscent of?

_____

_____

_____

8. After Israel escapes Jerusalem, what does Jesus do?

9. What is the physical result of Christ's defeat of Antichrist's army?

Discussion Questions

1. We hear the phrase, "Vengeance is the Lord's," often (Deuteronomy 32:35). It's also emphasized in this portion of Revelation 19. What does it mean for us as individual believers to leave vengeance to the Lord? How do we live considering this truth?

2. Trace the parallels between the Exodus through the Red Sea and the Jews fleeing Jerusalem prior to the final engagement of Armageddon. What can we learn about Jesus (who He is and what He does) from this comparison?

3. How does Jesus accomplish victory in this final phase of Armageddon? Who remains afterward? What can we learn about Jesus from His choice of weapon?

4. In the space below, record your takeaway from Session Sixty-Five and any questions you have that remain unanswered.

_____

_____

_____

Digging Deeper (Optional)

Should you choose to dig deeper, complete the following Digging Deeper section. Each meeting will open with discussion of what you've learned and observed in Scripture, and this section will prepare you for that discussion.

In a two-column graphic organizer, record what you observe in each passage and the questions you have about it. Things to look for: Who is speaking? To whom is he speaking? What does he say about God? Jesus? The church? Individual believers? What do readers of this text stand to gain?

Scripture Passage: Read Revelation 19:17–21

Scripture Passage: Isaiah 14:1–21

When the LORD will have compassion on Jacob and again choose Israel, and settle them in their own land, then strangers will join them and attach themselves to the house of Jacob. The peoples will take them along and bring them to their place, and the house of Israel will possess them as an inheritance in the land of the LORD as male servants and female servants; and they will take their captors captive and will rule over their oppressors. And it will be in the day when the LORD gives you rest from your pain and turmoil and harsh service in which you have been enslaved, that you will take up this taunt against the king of Babylon, and say, "How the oppressor has ceased, and how fury has ceased! The LORD has broken the staff of the wicked, the scepter of rulers which used to strike the peoples in fury with unceasing strokes, which subdued the nations in anger with unrestrained persecution. The whole earth is at rest and is quiet; they break forth into shouts of joy. Even the cypress trees rejoice over you, and the cedars of Lebanon, saying, 'Since you were laid low, no tree cutter comes up against us.' Sheol from beneath is excited over you to meet you when you come; it arouses for you the spirits of the dead, all the leaders of the earth; it raises all the kings of the nations from their thrones. They will all respond and say to you, 'Even you have been made weak as we, you have become like us. Your pomp and the music of your harps have been brought down to Sheol; maggots are spread out as your bed beneath you and worms are your covering.' How you have fallen from heaven, O star of the morning, son of the dawn! You have been cut down to the earth, you who have weakened the nations! But you said in your heart, 'I will ascend to heaven; I will raise my throne above the stars of God, and I will sit on the mount of assembly in the recesses of the north. I will ascend above the heights of the clouds; I will make myself like the Most High.' Nevertheless you will be thrust down to Sheol, to the recesses of the pit. Those who see you will gaze at you, they will ponder over you, saying, 'Is this the man who made the earth tremble, who shook kingdoms, who made the world like a wilderness and overthrew its cities, who did not allow his prisoners to go home?' All the kings of the nations lie in glory, each in his own tomb. But you have been cast out of your tomb like a rejected branch, clothed with the slain who are pierced with a sword, who go down to the stones of the pit like a trampled corpse. You will not be united with them in burial, because you have ruined your country, you have slain your people. May the offspring of evildoers not be mentioned forever. Prepare for his sons a place of slaughter because of the iniquity of their fathers. They must not arise and take possession of the earth and fill the face of the world with cities."

A Little Deeper...

1. Consider the fate of Antichrist as outlined here. Remember, at this point in time, Antichrist's body will physically contain Satan himself. Compare your idea of hell with what we find here. How are they similar, and how are they different? Consider specifically Satan's place in hell. Does this surprise you? Why or why not?

_____

_____

_____

SESSION SIXTY-SIX

Resolution of Armageddon

> ***Remember the Golden Rule:*** *When the plain sense of Scripture makes common sense, we seek no other sense.*

Video Sixty-Six

Topical overview: Resolution of Armageddon.
Learning goals: Examine what the lake of fire is, who ends up there, and when.

CORE QUESTIONS

Before watching video sixty-six, read Revelation 19:17–21. Use the two-column graphic organizer to help you organize your thoughts. Discuss your observations as a group.

As you watch the video, complete the following section. For many, reading the questions before watching the video will aid their understanding of the video content.

1. How did Christ defeat Antichrist's armies?

___

___

___

2. How does God clean up the carnage?

___

3. What is the state of the world after the resolution of Armageddon?

4. What happens when a physical body dies?

5. Why are the Antichrist and the False Prophet thrown alive into the lake of fire (hell)?

6. How is the Antichrist's fate different from that of His armies?

7. What is the lake of fire, and what do we know of it?

Discussion Questions

1. Review what happens when a physical body dies. Why is it significant that Antichrist

and the False Prophet are thrown alive into the lake of fire?

_____

_____

_____

2. Throughout Scripture, the word is portrayed as an offensive weapon, specifically a sword. Together, review the verses that come to mind in support of this truth. What does it mean to you that the word of God is a sword?

_____

_____

_____

3. In the space below, record your takeaway from Session Sixty-Six and any questions you have that remain unanswered.

_____

_____

_____

DIGGING DEEPER (OPTIONAL)

Should you choose to dig deeper, complete the following Digging Deeper section. Each meeting will open with discussion of what you've learned and observed in Scripture, and this section will prepare you for that discussion.

In a two-column graphic organizer, record what you observe in each passage and the questions you have about it. Things to look for: Who is speaking? To whom is he speaking? What does he say about God? Jesus? The church? Individual believers? What do readers of this text stand to gain?

Scripture Passage: Isaiah 2:2–3; 65:17–19

> *Now it will come about that in the last days the mountain of the house of the LORD will be established as the chief of the mountains, and will be raised above the hills; and all the nations will stream to it. And many peoples will come and say, "Come, let us go up to the mountain of the LORD, to the house of the God of Jacob; that He may teach us concerning His ways and that we may walk in His paths." For the law will go forth from Zion and the word of the LORD from Jerusalem. …*

"For behold, I create new heavens and a new earth; and the former things will not be remembered or come to mind. But be glad and rejoice forever in what I create; for behold, I create Jerusalem for rejoicing and her people for gladness. I will also rejoice in Jerusalem and be glad in My people; and there will no longer be heard in her the voice of weeping and the sound of crying."

Scripture Passage: Daniel 9:27; 12:11–12

And he will make a firm covenant with the many for one week, but in the middle of the week he will put a stop to sacrifice and grain offering; and on the wing of abominations will come one who makes desolate, even until a complete destruction, one that is decreed, is poured out on the one who makes desolate. ...

From the time that the regular sacrifice is abolished and the abomination of desolation is set up, there will be 1,290 days. How blessed is he who keeps waiting and attains to the 1,335 days!

A Little Deeper...

1. Consider the state of the world at the resolution of Armageddon. What do these passages seem to indicate occurs following Armageddon?

_____

_____

_____

SESSION SIXTY-SEVEN

The 75-Day Interval

> ***Remember the Golden Rule:*** *When the plain sense of Scripture makes common sense, we seek no other sense.*

Video Sixty-Seven

Topical overview: The 75-day interval, specifically the first 30 days.
Learning goals: Understand the purpose of and events within the first 30 days of the 75-day interval.

CORE QUESTIONS

Before watching video sixty-seven, read Revelation 19:17–21. Use the two-column graphic organizer to help you organize your thoughts. Discuss your observations as a group.

As you watch the video, complete the following section. For many, reading the questions before watching the video will aid their understanding of the video content.

Overview

1. What is the 75-day interval?

_____

_____

_____

2. What does Daniel 9:27 teach about the Tribulation timeline?

_____
_____
_____

3. Where do we learn of the interval period?

_____
_____
_____

4. What is the purpose of the first 30-day period after Tribulation ends?

_____
_____
_____

5. What is the purpose of the final 45-day period after the "desolation is abolished?"

_____
_____
_____

The First 30 Days of the 75-Day Interval

1. What does Isaiah 65 describe?

_____
_____
_____

2. Why is the remaking of the earth a necessity at this point?

_____
_____
_____

3. Where will Christ live in His 1,000-year kingdom?

_____
_____
_____

4. What is significant about the fact that it takes 30 days to repair the world and cleanse the temple?

_____
_____
_____

5. Where are Satan/ Antichrist and the False Prophet during this 30-day period?

_____
_____
_____

Discussion Questions

1. What do you imagine the remade world of the kingdom will be like?

_____
_____
_____

2. How is it fitting that the center of all things in the millennial kingdom will be a new and improved temple in Jerusalem?

_____
_____
_____

3. Consider the three defining events of Tribulation. What do they have in common, and what do they reveal about the theme and focus of Tribulation?

The 75-Day Interval

_____

_____

_____

4. In the space below, record your takeaway from Session Sixty-Seven and any questions you have that remain unanswered.

_____

_____

_____

Digging Deeper (Optional)

Should you choose to dig deeper, complete the following Digging Deeper section. Each meeting will open with discussion of what you've learned and observed in Scripture, and this section will prepare you for that discussion.

In a two-column graphic organizer, record what you observe in each passage and the questions you have about it. Things to look for: Who is speaking? To whom is he speaking? What does he say about God? Jesus? The church? Individual believers? What do readers of this text stand to gain?

Scripture Passage: Read Revelation 20:1–4

Scripture Passage: Daniel 12:1–2

> *Now at that time Michael, the great prince who stands guard over the sons of your people, will arise. And there will be a time of distress such as never occurred since there was a nation until that time; and at that time your people, everyone who is found written in the book, will be rescued. Many of those who sleep in the dust of the ground will awake, these to everlasting life, but the others to disgrace and everlasting contempt.*

Scripture Passage: Isaiah 26:13–19

> *O LORD our God, other masters besides You have ruled us; but through You alone we confess Your name. The dead will not live, the departed spirits will not rise; therefore You have punished and destroyed them, and You have wiped out all remembrance of them. You have increased the nation, O LORD, You have increased the nation, You are glorified; You have extended all the borders of the land. O LORD, they sought You in distress; they could only whisper a prayer, Your*

chastening was upon them. As the pregnant woman approaches the time to give birth, she writhes and cries out in her labor pains, thus were we before You, O LORD. We were pregnant, we writhed in labor, we gave birth, as it seems, only to wind. We could not accomplish deliverance for the earth, nor were inhabitants of the world born. Your dead will live; their corpses will rise. You who lie in the dust, awake and shout for joy, for your dew is as the dew of the dawn, and the earth will give birth to the departed spirits.

Scripture Passage: Jeremiah 24:7; 31:31–34; 50:19

"I will give them a heart to know Me, for I am the LORD; and they will be My people, and I will be their God, for they will return to Me with their whole heart."…

"Behold, days are coming," declares the LORD, "when I will make a new covenant with the house of Israel and with the house of Judah, not like the covenant which I made with their fathers in the day I took them by the hand to bring them out of the land of Egypt, My covenant which they broke, although I was a husband to them," declares the LORD. "But this is the covenant which I will make with the house of Israel after those days," declares the LORD, "I will put My law within them and on their heart I will write it; and I will be their God, and they shall be My people. They will not teach again, each man his neighbor and each man his brother, saying, 'Know the LORD,' for they will all know Me, from the least of them to the greatest of them," declares the LORD, "for I will forgive their iniquity, and their sin I will remember no more."…

"And I will bring Israel back to his pasture and he will graze on Carmel and Bashan, and his desire will be satisfied in the hill country of Ephraim and Gilead. 'In those days and at that time,' declares the LORD, 'search will be made for the iniquity of Israel, but there will be none; and for the sins of Judah, but they will not be found; for I will pardon those whom I leave as a remnant.'"

Scripture Passage: Ezekiel 11:19–20

And I will give them one heart and put a new spirit within them. And I will take the heart of stone out of their flesh and give them a heart of flesh, that they may walk in My statutes and keep My ordinances and do them. Then they will be My people, and I shall be their God.

A LITTLE DEEPER…

1. When we read these verses in the context of the 1,000-year kingdom, what do we learn about Israel as a nation?

_____

_____

_____

2. What do you imagine it will be like to reign with Christ in His kingdom?

SESSION SIXTY-EIGHT

Revelation 20:1–4

> ***Remember the Golden Rule:*** *When the plain sense of Scripture makes common sense, we seek no other sense.*

Video Sixty-Eight

Topical overview: The latter 45 days of the 75-day interval.
Learning goals: Explore the fates of believers, unbelievers, Satan, and his demons in the 75-day interval

CORE QUESTIONS

Before watching video sixty-eight, read Revelation 20:1–4. Use the two-column graphic organizer to help you organize your thoughts. Discuss your observations as a group.

As you watch the video, complete the following section. For many, reading the questions before watching the video will aid their understanding of the video content.

The Latter 45 Days of the 75 Day Interval

1. Why 45 days?

_____
_____
_____

2. Why can't God the Father be physically present on the earth at this point?

___

3. What is the mission of the angel sent to earth in Revelation 20?

___

4. What is the abyss?

___

5. What time is Daniel referring to the resurrection of saints in Daniel 12?

___

6. Who all is resurrected in this time period?

___

Revelation 20:4

1. Who remains alive in their natural bodies at this point?

___

2. What are the implications of this for the population of earth?

_____
_____
_____

3. Wat does the Old Testament teach about the nature of Israel during this time?

_____
_____
_____

DISCUSSION QUESTIONS

1. Does it surprise you that sin will still be present in the millennial kingdom? Why or why not?

_____
_____
_____

2. Does it surprise you that Satan and his demons will reside separately from unbelieving people in hell? Why or why not?

_____
_____
_____

3. How does what we learn of hell and judgment in this session differ from what is popularly believed? Consider what is commonly believed about Satan, too. How does the truth we learned in this session differ from popular belief, and what does this difference reveal about our beliefs about both God and Satan?

_____
_____
_____

4. In the millennial kingdom, Israel will finally believe in its Messiah, and they'll finally be able to worship by adhering to the Law.

_____
_____
_____

5. In the space below, record your takeaway from Revelation 20:1–4 and any questions you have that remain unanswered.

_____
_____
_____

DIGGING DEEPER (OPTIONAL)

Should you choose to dig deeper, complete the following Digging Deeper section. Each meeting will open with discussion of what you've learned and observed in Scripture, and this section will prepare you for that discussion.

In a two-column graphic organizer, record what you observe in each passage and the questions you have about it. Things to look for: Who is speaking? To whom is he speaking? What does he say about God? Jesus? The church? Individual believers? What do readers of this text stand to gain?

Scripture Passage: Read Revelation 20:5

Scripture Passage: Zephaniah 3:9–13

> *For then I will give to the peoples purified lips, that all of them may call on the name of the LORD, to serve Him shoulder to shoulder. From beyond the rivers of Ethiopia My worshipers, My dispersed ones, will bring My offerings. In that day you will feel no shame because of all your deeds by which you have rebelled against Me; for then I will remove from your midst Your proud, exulting ones, And you will never again be haughty on My holy mountain. But I will leave among you a humble and lowly people, and they will take refuge in the name of the LORD. The remnant of Israel will do no wrong and tell no lies, nor will a deceitful tongue be found in their mouths; for they will feed and lie down with no one to make them tremble.*

Scripture Passage: Mark 12:25–25

Jesus said to them, "Is this not the reason you are mistaken, that you do not understand the Scriptures or the power of God? For when they rise from the dead, they neither marry nor are given in marriage, but are like angels in heaven."

Scripture Passage: Ezekiel 44:21–26

Nor shall any of the priests drink wine when they enter the inner court. And they shall not marry a widow or a divorced woman but shall take virgins from the offspring of the house of Israel, or a widow who is the widow of a priest. Moreover, they shall teach My people the difference between the holy and the profane, and cause them to discern between the unclean and the clean. In a dispute they shall take their stand to judge; they shall judge it according to My ordinances. They shall also keep My laws and My statutes in all My appointed feasts and sanctify My Sabbaths. They shall not go to a dead person to defile themselves; however, for father, for mother, for son, for daughter, for brother, or for a sister who has not had a husband, they may defile themselves. After he is cleansed, seven days shall elapse for him.

Scripture Passage: 1 Peter 4:17–18

For it is time for judgment to begin with the household of God; and if it begins with us first, what will be the outcome for those who do not obey the gospel of God? AND IF IT IS WITH DIFFICULTY THAT THE RIGHTEOUS IS SAVED, WHAT WILL BECOME OF THE GODLESS MAN AND THE SINNER?

Scripture Passage: 2 Corinthians 5:9–10

Therefore, we also have as our ambition, whether at home or absent, to be pleasing to Him. For we must all appear before the judgment seat of Christ, so that each one may be recompensed for his deeds in the body, according to what he has done, whether good or bad.

Scripture Passage: 1 Corinthians 15:20

But now Christ has been raised from the dead, the first fruits of those who are asleep.

Scripture Passage: Matthew 25:31–46

But when the Son of Man comes in His glory, and all the angels with Him, then He will sit on His glorious throne. All the nations will be gathered before Him; and He will separate them from one another, as the shepherd separates the sheep from the goats; and He will put the sheep on His right, and the goats on the left. Then the King will say to those on His right, "Come, you who are blessed of My Father, inherit the kingdom prepared for you from the foundation of the world. For I was hungry, and you gave Me something to eat; I was thirsty, and you gave Me something to drink; I was a stranger, and you invited Me in; naked, and you clothed Me; I was sick, and you visited Me; I was in prison, and you came to Me." Then the righteous will answer Him, "Lord, when did we see You hungry, and feed You, or thirsty, and give You something to drink? And when did we see You a stranger, and invite You in, or naked, and clothe You? When did we see You sick, or in prison, and come to You?" The King will answer and say to them, "Truly I say to you, to the extent that you did it to one of these brothers of Mine, even the least of them, you did it to Me." Then He will also say to those on His left, "Depart from Me, accursed ones, into the eternal fire which has been prepared for the devil and his angels; for I was hungry, and you gave Me nothing to eat; I was thirsty, and you gave Me nothing to drink; I was a stranger, and you did not invite Me in; naked, and you did not clothe Me; sick, and in prison, and you did not visit Me." Then they themselves also will answer, "Lord, when did we see You hungry, or thirsty, or a stranger, or naked, or sick, or in prison, and did not take care of You?" Then He will answer them, "Truly I say to you, to the extent that you did not do it to one of the least of these, you did not do it to Me." These will go away into eternal punishment, but the righteous into eternal life.

A LITTLE DEEPER…

1. How might charity and kindness be the defining traits to determine faithfulness in Tribulation? (In the next session, you'll learn that this phase of judgment will specifically apply to Tribulation survivors.)

_____

_____

_____

2. Faith is a complex concept. We learn in the 1 Peter passage quoted here that it's difficult to be saved by faith. We know that without faith, it's impossible to please God (Hebrews 11:6). Do you struggle with faith? If so, why? What do you believe to be true about faith? What more does the Bible say about faith?

_____

_____

_____

3. What will the nation of Israel be like in the millennial kingdom? How is this even possible?

SESSION SIXTY-NINE

Revelation 20:5

> ***Remember the Golden Rule:*** *When the plain sense of Scripture makes common sense, we seek no other sense.*

Video Sixty-Nine

Topical overview: Who enters the kingdom, how, and in what state.
Learning goals: Identify the five groups who enter the kingdom and the one that does not.

Core Questions

Before watching video sixty-nine, read Revelation 20:5. Use the two-column graphic organizer to help you organize your thoughts. Discuss your observations as a group.

As you watch the video, complete the following section. For many, reading the questions before watching the video will aid their understanding of the video content.

Overview

1. Describe the conflict in how the surviving Jewish people enter the kingdom.

_____

_____

_____

Revelation

2. So, what's the answer?

Revelation 20:5

1. Who are the remaining dead to be resurrected after the 1,000-year kingdom?

The phases of resurrection also indicate phases of Judgment. Believers are judged in one phase, and unbelievers are judged in another.

2. What will happen to Gentiles who survive Tribulation?

3. What is the context of the Matthew 25 passage? Among whom do these works of mercy occur?

Discussion Questions

1. How is it possible for the Israel of the millennial kingdom to be sinless as a nation?

2. Have you ever heard this contextual application of Matthew 25 (sheep and goats) before? Does it affect your understanding of how to apply it to your life? Why or why not?

_____
_____
_____

3. We are saved on the basis of faith alone, not by works. Works are the evidence of faith, but they themselves are not saving faith. How do you balance the two (faith and works) in your own life?

_____
_____
_____

4. In the space below, record your takeaway from Revelation 20:5 and any questions you have that remain unanswered.

_____
_____
_____

DIGGING DEEPER (OPTIONAL)

Should you choose to dig deeper, complete the following Digging Deeper section. Each meeting will open with discussion of what you've learned and observed in Scripture, and this section will prepare you for that discussion.

In a two-column graphic organizer, record what you observe in each passage and the questions you have about it. Things to look for: Who is speaking? To whom is he speaking? What does he say about God? Jesus? The church? Individual believers? What do readers of this text stand to gain?

Scripture Passage: Read Revelation 11:15; 20:6–7

Scripture Passage: Hebrews 11:13

All these died in faith, without receiving the promises, but having seen them and having welcomed them from a distance, and having confessed that they were strangers and exiles on the earth.

Scripture Passage: Matthew 4:17, 28:19–20

From that time Jesus began to preach and say, "Repent for the kingdom of heaven is at hand." ...

"Go therefore and make disciples of all the nations, baptizing them in the name of the Father and the Son and the Holy Spirit, teaching them to observe all that I commanded you; and lo, I am with you always, even to the end of the age."

Scripture Passage: Genesis 3:17–19, 9:1–3

Then to Adam He said, "Because you have listened to the voice of your wife, and have eaten from the tree about which I commanded you, saying, 'You shall not eat from it'; cursed is the ground because of you; in toil you will eat of it all the days of your life. Both thorns and thistles it shall grow for you; and you will eat the plants of the field; by the sweat of your face You will eat bread, till you return to the ground, because from it you were taken; for you are dust, and to dust you shall return." ...

And God blessed Noah and his sons and said to them, "Be fruitful and multiply, and fill the earth. The fear of you and the terror of you will be on every beast of the earth and on every bird of the sky; with everything that creeps on the ground, and all the fish of the sea, into your hand they are given. Every moving thing that is alive shall be food for you; I give all to you, as I gave the green plant."

A LITTLE DEEPER...

1. In the two passages from Genesis, we see how God alters His original design of creation to accommodate humanity in their sin-altered state. If these circumstances are reversed and repaired in the kingdom, what will the world be like?

_____

_____

_____

2. The context of the passage in Hebrews is the "hall of faith" that lists many OT saints. Hebrews 11:1 says, "Now faith is the assurance of things hoped for the conviction of things not seen." What are these things we hope for but cannot see? How exactly are we blessed for believing without seeing (John 20:29)?

_____

_____

_____

SESSION SEVENTY

The 1,000-Year Kingdom

> ***Remember the Golden Rule:*** *When the plain sense of Scripture makes common sense, we seek no other sense.*

Video Seventy

Topical overview: The 1,000-year kingdom.
Learning goals: Identify the four phases of the kingdom throughout history. Explore how creation will be restored in the physical kingdom.

CORE QUESTIONS

Before watching video seventy, read Revelation 20:6–7. Use the two-column graphic organizer to help you organize your thoughts. Discuss your observations as a group.

As you watch the video, complete the following section. For many, reading the questions before watching the video will aid their understanding of the video content.

Overview

1. What do we learn about the kingdom period from Revelation?

_____

_____

_____

The 1,000-Year Kingdom

2. What does the term *kingdom* mean in the Bible?

_____

_____

_____

3. What was the promise?

_____

_____

_____

4. What was the proposal?

_____

_____

_____

5. What was the program?

_____

_____

_____

6. What is the place?

_____

_____

_____

7. What can we know for sure about the coming kingdom?

_____

_____

_____

The more real the kingdom gets, the less real this world will be.

REVELATION

Kingdom 101: How Creation Changes

1. What did God curse as a result of Adam's sin, and what did the curse do?

___

> Without sin, there is no death.

2. What does God provide in His blessing of Noah?

___

3. To what pattern is God restoring the earth?

___

DISCUSSION QUESTIONS

1. Discuss the statement "The more real the kingdom gets, the less real this world will be." How do you see this to be true in life? How do you live this way? What scriptures reveal the truth of this statement?

___

2. In which of the four stages of the kingdom do we reside? What is our purpose as citizens of the kingdom, and how do we accomplish this purpose? Use Scripture to support your answer.

___

The 1,000-Year Kingdom

3. What do you imagine Eden was like? What will it be like to live in a world restored to an Eden-like state?

_____

_____

_____

4. In the space below, record your takeaway from Session Seventy and any questions you have that remain unanswered.

DIGGING DEEPER (OPTIONAL)

Should you choose to dig deeper, complete the following Digging Deeper section. Each meeting will open with discussion of what you've learned and observed in Scripture, and this section will prepare you for that discussion.

In a two-column graphic organizer, record what you observe in each passage and the questions you have about it. Things to look for: Who is speaking? To whom is he speaking? What does he say about God? Jesus? The church? Individual believers? What do readers of this text stand to gain?

Scripture Passage: Isaiah 11:6–9; 14:1–2; 30:23–26; 54:3

And the wolf will dwell with the lamb, and the leopard will lie down with the young goat, and the calf and the young lion and the fatling together; and a little boy will lead them. Also the cow and the bear will graze, their young will lie down together, and the lion will eat straw like the ox. The nursing child will play by the hole of the cobra, and the weaned child will put his hand on the viper's den. They will not hurt or destroy in all My holy mountain, for the earth will be full of the knowledge of the LORD as the waters cover the sea. …

When the LORD will have compassion on Jacob and again choose Israel, and settle them in their own land, then strangers will join them and attach themselves to the house of Jacob. The peoples will take them along and bring them to their place, and the house of Israel will possess them as an inheritance in the land of the LORD as male servants and female servants; and they will take their captors captive and will rule over their oppressors. …

Then He will give you rain for the seed which you will sow in the ground, and bread from the yield of the ground, and it will be rich and plenteous; on that day your livestock will graze in a roomy pasture. Also the oxen and the donkeys which work the ground will eat salted fodder, which has been winnowed with shovel and fork. On every lofty mountain and on every high hill there will be streams running with water on the day of the great slaughter, when the towers fall. The light of the moon will be as the light of the sun, and the light of the sun will be seven times brighter, like the light of seven days, on the day the LORD binds up the fracture of His people and heals the bruise He has inflicted. …

"For you will spread abroad to the right and to the left. And your descendants will possess nations And will resettle the desolate cities.…"

Scripture Passage: Ezekiel 34:25–27; 36:27–30, 34–36; 65:25

"I will make a covenant of peace with them and eliminate harmful beasts from the land so that they may live securely in the wilderness and sleep in the woods. I will make them and the places around My hill a blessing. And I will cause showers to come down in their season; they will be showers of blessing. Also the tree of the field will yield its fruit and the earth will yield its increase, and they will be secure on their land. Then they will know that I am the LORD, when I have broken the bars of their yoke and have delivered them from the hand of those who enslaved them." …

"I will put My Spirit within you and cause you to walk in My statutes, and you will be careful to observe My ordinances. You will live in the land that I gave to your forefathers; so you will be My people, and I will be your God. Moreover, I will save you from all your uncleanness; and I will call for the grain and multiply it, and I will not bring a famine on you. I will multiply the fruit of the tree and the produce of the field, so that you will not receive again the disgrace of famine among the nations. …

"The desolate land will be cultivated instead of being a desolation in the sight of everyone who passes by. They will say, 'This desolate land has become like the garden of Eden; and the waste, desolate and ruined cities are fortified and inhabited.' Then the nations that are left round about you will know that I, the LORD, have rebuilt the ruined places and planted that which was desolate; I, the LORD, have spoken and will do it." …

"The wolf and the lamb will graze together, and the lion will eat straw like the ox; and dust will be the serpent's food. They will do no evil or harm in all My holy mountain," says the LORD.

Scripture Passage: Genesis 3:14; 15:18

The LORD God said to the serpent, "Because you have done this, cursed are you more than all cattle, and more than every beast of the field; on your belly you will go, and dust you will eat all the days of your life." …

On that day the LORD made a covenant with Abram, saying, "To your descendants I have given this land, from the river of Egypt as far as the great river, the river Euphrates.…"

Scripture Passage: Joshua 1:2–4

Moses My servant is dead; now therefore arise, cross this Jordan, you and all this people, to the land which I am giving to them, to the sons of Israel. Every place on which the sole of your foot treads, I have given it to you, just as I spoke to Moses. From the wilderness and this Lebanon, even as far as the great river, the river Euphrates, all the land of the Hittites, and as far as the Great Sea toward the setting of the sun will be your territory.

Scripture Passage: Ezekiel 47:15–20

This shall be the boundary of the land: on the north side, from the Great Sea by the way of Hethlon, to the entrance of Zedad; Hamath, Berothah, Sibraim, which is between the border of Damascus and the border of Hamath; Hazer-hatticon, which is by the border of Hauran. The boundary shall extend from the sea to Hazar-enan at the border of Damascus, and on the north toward the north is the border of Hamath. This is the north side. The east side, from between Hauran, Damascus, Gilead and the land of Israel, shall be the Jordan; from the north border to the eastern sea you shall measure. This is the east side. The south side toward the south shall extend from Tamar as far as the waters of Meribathkadesh, to the brook of Egypt and to the Great Sea. This is the south side toward the south. The west side shall be the Great Sea, from the south border to a point opposite Lebohamath. This is the west side.

A Little Deeper...

1. What would it look like for *all* the earth to have knowledge of the Lord, including animals? If you could have *any* animal as your pet, what would you choose and why?

_____

_____

_____

2. Several of the passages above are often quoted out of context. How so? To whom are the words of Ezekiel and Isaiah speaking? What does God promise the nation of Israel in the kingdom?

_____

_____

_____

SESSION SEVENTY-ONE

Changes to Nature and Israel

Remember the Golden Rule: When the plain sense of Scripture makes common sense, we seek no other sense.

Video Seventy-One

Topical overview: Changes to nature and changes to Israel.
Learning goals: Recognize exactly what it means for Eden to be restored in the time of the kingdom. Begin to explore the way boundaries and geography are changed within the kingdom.

CORE QUESTIONS

Before watching video seventy-one, read Revelation 20:6–7. Use the two-column graphic organizer to help you organize your thoughts. Discuss your observations as a group.

As you watch the video, complete the following section. For many, reading the questions before watching the video will aid their understanding of the video content.

Overview

1. What sort of relationships will cease to exist in the kingdom?

_____

_____

_____

2. Where is heaven specifically?

3. What will animals be like in the kingdom?

4. What will the land and plants be like in the kingdom?

5. How is the restored land a picture of grace?

6. What one part of creation is not restored to its state in Eden and why?

Changes to Borders and Geography

1. What happens to the physical boundaries of Israel?

2. What Gentile nation do we know will remain, what will it be like, and why?

Discussion Questions

1. Review what it means that the restored land of the kingdom is a picture of God's grace. Where else do you see this explanation of grace described in Scripture?

2. What do you imagine a world would be like without predatory relationships of any kind?

3. What is heaven, and how does this differ from our cultural understanding of heaven? In the space below, record your takeaway from Session Seventy-One and any questions you have that remain unanswered.

Digging Deeper (Optional)

Should you choose to dig deeper, complete the following Digging Deeper section. Each meeting will open with discussion of what you've learned and observed in Scripture, and this section will prepare you for that discussion.

In a two-column graphic organizer, record what you observe in each passage and the questions you have about it. Things to look for: Who is speaking? To whom is he speaking? What does he say about God? Jesus? The church? Individual believers? What do readers of this text stand to gain?

Scripture Passage: Read Revelation 20:4

Scripture Passage: Micah 4:1–3

And it will come about in the last days that the mountain of the house of the LORD will be established as the chief of the mountains. It will be raised above the hills, and the peoples will stream to it. Many nations will come and say, "Come and let us go up to the mountain of the LORD and to the house of the God of Jacob, that He may teach us about His ways and that we may walk in His paths." For from Zion will go forth the law, even the word of the LORD from Jerusalem. And He will judge between many peoples and render decisions for mighty, distant nations. Then they will hammer their swords into plowshares and their spears into pruning hooks; nation will not lift up sword against nation, and never again will they train for war.

Scripture Passage: Zechariah 14:8–11

And in that day living waters will flow out of Jerusalem, half of them toward the eastern sea and the other half toward the western sea; it will be in summer as well as in winter. And the LORD will be king over all the earth; in that day the LORD will be the only one, and His name the only one. All the land will be changed into a plain from Geba to Rimmon south of Jerusalem; but Jerusalem will rise and remain on its site from Benjamin's Gate as far as the place of the First Gate to the Corner Gate, and from the Tower of Hananel to the king's wine presses. People will live in it, and there will no longer be a curse, for Jerusalem will dwell in security.

Scripture Passage: Ezekiel 34:23–24; 47:8–11

"Then I will set over them one shepherd, My servant David, and he will feed them; he will feed them himself and be their shepherd. And I, the LORD, will be their God, and My servant David will be prince among them; I the LORD have spoken." ...

Then he said to me, "These waters go out toward the eastern region and go down into the Arabah; then they go toward the sea, being made to flow into the sea, and the waters of the sea become fresh. It will come about that every living creature which swarms in every place where the river goes, will live. And there will be very many fish, for these waters go there and the others become fresh; so everything will live where the river goes. And it will come about that fishermen will stand beside it; from Engedi to Eneglaim there will be a place for the spreading of nets. Their fish will be according to their kinds, like the fish of the Great Sea, very many. But its swamps and marshes will not become fresh; they will be left for salt."

Scripture Passage: Isaiah 9:6–7; 65:24

For a child will be born to us, a son will be given to us; and the government will rest on His shoulders; and His name will be called Wonderful Counselor, Mighty God, Eternal Father, Prince of Peace. There will be no end to the increase of His government or of peace, on the throne of David and over his kingdom, to establish it and to uphold it with justice and righteousness from then on and forevermore. The zeal of the LORD of hosts will accomplish this. ...

It will also come to pass that before they call, I will answer; and while they are still speaking, I will hear.

Scripture Passage: Psalm 2:6–11

"But as for Me, I have installed My King Upon Zion, My holy mountain." "I will surely tell of the decree of the LORD: He said to Me, 'You are My Son, today I have begotten You. Ask of Me, and I will surely give the nations as Your inheritance, and the very ends of the earth as Your possession. You shall break them with a rod of iron, You shall shatter them like earthenware.'" Now therefore, O kings, show discernment; take warning, O judges of the earth. Worship the LORD with reverence and rejoice with trembling.

Scripture Passage: Jeremiah 30:8–9

"It shall come about on that day," declares the LORD of hosts, "that I will break his yoke from off their neck and will tear off their bonds; and strangers will no longer make them their slaves. But they shall serve the LORD their God and David their king, whom I will raise up for them."

Scripture Passage: Matthew 19:28

And Jesus said to them, "Truly I say to you, that you who have followed Me, in the regeneration when the Son of Man will sit on His glorious throne, you also shall sit upon twelve thrones, judging the twelve tribes of Israel."

Scripture Passage: Deuteronomy 28:1

Now it shall be, if you diligently obey the LORD your God, being careful to do all His commandments which I command you today, the LORD your God will set you high above all the nations of the earth.

Changes to Nature and Israel

Scripture Passage: Isaiah 14:1–2

When the LORD will have compassion on Jacob and again choose Israel, and settle them in their own land, then strangers will join them and attach themselves to the house of Jacob. The peoples will take them along and bring them to their place, and the house of Israel will possess them as an inheritance in the land of the LORD as male servants and female servants; and they will take their captors captive and will rule over their oppressors.

A Little Deeper...

1. Imagine a world that has no need for weapons of any kind. What would it be like?

_____

_____

_____

2. What will life in the kingdom be like for Israel?

_____

_____

_____

3. Read Isaiah 65:24 again. How might this be quite literally true in the kingdom? How is the same true for the church today?

_____

_____

_____

SESSION SEVENTY-TWO

The State of Israel in the Kingdom

> *Remember the Golden Rule:* When the plain sense of Scripture makes common sense, we seek no other sense.

Video Seventy-Two

Topical overview: The physical and political state of Israel in the kingdom.
Learning goals: Envision the environmental changes to Israel. Explore Christ's millennial government.

CORE QUESTIONS

Before watching video seventy-two, read Revelation 20:6–7. Use the two-column graphic organizer to help you organize your thoughts. Discuss your observations as a group.

As you watch the video, complete the following section. For many, reading the questions before watching the video will aid their understanding of the video content.

1. What other specific Gentile nation will remain in the kingdom?

_____

_____

_____

2. What will be the tallest mountain in the kingdom, and what will be on top?

_____

3. What other changes will happen to physical Jerusalem?

4. What is significant about the eastern river?

5. What will happen to the land around Mt. Zion?

6. Where will the center of government of the kingdom be?

7. Why is it significant that nations will exist that require ruling?

    While there will be sin, there will be an all-knowing, all-powerful Ruler who can stop sin via His government before it's acted upon. Sin will have no material impact on life.

REVELATION

8. Who will compose Christ's perfect government?

9. Who will be the ruler over Israel, and who will be his lieutenants?

10. What do we know about the place of Gentiles in the kingdom?

11. Which nation will have primacy in the kingdom?

Discussion Questions

1. Who resides at the peak of the tallest place on earth? Where is he, what is he like, and what is this tallest place on earth?

2. Do you find it ironic that while the first century Jews expected a conquering king for their Messiah, Jesus came as the suffering servant prophesied in Isaiah. Had they accepted their suffering servant as Messiah as believers do, they would have received their conquering King as we will in the kingdom. What is the beauty of Israel's rejection of their Messiah the first time?

_____

_____

_____

3. Have you ever considered before that Christ's millennial kingdom will involve multiple nations under Christ's government, that there will be bureaucracy of which we will be a part? The Bible doesn't tell us much, but so far, what do we know about the place of the bride of Christ, believing Gentiles, and their place in the kingdom?

_____

_____

_____

4. In the space below, record your takeaway from Session Seventy-Two and any questions you have that remain unanswered.

_____

_____

_____

DIGGING DEEPER (OPTIONAL)

Should you choose to dig deeper, complete the following Digging Deeper section. Each meeting will open with discussion of what you've learned and observed in Scripture, and this section will prepare you for that discussion.

In a two-column graphic organizer, record what you observe in each passage and the questions you have about it. Things to look for: Who is speaking? To whom is he speaking? What does he say about God? Jesus? The church? Individual believers? What do readers of this text stand to gain?

Revelation

Scripture Passage: Romans 13:3–4

For rulers are not a cause of fear for good behavior, but for evil. Do you want to have no fear of authority? Do what is good and you will have praise from the same; for it is a minister of God to you for good. But if you do what is evil, be afraid; for it does not bear the sword for nothing; for it is a minister of God, an avenger who brings wrath on the one who practices evil.

Scripture Passage: Isaiah 65:20

No longer will there be in it an infant who lives but a few days, or an old man who does not live out his days; for the youth will die at the age of one hundred and the one who does not reach the age of one hundred will be thought accursed.

A Little Deeper...

1. Why will a government be required in the kingdom? What would a perfect (holy) government be like in nature and execution?

_____

_____

_____

2. What does Isaiah 65 reveal about the state of the human body in the kingdom?

_____

_____

_____

SESSION SEVENTY-THREE

Daily Life and Death in the Kingdom

> ***Remember the Golden Rule:*** *When the plain sense of Scripture makes common sense, we seek no other sense.*

Video Seventy-Three

Topical overview: Daily life and death in the kingdom.
Learning goals: Recognize the purpose and means of government. Explore the difference between righteousness and sinlessness, especially as it affects life in the kingdom.

CORE QUESTIONS

Before watching video seventy-three, read Revelation 20:6–7. Use the two-column graphic organizer to help you organize your thoughts. Discuss your observations as a group.

As you watch the video, complete the following section. For many, reading the questions before watching the video will aid their understanding of the video content.

1. What is the fundamental purpose of government?

_____

_____

_____

REVELATION

2. How does sin enter the kingdom?

_____
_____
_____

3. What are the conditions for entering the kingdom?

_____
_____
_____

Righteousness is not the same as sinlessness. Righteousness comes by faith alone.

4. What is significant about those in their natural bodies being able to repopulate the earth?

_____
_____
_____

5. How will Christ rule in response to sin?

_____
_____
_____

6. What will be the two classes of people in the kingdom?

_____
_____
_____

7. What does Isaiah 65 teach us about life in the kingdom?

_____
_____

DISCUSSION QUESTIONS

1. How would you define righteousness? Sinlessness? What is the difference between the two, and how does this difference affect how we live?

_____

_____

_____

2. Consider how Christ will deal with sin in the millennial kingdom versus how the Holy Spirit deals with sin now. How are the two similar? How are they different? Considering that recognizing sin is a necessary component to recognizing our need for a savior, in which environment do you think it would be easier to come to faith? Why?

_____

_____

_____

3. How do you respond to the idea of distinct social classes in the millennial kingdom? How might social classes in this context be different than our understanding of social classes today?

_____

_____

_____

4. In the space below, record your takeaway from Session Seventy-Three and any questions you have that remain unanswered.

_____

_____

_____

DIGGING DEEPER (OPTIONAL)

Should you choose to dig deeper, complete the following Digging Deeper section. Each meeting will open with discussion of what you've learned and observed in

Scripture, and this section will prepare you for that discussion.

In a two-column graphic organizer, record what you observe in each passage and the questions you have about it. Things to look for: Who is speaking? To whom is he speaking? What does he say about God? Jesus? The church? Individual believers? What do readers of this text stand to gain?

Scripture Passage: Ezekiel 43:4–7

And the glory of the L<small>ORD</small> came into the house by the way of the gate facing toward the east. And the Spirit lifted me up and brought me into the inner court; and behold, the glory of the L<small>ORD</small> filled the house. Then I heard one speaking to me from the house, while a man was standing beside me. He said to me, "Son of man, this is the place of My throne and the place of the soles of My feet, where I will dwell among the sons of Israel forever."

Scripture Passage: Hebrews 11:1

Now faith is the assurance of things hoped for, the conviction of things not seen.

Scripture Passage: Romans 8:24

For in hope we have been saved, but hope that is seen is not hope; for who hopes for what he already sees?

Scripture Passage: Philippians 2:9–11

For this reason also, God highly exalted Him, and bestowed on Him the name which is above every name, so that at the name of Jesus EVERY KNEE WILL BOW, of those who are in heaven and on earth and under the earth, and that every tongue will confess that Jesus Christ is Lord, to the glory of God the Father.

A LITTLE DEEPER...

1. Spend a little time in research. Trace the *shekinah* glory of God throughout Scripture. Know that the "glory of the Lord" in Ezekiel 43 is the *shekinah* glory of God during the millennial kingdom. Where had it been up until this point? Why? How had it interacted with people throughout biblical history?

SESSION SEVENTY-FOUR

Life and Faith in the Kingdom

> ***Remember the Golden Rule:*** *When the plain sense of Scripture makes common sense, we seek no other sense.*

Video Seventy-Four

Topical overview: Life and faith in the kingdom.
Learning goals: Answer the question: what are the mechanics of life, death, and faith in the kingdom?

CORE QUESTIONS

Before watching video seventy-four, read Revelation 20:6–7. Use the two-column graphic organizer to help you organize your thoughts. Discuss your observations as a group.

As you watch the video, complete the following section. For many, reading the questions before watching the video will aid their understanding of the video content.

1. What does Isaiah 65 teach us about life in the kingdom?

___

2. What is the message God is sending by the details of death in the kingdom?

___

3. When do kingdom believers receive their eternal bodies?

Supernatural displays do not create saving faith.

4. What will determine saving faith in the kingdom?

The Lord will remain in the holy of holies for the duration of the 1,000 years. He doesn't come out. He remains there in the form of the *shekinah* glory of God.

5. Who is allowed to enter into the temple courtyard?

6. What do we know is true because salvation remains the result of faith prior to the truth becoming self-evident?

Faith will remain on the basis of things unseen. When Christ—the truth—is self-evident, faith is no longer necessary for belief. As such, we can extrapolate much of what life in the kingdom will be like.

Discussion Questions

1. In your own words, how would you define faith? How would you define saving faith?

   _____
   _____
   _____

2. What does the Bible teach us about faith? Share the scriptures that come to mind.

   _____
   _____
   _____

3. Considering what determines saving faith, given the option, would you prefer to live in this present age or in the kingdom? Why?

   _____
   _____
   _____

4. In the space below, record your takeaway from Session Seventy-Four and any questions you have that remain unanswered.

   _____
   _____
   _____

Digging Deeper (Optional)

Should you choose to dig deeper, complete the following Digging Deeper section. Each meeting will open with discussion of what you've learned and observed in Scripture, and this section will prepare you for that discussion.

In a two-column graphic organizer, record what you observe in each passage and the questions you have about it. Things to look for: Who is speaking? To whom is he speaking? What does he say about God? Jesus? The church? Individual believers? What do readers of this text stand to gain?

Scripture Passage: Isaiah 4:2–6; 14:1–2; 56:6–7; 65:21–23; 66:18–21

In that day the Branch of the LORD will be beautiful and glorious, and the fruit of the earth will be the pride and the adornment of the survivors of Israel. It will come about that he who is left in Zion and remains in Jerusalem will be called holy—everyone who is recorded for life in Jerusalem. When the Lord has washed away the filth of the daughters of Zion and purged the bloodshed of Jerusalem from her midst, by the spirit of judgment and the spirit of burning, then the LORD will create over the whole area of Mount Zion and over her assemblies a cloud by day, even smoke, and the brightness of a flaming fire by night; for over all the glory will be a canopy. There will be a shelter to give shade from the heat by day, and refuge and protection from the storm and the rain. …

When the LORD will have compassion on Jacob and again choose Israel, and settle them in their own land, then strangers will join them and attach themselves to the house of Jacob. The peoples will take them along and bring them to their place, and the house of Israel will possess them as an inheritance in the land of the LORD as male servants and female servants; and they will take their captors captive and will rule over their oppressors. …

"Also the foreigners who join themselves to the LORD, to minister to Him, and to love the name of the LORD, to be His servants, every one who keeps from profaning the sabbath and holds fast My covenant; even those I will bring to My holy mountain and make them joyful in My house of prayer. Their burnt offerings and their sacrifices will be acceptable on My altar; for My house will be called a house of prayer for all the peoples." …

"They will build houses and inhabit them; they will also plant vineyards and eat their fruit. They will not build and another inhabit, they will not plant and another eat; for as the lifetime of a tree, so will be the days of My people, and My chosen ones will wear out the work of their hands. They will not labor in vain, or bear children for calamity; for they are the offspring of those blessed by the LORD, and their descendants with them." …

"For I know their works and their thoughts; the time is coming to gather all nations and tongues. And they shall come and see My glory. I will set a sign among them and will send survivors from them to the nations: Tarshish, Put, Lud, Meshech, Tubal and Javan, to the distant coastlands that have neither heard My fame nor seen My glory. And they will declare My glory among the nations. Then they shall bring all your brethren from all the nations as a grain offering to the LORD, on horses, in chariots, in litters, on mules and on camels, to My holy mountain Jerusalem," says the LORD, "just as the sons of Israel bring their grain offering in a clean vessel to the house of the LORD. I will also take some of them for priests and for Levites," says the LORD.

Scripture Passage: Zechariah 14:16–18

Then it will come about that any who are left of all the nations that went against Jerusalem will go up from year to year to worship the King, the LORD of hosts, and to celebrate the Feast of Booths. And it will be that whichever of the families of the earth does not go up to Jerusalem to worship the King, the LORD of hosts, there will be no rain on them. If the family of Egypt does not go up or enter, then no rain will fall on them; it will be the plague with which the LORD smites the nations who do not go up to celebrate the Feast of Booths.

Revelation

A Little Deeper...

1. As you read about what life will be like in the kingdom, what do you look forward to the most, or what do you think will be the best part?

_____

_____

_____

2. In Zechariah, we learn there will be consequences in the kingdom for nations/ families/ individuals who refuse to celebrate the Feast of Booths. What does this proclamation reveal about the people in the kingdom?

_____

_____

_____

SESSION SEVENTY-FIVE

Overview of Life in the Kingdom

Remember the Golden Rule: *When the plain sense of Scripture makes common sense, we seek no other sense.*

Video Seventy-Five

Topical overview: Overview of life in the kingdom.
Learning goals: Reconcile our hope of the future with Jesus with the reality of the kingdom.

CORE QUESTIONS

Before watching video seventy-five, read Revelation 20:6–7. Use the two-column graphic organizer to help you organize your thoughts. Discuss your observations as a group.

As you watch the video, complete the following section. For many, reading the questions before watching the video will aid their understanding of the video content.

1. Will the sinlessness of glorified saints lead people to saving faith?

_____
_____
_____

2. What will it be like for the saints in the kingdom?

_____

_____

_____

It's going to be everything we like about life today and nothing we don't. It's going to be a life with fulfillment in place of disappointment. It will be a life with meaning instead of one that sometimes seems senseless. It's a life with a rhythm and stability that eliminates fear or worry.

3. What does Isaiah 4 teach us about what life will be like for Jews in the kingdom?

_____

_____

_____

4. What will be different for Gentiles in the temple in the kingdom?

_____

_____

_____

5. What will be the responsibility of believing Gentiles in the kingdom?

_____

_____

_____

6. What will be the punishment for failing to attend the festival of booths?

_____

_____

_____

The life you have here will always pale in comparison to the one you'll have in the kingdom.

DISCUSSION QUESTIONS

1. The details of the kingdom create an idyllic picture. What will be the best part in your opinion?

_____

_____

_____

2. What does it mean that the life you have presently will always pale in comparison to the life you'll have in the kingdom? What does it mean and what does it look like to live with this truth in view?

_____

_____

_____

3. In the space below, record your takeaway from Session Seventy-Five and any questions you have that remain unanswered.

_____

_____

_____

DIGGING DEEPER (OPTIONAL)

Should you choose to dig deeper, complete the following Digging Deeper section. Each meeting will open with discussion of what you've learned and observed in Scripture, and this section will prepare you for that discussion.

In a two-column graphic organizer, record what you observe in each passage and the questions you have about it. Things to look for: Who is speaking? To whom is he speaking? What does he say about God? Jesus? The church? Individual believers? What do readers of this text stand to gain?

Scripture Passage: Ezekiel 40:2–4

In the visions of God He brought me into the land of Israel and set me on a very high mountain, and on it to the south there was a structure like a city. So He brought me there; and behold, there was a man whose appearance was like the appearance of bronze, with a line of flax and a measuring rod in his hand; and he was standing in the gateway. The man said to me, "Son of man, see with your eyes, hear with your ears, and give attention to all that I am going to show you; for you have been brought here in order to show it to you. Declare to the house of Israel all that you see."

A Little Deeper…

1. We learn more of the kingdom in Old Testament prophecy than we do in Revelation itself. How much do you know of Old Testament history and prophecy? Can you recognize the relationships between these Old Testament elements and our New Covenant theology? Summarize your understanding of the relationship between Old Testament prophecy and New Covenant theology.

_____

_____

_____

SESSION SEVENTY-SIX

The Temple in the Kingdom

> ***Remember the Golden Rule:*** *When the plain sense of Scripture makes common sense, we seek no other sense.*

Video Seventy-Six

Topical overview: The temple in the kingdom.
Learning goals: Understand the structure and function of the temple in the kingdom.

CORE QUESTIONS

Before watching video seventy-six, read Revelation 20:5–6. Use the two-column graphic organizer to help you organize your thoughts. Discuss your observations as a group.

As you watch the video, complete the following section. For many, reading the questions before watching the video will aid their understanding of the video content.

1. Which prophet tells us most of what we know of the temple, worship, and sacrifice in the kingdom?

2. Why are Ezekiel's dimensions significant?

3. What is the significance of the great size of this structure?

4. What is the symbolic significance of the building's various dimensions?

5. How does the millennial temple differ from previous ones?

6. Why are most of the temple implements no longer necessary in the kingdom?

7. Why is the table of incense still present in the temple?

8. Where does the river emerge from the temple, and how does it flow?

DISCUSSION QUESTIONS

1. *Everything* God does and commands is precise and intentional, as evidenced by Ezekiel's vision of the millennial temple. How does understanding this aspect of God's character affect your interaction with and response to Him?

2. Have you ever considered the symbolic significance of temple implements before? What is the meaning of the presence and absence of various temple implements in the millennial temple? What does the current significance of temple elements (showbread, lampstands, laver, altar, incense, etc.) reveal about who Christ is to us today?

3. Where do we first read of symbolic living water? How is this symbolism carried into physical existence in the millennial kingdom, and what does the persistence of the symbol teach us about who Jesus is? How do we respond?

4. In the space below, record your takeaway from Session Seventy-Six and any questions you have that remain unanswered.

Revelation

DIGGING DEEPER (OPTIONAL)

Should you choose to dig deeper, complete the following Digging Deeper section. Each meeting will open with discussion of what you've learned and observed in Scripture, and this section will prepare you for that discussion.

In a two-column graphic organizer, record what you observe in each passage and the questions you have about it. Things to look for: Who is speaking? To whom is he speaking? What does he say about God? Jesus? The church? Individual believers? What do readers of this text stand to gain?

Scripture Passage: Ezekiel 10:4, 18–19; 11:23–24; 43:1–9; 44:1–3, 8–10, 13–16; 46:9

Then the glory of the LORD went up from the cherub to the threshold of the temple, and the temple was filled with the cloud and the court was filled with the brightness of the glory of the LORD. ...

Then the glory of the LORD departed from the threshold of the temple and stood over the cherubim. When the cherubim departed, they lifted their wings and rose up from the earth in my sight with the wheels beside them; and they stood still at the entrance of the east gate of the LORD's house, and the glory of the God of Israel hovered over them. ...

The glory of the LORD went up from the midst of the city and stood over the mountain which is east of the city. And the Spirit lifted me up and brought me in a vision by the Spirit of God to the exiles in Chaldea. So the vision that I had seen left me. ...

Then he led me to the gate, the gate facing toward the east; and behold, the glory of the God of Israel was coming from the way of the east. And His voice was like the sound of many waters; and the earth shone with His glory. And it was like the appearance of the vision which I saw, like the vision which I saw when He came to destroy the city. And the visions were like the vision which I saw by the river Chebar; and I fell on my face. And the glory of the LORD came into the house by the way of the gate facing toward the east. And the Spirit lifted me up and brought me into the inner court; and behold, the glory of the LORD filled the house. Then I heard one speaking to me from the house, while a man was standing beside me. He said to me, "Son of man, this is the place of My throne and the place of the soles of My feet, where I will dwell among the sons of Israel forever. And the house of Israel will not again defile My holy name, neither they nor their kings, by their harlotry and by the corpses of their kings when they die, by setting their threshold by My threshold and their door post beside My door post, with only the wall between Me and them. And they have defiled My holy name by their abominations which they have committed. So I have consumed them in My anger. "Now let them put away their harlotry and the corpses of their kings far from Me; and I will dwell among them forever." ...

Then He brought me back by the way of the outer gate of the sanctuary, which faces the east; and it was shut. The LORD said to me, "This gate shall be shut; it shall not be opened, and no one shall enter by it, for the LORD God of Israel has entered by it; therefore it shall be shut. As for the prince, he shall sit in it as prince to eat bread before the LORD; he shall enter by way of the porch of the gate and shall go out by the same way." ...

"And you have not kept charge of My holy things yourselves, but you have set foreigners to keep

charge of My sanctuary." Thus says the Lord GOD, "No foreigner uncircumcised in heart and uncircumcised in flesh, of all the foreigners who are among the sons of Israel, shall enter My sanctuary. But the Levites who went far from Me when Israel went astray, who went astray from Me after their idols, shall bear the punishment for their iniquity." …

"And they shall not come near to Me to serve as a priest to Me, nor come near to any of My holy things, to the things that are most holy; but they will bear their shame and their abominations which they have committed. Yet I will appoint them to keep charge of the house, of all its service and of all that shall be done in it. But the Levitical priests, the sons of Zadok, who kept charge of My sanctuary when the sons of Israel went astray from Me, shall come near to Me to minister to Me; and they shall stand before Me to offer Me the fat and the blood," declares the Lord GOD. "They shall enter My sanctuary; they shall come near to My table to minister to Me and keep My charge." …

But when the people of the land come before the LORD at the appointed feasts, he who enters by way of the north gate to worship shall go out by way of the south gate. And he who enters by way of the south gate shall go out by way of the north gate. No one shall return by way of the gate by which he entered but shall go straight out.

Scripture Passage: 1 Peter 2:9

But you are A CHOSEN RACE, A royal PRIESTHOOD, A HOLY NATION, A PEOPLE FOR God's OWN POSSESSION, so that you may proclaim the excellencies of Him who has called you out of darkness into His marvelous light….

A LITTLE DEEPER…

1. What do we learn of God's glory from Ezekiel?

_____
_____
_____

2. Where is God's glory presently, and what are we to do in response?

_____
_____
_____

SESSION SEVENTY-SEVEN

The Glory of God

> ***Remember the Golden Rule:*** *When the plain sense of Scripture makes common sense, we seek no other sense.*

Video Seventy-Seven

Topical overview: The glory of God and millennial temple worship.
Learning goals: Trace the movement of God's glory throughout history.

CORE QUESTIONS

Before watching video seventy-seven, read Revelation 20:5–6. Use the two-column graphic organizer to help you organize your thoughts. Discuss your observations as a group.

As you watch the video, complete the following section. For many, reading the questions before watching the video will aid their understanding of the video content.

1. What is Christ's physical location in the temple?

_____

_____

_____

Any physical representation of God is a form of the second person of the Trinity: Jesus.

2. When did the *shekinah* glory of God depart the temple and why?

_____

_____

_____

3. Where did God's glory go when it departed, and why does this matter?

_____

_____

_____

4. Where is the Glory of the Lord during the millennium?

_____

_____

_____

5. How is Christ's entry to the temple symbolic?

_____

_____

_____

6. Because the East Gate is permanently closed, who uses this space?

_____

_____

_____

7. When will those in the kingdom be able to see Jesus?

_____

_____

_____

8. How are the seven feasts of Scripture symbolic?

9. Which two feasts survive to be celebrated purposefully in the millennium?

10. Why does God create a one-way route through the temple?

11. What are unbelievers allowed in the temple, and what are they forbidden?

12. Why do Levites have a new job in the kingdom temple, and who will be its priests?

DISCUSSION QUESTIONS

1. Where does God's glory presently reside, and what does it mean for us to come face to face with it? What will be the difference to individual worship caused by physically passing God's visible glory in the millennial temple versus our current experience?

2. What do we learn of Christ through Jewish feasts and festivals? How does this inform our understanding of who He is today? Which two feasts/ festivals persist into the millennial kingdom, and why is this significant?

_____

3. How does temple admittance differ between the Old Testament and the millennial kingdom? Why is this distinction significant?

_____

4. In the space below, record your takeaway from Session Seventy-Seven and any questions you have that remain unanswered.

_____

DIGGING DEEPER (OPTIONAL)

Should you choose to dig deeper, complete the following Digging Deeper section. Each meeting will open with discussion of what you've learned and observed in Scripture, and this section will prepare you for that discussion.

In a two-column graphic organizer, record what you observe in each passage and the questions you have about it. Things to look for: Who is speaking? To whom is he speaking? What does he say about God? Jesus? The church? Individual believers? What do readers of this text stand to gain?

Scripture Passage: Hebrews 10:10–14

By this will we have been sanctified through the offering of the body of Jesus Christ once for all. Every priest stands daily ministering and offering time after time the same sacrifices, which can never take away sins; but He, having offered one sacrifice for sins for all time, SAT DOWN AT THE RIGHT HAND OF GOD, waiting from that time onward UNTIL HIS ENEMIES BE MADE A FOOTSTOOL FOR HIS FEET. For by one offering He has perfected for all time those who are sanctified.

Scripture Passage: Genesis 3:7–8, 15, 21

Then the eyes of both of them were opened, and they knew that they were naked; and they sewed fig leaves together and made themselves loin coverings. They heard the sound of the LORD God walking in the garden in the cool of the day, and the man and his wife hid themselves from the presence of the LORD God among the trees of the garden. …

"And I will put enmity between you and the woman, and between your seed and her seed; he shall bruise you on the head, and you shall bruise him on the heel." …

The LORD God made garments of skin for Adam and his wife, and clothed them.

Scripture Passage: 1 Corinthians 6:19

Or do you not know that your body is a temple of the Holy Spirit who is in you, whom you have from God, and that you are not your own?

Scripture Passage: Romans 12:1–2

Therefore I urge you, brethren, by the mercies of God, to present your bodies a living and holy sacrifice, acceptable to God, which is your spiritual service of worship. And do not be conformed to this world, but be transformed by the renewing of your mind, so that you may prove what the will of God is, that which is good and acceptable and perfect.

Scripture Passage: Philippians 2:5–8

Have this attitude in yourselves which was also in Christ Jesus, who, although He existed in the form of God, did not regard equality with God a thing to be grasped, but emptied Himself, taking the form of a bond-servant, and being made in the likeness of men. Being found in appearance as a man, He humbled Himself by becoming obedient to the point of death, even death on a cross.

A LITTLE DEEPER...

1. Under the current covenant in Jesus' blood (the one in which we presently participate by faith), how do we make sacrifice or atone for our sins? How is this similar to sacrifices made under the old covenant, and how is it different?

_____

_____

_____

2. How do we, in practice, present our bodies as living sacrifices? How is God leading you, specifically, to repent and offer Him the sacrifice of your body?

_____

_____

_____

SESSION SEVENTY-EIGHT

The Millennial Kingdom

> ***Remember the Golden Rule:*** *When the plain sense of Scripture makes common sense, we seek no other sense.*

Video Seventy-Eight

Topical overview: Sacrifice and worship in the millennial kingdom.
Learning goals: Answer: what is the effect of sin on relationships, and how does sacrifice repair the breach sin causes?

CORE QUESTIONS

Before watching video seventy-eight, read Revelation 20:5–6. Use the two-column graphic organizer to help you organize your thoughts. Discuss your observations as a group.

As you watch the video, complete the following section. For many, reading the questions before watching the video will aid their understanding of the video content.

1. Who was Zadok?

_____

_____

_____

Faithfulness to God now is a measuring stick for assigned opportunities in the kingdom.

2. How will the role of priests be different in the kingdom?

3. If Jesus is back in the kingdom, why does the sacrificial system return?

4. What were the two fundamental effects of sin on the human condition?

5. How does the Lord cover the spiritual lack caused by sin?

6. How does the Lord cover the physical lack caused by sin?

We *first* reconcile with God by faith in the provision of His Son. *Then* He may accept our physical sacrifices made in His presence to grant us reconciliation with each other.

7. How do we currently participate in a physical sacrificial system?

8. What does it mean to make a sacrifice *in our body*?

9. Where does God dwell in the kingdom, and what does that mean for sacrifice?

10. What is the role of the saints in this whole system?

Discussion Questions

1. What is sin, and how does it affect the relationship between the individual and God? How does our experience of grace, being covered by the blood of Jesus, alter this relationship, and why is this the exception rather than the rule?

2. Have you ever considered the interpersonal element of sacrifice? How does a blood sacrifice, or the present means of dying to self, restore broken interpersonal relationships?

3. In your current faith context, how can you actively strive to restore broken relationships within your local body of believers?

_____

_____

_____

4. In the space below, record your takeaway from Session Seventy-Eight and any questions you have that remain unanswered.

_____

_____

_____

DIGGING DEEPER (OPTIONAL)

Should you choose to dig deeper, complete the following Digging Deeper section. Each meeting will open with discussion of what you've learned and observed in Scripture, and this section will prepare you for that discussion.

In a two-column graphic organizer, record what you observe in each passage and the questions you have about it. Things to look for: Who is speaking? To whom is he speaking? What does he say about God? Jesus? The church? Individual believers? What do readers of this text stand to gain?

Scripture Passage: Read Revelation 12:9; 20:1–2, 7–9

Scripture Passage: Zechariah 14:9–10

> And the LORD will be king over all the earth; in that day the LORD will be the only one, and His name the only one. All the land will be changed into a plain from Geba to Rimmon south of Jerusalem; but Jerusalem will rise and remain on its site from Benjamin's Gate as far as the place of the First Gate to the Corner Gate, and from the Tower of Hananel to the king's wine presses.

Scripture Passage: Romans 7:18

> For I know that nothing good dwells in me, that is, in my flesh; for the willing is present in me, but the doing of the good is not.

Revelation

Scripture Passage: 1 Corinthians 10:13; 15:24–28

For I know that nothing good dwells in me, that is, in my flesh; for the willing is present in me, but the doing of the good is not.

…then comes the end, when He hands over the kingdom to the God and Father, when He has abolished all rule and all authority and power. For He must reign until He has put all His enemies under His feet. The last enemy that will be abolished is death. For HE HAS PUT ALL THINGS IN SUBJECTION UNDER HIS FEET. But when He says, "All things are put in subjection," it is evident that He is excepted who put all things in subjection to Him. When all things are subjected to Him, then the Son Himself also will be subjected to the One who subjected all things to Him, so that God may be all in all.

Note: for a complete explanation of this passage, refer to the VBVMI 1 Corinthians study online: https://www.versebyverseministry.org/bible-studies/first-corinthians episode 15C.

A LITTLE DEEPER…

1. Considering all we've learned to this point, why must Satan be allowed an opportunity to deceive again? What is the purpose of this final war of Gog and Magog?

_____

_____

_____

2. Listen to episode 15C of the 1 Corinthians study on VBVMI's website linked above. The passage is complex, and Pastor Armstrong doesn't go into much detail in Session Seventy-Nine regarding it. Spending some time this way in preparation will be well worth the investment.

_____

_____

_____

SESSION SEVENTY-NINE

Revelation 20:7–9

> ***Remember the Golden Rule:*** *When the plain sense of Scripture makes common sense, we seek no other sense.*

Video Seventy-Nine

Topical overview: Gog, Magog, and the release of Satan from his prison.
Learning goals: Recognize how and why the war of Gog and Magog will be fought and won.

CORE QUESTIONS

Before watching video seventy-nine, read Revelation 20:7–9. Use the two-column graphic organizer to help you organize your thoughts. Discuss your observations as a group.

As you watch the video, complete the following section. For many, reading the questions before watching the video will aid their understanding of the video content.

The Final War of Gog and Magog

1. In our timeline, what follows the millennial kingdom?

_____

_____

_____

REVELATION

2. What event begins the war?

_____
_____
_____

3. What is the target of the war?

_____
_____
_____

4. How does the war end?

_____
_____
_____

5. Why was Satan bound in the first place?

_____
_____
_____

6. How does Satan provoke sin?

_____
_____
_____

7. What is Satan able to do, and what is he not able to do?

_____
_____
_____

To ensure Satan has no opportunity to gain a foothold in Christ's kingdom, he is imprisoned throughout the kingdom so as not to move in opposition to the ordained ruler.

DISCUSSION QUESTIONS

1. When it comes to sin, what *is* Satan allowed to do, and what is he *not* allowed to do? How does this differ from the popular understanding of his power?

2. Why was Satan bound rather than destroyed at the end of Tribulation? And what is the purpose of releasing him for the war of Gog and Magog?

3. What does it look like for Satan to "gain a foothold" in our world today? How does Scripture teach us to prevent him from gaining a foothold in our lives today? How is this similar to or different from the way in which Jesus prevents Satan gaining a foothold in the lives of those who live in the millennial kingdom?

4. In the space below, record your takeaway from Revelation 20:7–9 and any questions you have that remain unanswered.

Revelation

DIGGING DEEPER (OPTIONAL)

Should you choose to dig deeper, complete the following Digging Deeper section. Each meeting will open with discussion of what you've learned and observed in Scripture, and this section will prepare you for that discussion.

In a two-column graphic organizer, record what you observe in each passage and the questions you have about it. Things to look for: Who is speaking? To whom is he speaking? What does he say about God? Jesus? The church? Individual believers? What do readers of this text stand to gain?

Scripture Passage: 1 Corinthians 15:24–28

...then comes the end, when He hands over the kingdom to the God and Father, when He has abolished all rule and all authority and power. For He must reign until He has put all His enemies under His feet. The last enemy that will be abolished is death. For HE HAS PUT ALL THINGS IN SUBJECTION UNDER HIS FEET. But when He says, "All things are put in subjection," it is evident that He is excepted who put all things in subjection to Him. When all things are subjected to Him, then the Son Himself also will be subjected to the One who subjected all things to Him, so that God may be all in all.

Scripture Passage: Jeremiah 17:5–7, 9

Thus says the LORD, "Cursed is the man who trusts in mankind and makes flesh his strength, and whose heart turns away from the LORD. For he will be like a bush in the desert and will not see when prosperity comes, but will live in stony wastes in the wilderness, a land of salt without inhabitant. Blessed is the man who trusts in the LORD and whose trust is the LORD. ...

"The heart is more deceitful than all else and is desperately sick; who can understand it?"

Scripture Passage: Ezekiel 38:1–8

And the word of the LORD came to me saying, "Son of man, set your face toward Gog of the land of Magog, the prince of Rosh, Meshech and Tubal, and prophesy against him and say, 'Thus says the Lord GOD, "Behold, I am against you, O Gog, prince of Rosh, Meshech and Tubal. I will turn you about and put hooks into your jaws, and I will bring you out, and all your army, horses and horsemen, all of them splendidly attired, a great company with buckler and shield, all of them wielding swords; Persia, Ethiopia and Put with them, all of them with shield and helmet; Gomer with all its troops; Beth-togarmah from the remote parts of the north with all its troops—many peoples with you. Be prepared, and prepare yourself, you and all your companies that are assembled about you, and be a guard for them. After many days you will be summoned; in the latter years you will come into the land that is restored from the sword, whose inhabitants have been gathered from many nations to the mountains of Israel which had been a continual waste;

REVELATION 20:7–9

but its people were brought out from the nations, and they are living securely, all of them.""

A LITTLE DEEPER...

1. What truth do you learn from the passage in Jeremiah that applies to life today, not just life in the kingdom? How can you live with that truth in mind?

_____

_____

_____

2. What does it mean that the final enemy for Christ to defeat is death? How/ why is the defeat of death a prerequisite for the coming of the new heaven and new earth?

_____

_____

_____

SESSION EIGHTY

The Purpose of the War of Gog and Magog

***Remember the Golden Rule:** When the plain sense of Scripture makes common sense, we seek no other sense.*

Video Eighty

Topical overview: The process and end of the war of Gog and Magog. Transition from the millennial kingdom to new heavens and earth.

Learning goals: Recognize the purpose and plan of God in the war of Gog and Magog.

CORE QUESTIONS

Before watching video eighty, read Revelation 20:7–9. Use the two-column graphic organizer to help you organize your thoughts. Discuss your observations as a group.

As you watch the video, complete the following section. For many, reading the questions before watching the video will aid their understanding of the video content.

1. Summarize the interpretation and significance of 1 Corinthians 15:24–28.

_____
_____
_____

2. What is the purpose of the millennial kingdom?

_____

The Purpose of the War of Gog and Magog

3. How long is the earth ruled by sinful people?

4. Why is Satan released?

5. What are the details of Satan's deception and this final battle?

6. Other than Revelation 20, where do we read of Gog and Magog?

7. How much of Ezekiel is devoted to kingdom prophecy?

8. How are the chapters of Ezekiel organized?

9. Who are Gog and Magog?

10. How was the area of Magog named?

11. Who starts this war?

12. Why is it significant that the war of Gog and Magog is fought with wooden weapons?

13. What conclusion do we draw from the key details presented from Ezekiel 38 and 39?

DISCUSSION QUESTIONS

1. What do we know of the state of the world and those in it at the beginning of the war of Gog and Magog?

_____

_____

_____

2. God starts the war of Gog and Magog by releasing Satan from prison. What does this reveal of God's character, plan, and purposes?

_____

_____

_____

3. Ezekiel was a priest and prophet during the time of Babylonian exile. A large portion of the prophecies he received tell us of life in the millennial kingdom and the transition to a new heaven and new earth. Recall: how does Ezekiel order or organize his prophecies, and why might this be?

_____

_____

_____

4. In the space below, record your takeaway from Session Eighty and any questions you have that remain unanswered.

_____

_____

_____

DIGGING DEEPER (OPTIONAL)

Should you choose to dig deeper, complete the following Digging Deeper section. Each meeting will open with discussion of what you've learned and observed in Scripture, and this section will prepare you for that discussion.

Revelation

In a two-column graphic organizer, record what you observe in each passage and the questions you have about it. Things to look for: Who is speaking? To whom is he speaking? What does he say about God? Jesus? The church? Individual believers? What do readers of this text stand to gain?

Scripture Passage: Ezekiel 38:9–16; 39:1–6, 9–21

"'You will go up, you will come like a storm; you will be like a cloud covering the land, you and all your troops, and many peoples with you.' Thus says the Lord GOD, 'It will come about on that day, that thoughts will come into your mind and you will devise an evil plan, and you will say, "I will go up against the land of unwalled villages. I will go against those who are at rest, that live securely, all of them living without walls and having no bars or gates, to capture spoil and to seize plunder, to turn your hand against the waste places which are now inhabited, and against the people who are gathered from the nations, who have acquired cattle and goods, who live at the center of the world." Sheba and Dedan and the merchants of Tarshish with all its villages will say to you, "Have you come to capture spoil? Have you assembled your company to seize plunder, to carry away silver and gold, to take away cattle and goods, to capture great spoil?"'" Therefore prophesy, son of man, and say to Gog, "Thus says the Lord GOD, 'On that day when My people Israel are living securely, will you not know it? You will come from your place out of the remote parts of the north, you and many peoples with you, all of them riding on horses, a great assembly and a mighty army; and you will come up against My people Israel like a cloud to cover the land. It shall come about in the last days that I will bring you against My land, so that the nations may know Me when I am sanctified through you before their eyes, O Gog.'" ...

And you, son of man, prophesy against Gog and say, "Thus says the Lord GOD, 'Behold, I am against you, O Gog, prince of Rosh, Meshech and Tubal; and I will turn you around, drive you on, take you up from the remotest parts of the north and bring you against the mountains of Israel. I will strike your bow from your left hand and dash down your arrows from your right hand. You will fall on the mountains of Israel, you and all your troops and the peoples who are with you; I will give you as food to every kind of predatory bird and beast of the field. You will fall on the open field; for it is I who have spoken,' declares the Lord GOD. 'And I will send fire upon Magog and those who inhabit the coastlands in safety; and they will know that I am the LORD. ...

'Then those who inhabit the cities of Israel will go out and make fires with the weapons and burn them, both shields and bucklers, bows and arrows, war clubs and spears, and for seven years they will make fires of them. They will not take wood from the field or gather firewood from the forests, for they will make fires with the weapons; and they will take the spoil of those who despoiled them and seize the plunder of those who plundered them,' declares the Lord GOD. 'On that day I will give Gog a burial ground there in Israel, the valley of those who pass by east of the sea, and it will block off those who would pass by. So they will bury Gog there with all his horde, and they will call it the valley of Hamon-gog. For seven months the house of Israel will be burying them in order to cleanse the land. Even all the people of the land will bury them; and it will be to their renown on the day that I glorify Myself,' declares the Lord GOD. 'They will set apart men who will constantly pass through the land, burying those who were passing through, even those left on the surface of the ground, in order to cleanse it. At the end of seven months they will make a search. As those who pass through the land pass through and anyone sees a man's bone, then he will set up a marker by it until the buriers have buried it in the valley of Hamon-gog. And even the name of the city will be Hamonah. So they will cleanse the land.'" As for you, son of man, thus says the Lord GOD, "Speak to every kind of bird and to every beast of the field, 'Assemble and come, gather from every side to My sacrifice which I am going to sacrifice for you, as a great

sacrifice on the mountains of Israel, that you may eat flesh and drink blood. You will eat the flesh of mighty men and drink the blood of the princes of the earth, as though they were rams, lambs, goats and bulls, all of them fatlings of Bashan. So you will eat fat until you are glutted, and drink blood until you are drunk, from My sacrifice which I have sacrificed for you. You will be glutted at My table with horses and charioteers, with mighty men and all the men of war,' declares the Lord GOD. 'And I will set My glory among the nations; and all the nations will see My judgment which I have executed and My hand which I have laid on them.'"

Scripture Passage: Isaiah 2:4

And He will judge between the nations, and will render decisions for many peoples; and they will hammer their swords into plowshares and their spears into pruning hooks. Nation will not lift up sword against nation, and never again will they learn war.

A LITTLE DEEPER...

1. Who receives the sacrifice prophesied in Ezekiel? Why might that be (consider connections to Genesis)?

_____

_____

_____

2. What exactly happens in the war of Gog and Magog? Summarize the phases and its consequences in the space below.

_____

_____

_____

SESSION EIGHTY-ONE

The Resolution of the War of Gog and Magog

> ***Remember the Golden Rule:*** *When the plain sense of Scripture makes common sense, we seek no other sense.*

Video Eighty-One

Topical overview: The progress and resolution of the war of Gog and Magog.
Learning goals: Trace the purpose and plan of God through the events and aftermath of the war of Gog and Magog.

CORE QUESTIONS

Before watching video eighty-one, read Revelation 20:7–9. Use the two-column graphic organizer to help you organize your thoughts. Discuss your observations as a group.

As you watch the video, complete the following section. For many, reading the questions before watching the video will aid their understanding of the video content.

1. What does Ezekiel 38 tell us about the movement of Gog and his army?

_____
_____
_____

2. Where do these thoughts of Gog's originate?

_____

3. In the kingdom, how will God demonstrate His faithfulness in keeping His promise to keep Israel safe from enemies?

4. How is the war of Gog and Magog resolved?

5. What happens to the fallen soldiers and their weapons?

6. What's the significance of God's words to the animal kingdom in Ezekiel 39?

DISCUSSION QUESTIONS

1. What motivates Gog to war? How is Satan using the same tactics he's always used to incite violence?

Revelation

2. Have you ever considered that God creates, instigates, or allows opportunities to prove Himself faithful? Where else in Scripture do we find this to be true? Where in your own life do you find this to be true?

_____

_____

_____

3. How does God place bookends on the history of humanity? Why are these specific bookends significant in His grand plan?

_____

_____

_____

4. In the space below, record your takeaway from Session Eighty-One and any questions you have that remain unanswered.

_____

_____

_____

Digging Deeper (Optional)

Should you choose to dig deeper, complete the following Digging Deeper section. Each meeting will open with discussion of what you've learned and observed in Scripture, and this section will prepare you for that discussion.

In a two-column graphic organizer, record what you observe in each passage and the questions you have about it. Things to look for: Who is speaking? To whom is he speaking? What does he say about God? Jesus? The church? Individual believers? What do readers of this text stand to gain?

Scripture Passage: Revelation 14:9–10; 20:5–6, 10–15

> *Then another angel, a third one, followed them, saying with a loud voice, "If anyone worships the beast and his image, and receives a mark on his forehead or on his hand, he also will drink of the wine of the wrath of God, which is mixed in full strength in the cup of His anger; and he will be tormented with fire and brimstone in the presence of the holy angels and in the presence of the Lamb. ..."*

The rest of the dead did not come to life until the thousand years were completed. This is the first resurrection. Blessed and holy is the one who has a part in the first resurrection; over these the second death has no power, but they will be priests of God and of Christ and will reign with Him for a thousand years. …

And the devil who deceived them was thrown into the lake of fire and brimstone, where the beast and the false prophet are also; and they will be tormented day and night forever and ever. Then I saw a great white throne and Him who sat upon it, from whose presence earth and heaven fled away, and no place was found for them. And I saw the dead, the great and the small, standing before the throne, and books were opened; and another book was opened, which is the book of life; and the dead were judged from the things which were written in the books, according to their deeds. And the sea gave up the dead which were in it, and death and Hades gave up the dead which were in them; and they were judged, every one of them according to their deeds. Then death and Hades were thrown into the lake of fire. This is the second death, the lake of fire. And if anyone's name was not found written in the book of life, he was thrown into the lake of fire.

Scripture Passage: 2 Thessalonians 1:6–9

For after all it is only just for God to repay with affliction those who afflict you, and to give relief to you who are afflicted and to us as well when the Lord Jesus will be revealed from heaven with His mighty angels in flaming fire, dealing out retribution to those who do not know God and to those who do not obey the gospel of our Lord Jesus. These will pay the penalty of eternal destruction, away from the presence of the Lord and from the glory of His power….

Scripture Passage: John 5:21–22

For just as the Father raises the dead and gives them life, even so the Son also gives life to whom He wishes. For not even the Father judges anyone, but He has given all judgment to the Son….

Scripture Passage: Acts 10:42

And He ordered us to preach to the people, and solemnly to testify that this is the One who has been appointed by God as Judge of the living and the dead.

Scripture Passage: Luke 21:33

Heaven and earth will pass away, but My words will not pass away.

Revelation

A Little Deeper...

1. Consider all the timelines we've studied up to this point. What points on the timeline might the first and second deaths represent? What points on the timeline might the first and second resurrections represent? In which of these things will today's believers take part?

_____
_____
_____

2. According to these passages, what is the book of life, and what is it used for?

_____
_____
_____

3. How is eternal punishment in the lake of fire justified? Do you struggle to accept this? Why or why not?

_____
_____
_____

4. Focus on Luke 21:33. How do we live in view of the truth of this Scripture?

_____
_____
_____

SESSION EIGHTY-TWO

Revelation 20:10–15

***Remember the Golden Rule:** When the plain sense of Scripture makes common sense, we seek no other sense.*

Video Eighty-Two

Topical overview: The lake of fire and the Great White Throne Judgment.
Learning goals: Discern the distinction between physical and spiritual death. Recognize the role of Jesus in the seven years between His millennial kingdom and the new heavens and earth.

CORE QUESTIONS

Before watching video eighty-two, read Revelation 20:10–15. Use the two-column graphic organizer to help you organize your thoughts. Discuss your observations as a group.

As you watch the video, complete the following section. For many, reading the questions before watching the video will aid their understanding of the video content.

1. What will the seven years following the millennial kingdom most closely resemble?

_____

_____

_____

REVELATION

2. What occurs between this seven-year interim and the new heavens and earth?

3. Where does Satan go at the time of judgment?

4. Where is this lake of fire currently?

5. Who will be in the lake of fire during the millennial kingdom?

The lake of fire is the home of the ungodly and unbelieving for all of eternity.

6. What is the purpose of eternal punishment?

7. What is spiritual death?

REVELATION 20:10–15

Sin is a function of *identity*, not just actions. Evil, the fallen nature of Satan, his demons, and all unbelieving humanity last forever.

8. What are the two kinds of resurrection?

_____
_____
_____

9. Who sits on the Great White Throne and why?

_____
_____
_____

10. What disappears at the beginning of this time of judgment?

_____
_____
_____

11. Who will be present around the throne in this moment and for what purpose?

_____
_____
_____

DISCUSSION QUESTIONS

1. What is the difference between the lake of fire and hell? How do you know? Support your answer with Scripture.

_____
_____
_____

2. What did you learn about judgment in this session? How does the truth of Christ's authority to judge affect how we live our lives today?

_____

_____

_____

3. In the last session, we learned of the "bookends" of sacrifice on the course of human history. In the seven years following the millennial kingdom, how does the physical world "bookend" human history? Why does God consistent follow this pattern, and how does this expression of "making all things new" give you hope?

_____

_____

_____

4. In the space below, record your takeaway from Revelation 20:10–15 and any questions you have that remain unanswered.

_____

_____

_____

DIGGING DEEPER (OPTIONAL)

Should you choose to dig deeper, complete the following Digging Deeper section. Each meeting will open with discussion of what you've learned and observed in Scripture, and this section will prepare you for that discussion.

In a two-column graphic organizer, record what you observe in each passage and the questions you have about it. Things to look for: Who is speaking? To whom is he speaking? What does he say about God? Jesus? The church? Individual believers? What do readers of this text stand to gain?

Scripture Passage: Read Revelation 3:5; 13:8

Scripture Passage: Matthew 8:28–29

When He came to the other side into the country of the Gadarenes, two men who were demon-

possessed met Him as they were coming out of the tombs. They were so extremely violent that no one could pass by that way. And they cried out, saying, "What business do we have with each other, Son of God? Have You come here to torment us before the time?"

Scripture Passage: Philippians 2:9–11; 4:3

For this reason also, God highly exalted Him, and bestowed on Him the name which is above every name, so that at the name of Jesus EVERY KNEE WILL BOW, of those who are in heaven and on earth and under the earth, and that every tongue will confess that Jesus Christ is Lord, to the glory of God the Father. So if all their tongues confess Jesus as Lord, why are they still subject to His judgment? …

Indeed, true companion, I ask you also to help these women who have shared my struggle in the cause of the gospel, together with Clement also and the rest of my fellow workers, whose names are in the book of life.

A LITTLE DEEPER…

1. Recall: what is the symbolic significance of white garments?

_____

_____

_____

2. The words of the demons in Matthew 8 reveal their understanding of what truth found in Revelation 20?

_____

_____

_____

3. In the time of the Great White Throne judgment, Jesus will finally receive His due from all creation. So answer the question of Philippians 2:11: "…if all their tongues confess Jesus as Lord, why are they still subject to His judgment?"

_____

_____

_____

SESSION EIGHTY-THREE

Revelation 20:21

> ***Remember the Golden Rule:*** *When the plain sense of Scripture makes common sense, we seek no other sense.*

Video Eighty-Three

Topical overview: The Great White Throne Judgment and the book of life.
Learning goals: Recognize the place of Jesus and that of humanity in this moment of final judgment.

CORE QUESTIONS

Before watching video eighty-three, read Revelation 20:21. Use the two-column graphic organizer to help you organize your thoughts. Discuss your observations as a group.

As you watch the video, complete the following section. For many, reading the questions before watching the video will aid their understanding of the video content.

1. During the Great White Throne judgment, where exactly will we be?

___

___

___

2. What are the two parts of human existence?

___

3. Who are the only two people who miss out on the Great White Throne Judgment and why?

4. What are the two areas of hell, and who resides there?

5. What is significant about the demons' words to Christ is Matthew 8?

All the unrepentant sin of all time will be on display in this one moment as unbelievers face judgment. Remember: there, *but for the grace of God*, go I.

6. Why will bowing to Jesus at this moment of judgment not be sufficient for salvation?

7. What is in the Book of Life?

8. Why is the Book of Life present at the Great White Throne judgment?

___

9. By what criteria are these unbelievers judged?

___

DISCUSSION QUESTIONS

1. What scriptures come to mind when you consider the two parts of human existence, body and soul? What does Scripture teach of these parts of ourselves?

___

2. Focus on the phrase, "There, but for the grace of God, go I." How does the truth of this statement affect your understanding of the Great White Throne judgment? How does the truth of this statement affect how you live your life today?

___

3. How does learning the realities of sin, hell, and judgment affect your desire to share Jesus? What will you do about it?

___

REVELATION 20:21

4. In the space below, record your takeaway from Session Eighty-Three and any questions you have that remain unanswered.

_____

_____

_____

DIGGING DEEPER (OPTIONAL)

Should you choose to dig deeper, complete the following Digging Deeper section. Each meeting will open with discussion of what you've learned and observed in Scripture, and this section will prepare you for that discussion.

In a two-column graphic organizer, record what you observe in each passage and the questions you have about it. Things to look for: Who is speaking? To whom is he speaking? What does he say about God? Jesus? The church? Individual believers? What do readers of this text stand to gain?

Scripture Passage: Revelation 21:1–8

Scripture Passage: Genesis 1:1; 2:7–8

In the beginning God created the heavens and the earth….

Then the LORD God formed man of dust from the ground, and breathed into his nostrils the breath of life; and man became a living being. The LORD God planted a garden toward the east, in Eden; and there He placed the man whom He had formed….

Scripture Passage: Hebrews 1:1–2; 11:15–16; 12:22–24

God, after He spoke long ago to the fathers in the prophets in many portions and in many ways, in these last days has spoken to us in His Son, whom He appointed heir of all things, through whom also He made the world. …

And indeed if they had been thinking of that country from which they went out, they would have had opportunity to return. But as it is, they desire a better country, that is, a heavenly one. Therefore God is not ashamed to be called their God; for He has prepared a city for them. …

But you have come to Mount Zion and to the city of the living God, the heavenly Jerusalem, and to myriads of angels, to the general assembly and church of the firstborn who are enrolled in heaven, and to God, the Judge of all, and to the spirits of the righteous made perfect, and to Jesus, the mediator of a new covenant, and to the sprinkled blood, which speaks better than the

REVELATION

blood of Abel.

Scripture Passage: Philippians 3:20

For our citizenship is in heaven, from which also we eagerly wait for a Savior, the Lord Jesus Christ....

A Little Deeper...

1. What does it mean to fix our eyes on Jesus, to live with our future hope in view? What does this look like practically?

_____

_____

_____

2. Throughout these passages, trace what God *does*. Look at the verbs. Pay specific attention to things He does in relationship to us. What do we learn about who God is and how He relates to us in these passages?

_____

_____

_____

SESSION EIGHTY-FOUR

Revelation 21:1–8

> ***Remember the Golden Rule:*** *When the plain sense of Scripture makes common sense, we seek no other sense.*

Video Eighty-Four

Topical overview: The message of Revelation. The Final judgment and what comes next.

Learning goals: Identify the fate of unbelievers after judgment, what remains, and what comes next.

CORE QUESTIONS

Before watching video eighty-four, read Revelation 21:1–8. Use the two-column graphic organizer to help you organize your thoughts. Discuss your observations as a group.

As you watch the video, complete the following section. For many, reading the questions before watching the video will aid their understanding of the video content.

1. How are the unbelievers convicted at judgment?

_____

_____

_____

Revelation

2. What is the punishment of unbelievers?

___

3. After unbelievers are judged, what remains?

___

4. What scriptural principle is on display by the rather vague content of Revelation 21–22?

___

5. To what two chapters of Scripture are Revelation 21–22 closely connected and in what way?

___

6. What are two specific details we learn of the new heavens and earth?

___

7. What is the counterpart of the new Jerusalem in Genesis?

___

8. What does Jesus say is the significance of the new Jerusalem?

9. Where does God the Father dwell in the new heavens and earth?

10. There will be no tears, death, mourning, crying, pain—what does their absence signify?

11. What is the message of Revelation to the present reader?

DISCUSSION QUESTIONS

1. The lack of tears, death, mourning, pain in the new earth signifies a lack of sin as well. Do you attribute the presence of these things in your own life or the lives of others to sin? Why or why not? How does attributing the pain of life affect how we deal with our own pain and that of others?

REVELATION

2. The message of Revelation can be summarized as "Seek Jesus while you still can." Do you believe this is true? Why or why not? For those who know Jesus already, what is the message or purpose of Revelation?

_____
_____
_____

3. When Jesus tells us He's making all things new, to what is He referring? How can we read this verse to have significance both in the present and prophetic senses?

_____
_____
_____

4. In the space below, record your takeaway from Revelation 21:1–8 and any questions you have that remain unanswered.

_____
_____
_____

DIGGING DEEPER (OPTIONAL)

Should you choose to dig deeper, complete the following Digging Deeper section. Each meeting will open with discussion of what you've learned and observed in Scripture, and this section will prepare you for that discussion.

In a two-column graphic organizer, record what you observe in each passage and the questions you have about it. Things to look for: Who is speaking? To whom is he speaking? What does he say about God? Jesus? The church? Individual believers? What do readers of this text stand to gain?

Scripture Passage: Revelation 21:9–21

Scripture Passage: Romans 9:4–5

> ...who are Israelites, to whom belongs the adoption as sons, and the glory and the covenants and the giving of the Law and the temple service and the promises, whose are the fathers, and

from whom is the Christ according to the flesh, who is over all, God blessed forever. Amen.

Scripture Passage: Ephesians 2:12–21

…remember that you [Gentiles] were at that time separate from Christ, excluded from the commonwealth of Israel, and strangers to the covenants of promise, having no hope and without God in the world. But now in Christ Jesus you who formerly were far off have been brought near by the blood of Christ. For He Himself is our peace, who made both groups into one and broke down the barrier of the dividing wall, by abolishing in His flesh the enmity, which is the Law of commandments contained in ordinances, so that in Himself He might make the two into one new man, thus establishing peace, and might reconcile them both in one body to God through the cross, by it having put to death the enmity. AND HE CAME AND PREACHED PEACE TO YOU WHO WERE FAR AWAY, AND PEACE TO THOSE WHO WERE NEAR; for through Him we both have our access in one Spirit to the Father. So then you are no longer strangers and aliens, but you are fellow citizens with the saints, and are of God's household, having been built on the foundation of the apostles and prophets, Christ Jesus Himself being the corner stone, in whom the whole building, being fitted together, is growing into a holy temple in the Lord….

A LITTLE DEEPER…

1. Ephesians chapter 2 presents a spiritual reality made physical in the new Jerusalem of Revelation 22. How so?

_____

_____

_____

2. Find a unit of measure to help you understand how large 1,500 square (cubed) miles is. To what does a city of this size compare? Why might new Jerusalem be so large?

_____

_____

_____

3. Spend some time researching the elements described in the construction of the new Jerusalem. What do they look like?

_____

_____

_____

SESSION EIGHTY-FIVE

Revelation 21:9–21

> ***Remember the Golden Rule:*** *When the plain sense of Scripture makes common sense, we seek no other sense.*

Video Eighty-Five

Topical overview: Describing the new earth.
Learning goals: Identify how the new earth and its Jerusalem are structured and why.

CORE QUESTIONS

Before watching video eighty-five, read Revelation 21:9–21. Use the two-column graphic organizer to help you organize your thoughts. Discuss your observations as a group.

As you watch the video, complete the following section. For many, reading the questions before watching the video will aid their understanding of the video content.

1. What is the capital of the new earth, and what do we know about it?

___

2. In the new earth, to what will the "bride of Christ" refer and why?

___

REVELATION 21:9–21

3. What is the shape of the City?

4. What do we know about the earth at this point?

5. What is the purpose of the walls and gates of the new Jerusalem?

6. Why the focus on Israel in the new creation?

7. What are the symbolic significances of 12 and 3?

8. Who is memorialized in the foundations of the new Jerusalem?

Revelation

_____

_____

In the new heavens and earth, we will live in a city constructed to remind us of Israel's role in allowing all people to enter God's grace.

9. What is the purpose of John's description of the new Jerusalem?

_____

_____

_____

10. What is significant about the city's dimensions other than their large proportions?

_____

_____

_____

DISCUSSION QUESTIONS

1. The phrase "bride of Christ" takes on new meaning in the new heavens and earth. How so and why?

_____

_____

_____

2. Consider all the memorializing encompassed in the new heavens and earth. Why does God do things this way? How is this consistent with His actions throughout Scripture?

_____

_____

_____

REVELATION 21:9–21

3. What is Israel's role in the new creation and why?

___

4. God gives John a glimpse of the new Jerusalem as recorded in Revelation just as God gave Ezekiel a glimpse of the millennial temple. Why show us at all, why just a glimpse? Why are these visions preserved for our benefit?

___

5. In the space below, record your takeaway from Revelation 20:9–21 and any questions you have that remain unanswered.

___

DIGGING DEEPER (OPTIONAL)

Should you choose to dig deeper, complete the following Digging Deeper section. Each meeting will open with discussion of what you've learned and observed in Scripture, and this section will prepare you for that discussion.

In a two-column graphic organizer, record what you observe in each passage and the questions you have about it. Things to look for: Who is speaking? To whom is he speaking? What does he say about God? Jesus? The church? Individual believers? What do readers of this text stand to gain?

Scripture Passage: Revelation 21:22–27, 22:1–5

Scripture Passage: 1 Corinthians 15:24, 28

> ...then comes the end, when He hands over the kingdom to the God and Father, when He has abolished all rule and all authority and power. ...

When all things are subjected to Him, then the Son Himself also will be subjected to the One who subjected all things to Him, so that God may be all in all.

Scripture Passage: 2 Peter 3:5–6

For when they maintain this, it escapes their notice that by the word of God the heavens existed long ago and the earth was formed out of water and by water, through which the world at that time was destroyed, being flooded with water.

Scripture Passage: Genesis 1:2–5, 14–15; 2:2–9; 3:22–24

The earth was formless and void, and darkness was over the surface of the deep, and the Spirit of God was moving over the surface of the waters. Then God said, "Let there be light"; and there was light. God saw that the light was good; and God separated the light from the darkness. God called the light day, and the darkness He called night. And there was evening and there was morning, one day. ...

Then God said, "Let there be lights in the expanse of the heavens to separate the day from the night, and let them be for signs and for seasons and for days and years; and let them be for lights in the expanse of the heavens to give light on the earth"; and it was so. ...

By the seventh day God completed His work which He had done, and He rested on the seventh day from all His work which He had done. Then God blessed the seventh day and sanctified it, because in it He rested from all His work which God had created and made. This is the account of the heavens and the earth when they were created, in the day that the LORD God made earth and heaven. Now no shrub of the field was yet in the earth, and no plant of the field had yet sprouted, for the LORD God had not sent rain upon the earth, and there was no man to cultivate the ground. But a mist used to rise from the earth and water the whole surface of the ground. Then the LORD God formed man of dust from the ground, and breathed into his nostrils the breath of life; and man became a living being. The LORD God planted a garden toward the east, in Eden; and there He placed the man whom He had formed. Out of the ground the LORD God caused to grow every tree that is pleasing to the sight and good for food; the tree of life also in the midst of the garden, and the tree of the knowledge of good and evil. ...

Then the LORD God said, "Behold, the man has become like one of Us, knowing good and evil; and now, he might stretch out his hand, and take also from the tree of life, and eat, and live forever"—therefore the LORD God sent him out from the garden of Eden, to cultivate the ground from which he was taken. So He drove the man out; and at the east of the garden of Eden He stationed the cherubim and the flaming sword which turned every direction to guard the way to the tree of life.

REVELATION 21:9–21

A LITTLE DEEPER…

1. What does it mean for God to be "all in all" generally? Personally?

_____

_____

_____

2. What do we learn of the tree of life from these passages?

_____

_____

_____

3. What do we learn of the new earth as described in Revelation 22?

_____

_____

_____

SESSION EIGHTY-SIX

Revelation 21:22–22:5

> ***Remember the Golden Rule:*** *When the plain sense of Scripture makes common sense, we seek no other sense.*

Video Eighty-Six

Topical overview: New heavens and earth.
Learning goals: Discern what will and will not be present in the new earth and why.

CORE QUESTIONS

Before watching video eighty-six, read Revelation 21:22–22:5. Use the two-column graphic organizer to help you organize your thoughts. Discuss your observations as a group.

As you watch the video, complete the following section. For many, reading the questions before watching the video will aid their understanding of the video content.

1. Why will there be no temple in the new Jerusalem?

_____

_____

_____

2. What is the light source in the new heavens and earth?

_____

REVELATION 21:22–22:5

3. What will be noticeably absent from the new world?

4. Why specifically did God create water/ seas the first time?

5. Why specifically did God create light and dark the first time?

6. So why will seas and darkness be absent from the new earth?

7. What does the Bible teach us about the passing of time in this creation?

8. What is significant about the tree we see in Revelation 22?

9. Why did God forbid access to the tree of life in Eden?

10. Why has the tree of life existed throughout various phases of creation?

Mortality reminds us of our dependence on God.

11. What is the purpose of the tree of life?

Discussion Questions

1. What does the Bible teach us about how time is moving? How does this differ from the popular social understanding of time? And how does adopting a biblical worldview on this issue affect how you live your life presently?

2. Even in the new earth, God will be glorified in all things. How so and why?

3. In this session's discussion of mortality, we learned that mortality reminds us of our dependence on God. How so? How do we live in light of this truth? Considering current events, how might society change if humanity, as a whole, or even just the church as a whole, lived in awareness of our dependence on God?

_____

_____

_____

4. In the space below, record your takeaway from Revelation 21:22–22:5 and any questions you have that remain unanswered.

_____

_____

_____

DIGGING DEEPER (OPTIONAL)

Should you choose to dig deeper, complete the following Digging Deeper section. Each meeting will open with discussion of what you've learned and observed in Scripture, and this section will prepare you for that discussion.

In a two-column graphic organizer, record what you observe in each passage and the questions you have about it. Things to look for: Who is speaking? To whom is he speaking? What does he say about God? Jesus? The church? Individual believers? What do readers of this text stand to gain?

Scripture Passage: Revelation 22:6–21

Scripture Passage: John 8:12

> *Then Jesus again spoke to them, saying, "I am the Light of the world; he who follows Me will not walk in the darkness, but will have the Light of life."*

Revelation

Scripture Passage: Genesis 49:25

From the God of your father who helps you, and by the Almighty who blesses you with blessings of heaven above, blessings of the deep that lies beneath, blessings of the breasts and of the womb.

Scripture Passage: Ephesians 1:4–6

...just as He chose us in Him before the foundation of the world, that we would be holy and blameless before Him. In love He predestined us to adoption as sons through Jesus Christ to Himself, according to the kind intention of His will, to the praise of the glory of His grace, which He freely bestowed on us in the Beloved.

A Little Deeper...

1. Daniel's angel has him seal up the last of his prophecies, while John's commands the opposite—that John should *not* seal up the prophecies of Revelation. Why? How are the circumstances different between their experiences and prophecies?

_____

_____

_____

2. What do we learn from these passages about our identity as believers? Reflect on how you live. Is your identity grounded in Christ and the truth of His word? Spend time in prayer asking God to help you live the truth of your identity in Him.

_____

_____

_____

SESSION EIGHTY-SEVEN

Revelation 22:6–21

Remember the Golden Rule: When the plain sense of Scripture makes common sense, we seek no other sense.

Video Eighty-Seven

Topical overview: The benediction, invitation, and warning.
Learning goals: Contextualize the events of Revelation in God's purpose and plan for His creation.

CORE QUESTIONS

Before watching video eighty-seven, read Revelation 22:6–21. Use the two-column graphic organizer to help you organize your thoughts. Discuss your observations as a group.

As you watch the video, complete the following section. For many, reading the questions before watching the video will aid their understanding of the video content.

In the design of creation the first time, He anticipated the arrival of sin and the necessity to teach humanity of sin and redemption. God's plan for the first creation fully anticipated the arrival of sin and His design made accommodations for it.

1. Why does God not reinstitute some aspects of the first creation in His second creation?

_____

_____

2. What was the purpose of the first creation?

3. What literary purpose does the final portion of Revelation 22 serve?

We can trust the record of this book and receive it in complete confidence that this is the future, and that future is not long away; the same Spirit who gave the prophets their words is the One Who gave John these words.

4. What that knowledge, what are we to do in the meantime?

5. What is the only possible interruption to the path of the unbeliever?

6. Where is the lake of fire in physical relationship to the new Jerusalem?

7. Why does Jesus testify to His own identity?

8. What is the invitation of Revelation 22?

9. What is the warning of Revelation 22?

Discussion Questions

1. What defines the difference between the first and new creations? Why was the first, the sinful world we live in today, necessary?

2. What is a benediction, and why is there one at this point (the end) in Revelation?

3. Recall the warning of Revelation 22. Where else in Scripture do we find the same caution? How do we practically adhere to the wisdom of this caution?

Revelation

4. In the space below, record your takeaway from Revelation 22:6–21 and any questions you have that remain unanswered.

DIGGING DEEPER
FINAL REFLECTION

Complete the following Digging Deeper section to reflect on and process all you've learned in this study. Each meeting will open with discussion of what you've learned and observed in Scripture, and this section will prepare you for that discussion.

1. As a group, discuss the one thing you'll take with you from this study. How will it impact your daily life?

2. How do we use what we've learned in this study of Revelation to, in turn, offer the invitation of Revelation 22 to a thirsty, broken world?

A LITTLE DEEPER…

On a personal level, reflect (share with the group if you feel so led):

1. How did this study affect your understanding of the Godhead (Father, Son, and Spirit)?

2. How did this study affect your understanding of your identity as a believer?

3. How has this study called you to repentance? What will you do about it?

APPENDIX

Answer Key

INTRODUCTION ANSWERS
LISTENING GUIDE

1. Why do we study with rigor? Because when we don't, there is controversy.

2. What is the proof that the enemy doesn't want you to study Revelation? Controversy—people avoid it. Spiritual warfare—it can change your life.

3. What does 1 Corinthians 14:33, which says, "For God is not a God of confusion but of peace, as in all the churches of the saints," teach us? Our God is not a God of confusion. We have everything we need to understand the Bible.

4. How is the Bible like a novel? Sixty-six chapters (books) with one author (God).

5. Why is Revelation the last book of the Bible? It is the summation/ culmination of everything that came before.

6. What is Pastor Armstrong's job? It is to provide the background information necessary so that you can understand Revelation.

7. Why has this study been called a survey of the whole Bible masquerading as a study of Revelation? 1) There is a lot of cross-referencing in this study. 2) There are rules of interpretation.

8. What is the purpose of having rules of interpretation? Rules are there to protect us from our own biases, blind spots, and imaginations.

9. What will we *not* do? We will not make it up as we go; fill in gaps with our own understanding.

10. When we get to a place where we have an unanswered question, what will the answer be? The answer will just be "I don't know" until God reveals otherwise.

Two Rules for Interpretation

11. If you follow the golden rule of interpretation, how often will you steer clear of trouble? 95% of the time.

12. If a symbol has significance, where will its meaning be already established? The Bible.

13. How do the rules of interpretation work? You look in the immediate context, then move backward in the Bible if necessary.

14. Why do you only look backward? The Lord knows how we read: from front to back.

15. What leads to confusion? Poor scholarship.

SESSION ONE ANSWERS
REVELATION 1:1–3

1. What does the Greek word for Revelation teach us? It is where we get the word apocalypse, which means to be revealed.

2. Of whom is this book said to be the direct revelation? Jesus Christ.

3. Which entities make up the "chain of custody" for this letter? God the Father > Jesus the Son > His Angel > John the Apostle > bondservants.

4. Why does God include this "chain of custody" information? To encourage the church to believe the content of this Revelation, which resolves dispute and excludes false teaching regarding the return of Christ.

5. How does Jesus communicate the details of this letter (verse 1)? He showed them to John.

6. What is this letter a testimony about (verse 3)? A testimony to what John saw.

7. Why are these two verbs so crucial to our understanding of Revelation? John has to explain what he *saw*, not what he was told, so much of the book is shrouded in mystery. It obscures the meaning to those outside the church. It makes this study a bit of a reward to the student who pursues it diligently.

8. What does Revelation specifically promise to those who study it? Blessing.

9. What does it mean to "heed" the teaching in Revelation? Doesn't mean "to understand," it means to give it your attention and your heart, to whatever level of understanding you gain.

Revelation

SESSION TWO ANSWERS
INTRODUCTION TO REVELATION

Revelation 1:4–8

1. To whom does John write? The seven churches of Asia.

2. In the Bible, what does the number seven generally convey? 100%.

3. So, what is the symbolic meaning of "the seven churches of Asia?" 100% of the church throughout the history of time.

4. Who does John's greeting come from? God the Father, 100% of the Spirit, and Jesus.

5. What do the descriptions of Jesus point to? The three periods of His ministry: witness of creation; resurrection at the culmination of His earthly ministry; and the ruler of earth after His second coming.

6. What is the book of Revelation about? The circumstances that take us from Jesus as the firstborn of the dead to the Ruling King after His second coming.

7. What it the significance of the phrase "kingdom of priests?" A priest is an intercessor; we are representatives (intercessors) between Christ and the unbelieving world.

Revelation 1:9–16

1. Where was John moved from when he was exiled to Patmos? Ephesus, in present-day Turkey.

2. Who are the Church Fathers? Early church leaders following the disciples; second century.

3. How old was John when he wrote this text? Likely in his eighties.

4. How did the letter, Revelation, get off Patmos? John took it with him when he was released after Domitian's death.

5. What is John commanded to do? Record what he *sees* and give it to the churches.

6. What should a "lampstand" look like? A menorah. Exodus describes them clearly.

7. What does a lampstand mean? Apply the rule about interpreting symbols.

SESSION THREE ANSWERS
REVELATION 1:17–20

Revelation 1:20

1. What do the seven stars represent? The seven angels of the seven churches.

2. What do the seven lampstands represent? The seven churches.

3. What do lampstands commonly represent? The illumination of truth reaching into the darkness.

4. What is the mission of the whole church? We bring light to darkness.

5. How does John's description of Jesus compare with that of the rest of Scripture? It is consistent.

Revelation 1:17–18

1. What is John's response to seeing Jesus again after 60 years? He falls flat on his face terrified. Accompanying scriptures: Joshua 5:13–14; Ezekiel 1:28; Daniel 8:15–17.

2. Philippians 2:5–9 illustrates what about Jesus' incarnate form? The period in which incarnate Jesus appears in a form in which we can hug Him is historically unique.

3. If you can hug your God when you see Him in His glory, what kind of god do you have? Not a very powerful one.

4. What do we learn about Jesus here? He is to be known and worshiped for who and what He is.

5. How does Jesus describe Himself? By His eternal characteristics: first and last, dead and alive forevermore, holding the keys of death and Hades.

Revelation 1:19

1. What is John's task? Write the letter describing what he sees.

2. What are the three parts of his task? 1. Write what he saw (Chapters 1); 2. Write the things that are (Chapters 2–3); 3. Write the things that happen after these things which refers to the things that happen after the things that are (Chapters 4–22). Revelation 4:1 literally says, "after these things."

Revelation

SESSION FOUR ANSWERS
REVELATION 2 INTRODUCTION

Revelation 1:19

1. The outline of Revelation includes which three parts? Things you saw (Chapter 1), things which are (chapters 2–3), and things after these things (Chapters 4–22).

2. What did John see (Review Revelation chapter 1)? Jesus, stars, lampstands.

3. What is the purpose of these descriptions? To authenticate John's coming prophetic message.

4. Who is the "are" in the "things that are" applicable to? Who in history falls into the time period John calls "the things that are?" From first century until present day, until the events of chapters 4 and onward begin.

Interpreting the Letters

1. How many methods are there for interpreting the letters? What are the three methods? Three complementary interpretive methods: literally (real letters to real people about real things), universally (the content of these letters remain true for churches throughout history; they're timeless), and prophetically.

2. What might the clockwise naming of the churches indicate? That the messages might also apply to churches throughout history.

3. The "times that are" might prophetically represent what? The nature of the church over time.

SESSION FIVE ANSWERS
BACKGROUND OF THE LETTERS

Overview

1. Prophetic reading of the letters indicates a symbolic, eschatological meaning. What does this mean? These letters point to the end, the second coming.

2. What do chapters 2 and 3 explain? How the Lord fills the time between John's Revelation and Jesus' second coming.

3. When did the first mention of a prophetic reading of the letters to the churches occur? Only 150 years ago.

4. So the seven churches represent not only 100% of the church but also what? 100% of the time of the church.

5. What will the church age look like? It will have seven periods defined by the characteristics ascribed to the churches in the seven letters.

6. The prophetic reading of this text will reveal what two things? History will validate it, and it suggests that just as the church began at Pentecost, it will have an end. There will be a time in which the church as we know it will no longer exist.

7. If there are only seven stages in the letters, what is possible? Determining which stage we are in ourselves.

8. How does Scripture refer to Christ's second coming? Imminent, always possible, and dependent on nothing when it comes to the church.

Letter to the Church in Ephesus

1. What was historical Ephesus like? Ephesus was a metropolitan, worldly city. Prominent in both Scripture and the world at that time.

2. What symbols appear in this letter, and what do they represent? Jesus assigns symbols of stars and lampstands—all the angels over all the churches—it's a picture of authority. And it's a reminder that Jesus has authority over all the churches.

3. What is Jesus' assessment of the Ephesian church? He says they're doing a pretty of good job testing apostles and teachers.

4. Summarize Pastor Armstrong's teaching about apostleship: Apostles were made so physically by Jesus Himself, and they proved it by acts requiring apostolic authority. Apostles had a specific purpose in time: to write the canon of Scripture and to lead Christians and the church when the canon of Scripture was not yet fully established. It's no coincidence that the last living apostle wrote the last book of the Bible.

5. Who were the Nicolaitans, and what was Jesus' problem with them? The Nicolaitans were propagating the idea of a church ruling class, clergy intermediaries like Pharisees; it's heresy to say any believer is more special than another.

6. How can we imitate the Ephesian church? We, too, should test everything.

7. These people had a history of perseverance. What does the Bible say about perseverance? It results in spiritual maturity and eternal reward.

SESSION SIX ANSWERS
REVELATION 2:1–7

Letter to the Church in Ephesus

1. How do we bring ourselves to where God is trying to bring us? We practice endurance.

2. What sort of good example is Ephesus to us? In discernment in false teaching, unity of clergy/ laity, and endurance when it comes to serving Christ.

3. Jesus critiques them for leaving their first love (Jesus)—but how can this be true considering their commendations? It begins in the description—Jesus reminds them who's in charge. They moved from appreciating Jesus' care to chafing under His authority.

4. What is the remedy outlined in the letter? Remember where they've fallen (repent of mistakes) and do as they did before (they were doing the right things for the wrong reasons; they'd lost sight of the gospel).

5. The Ephesians were practicing "self-satisfied Christianity." How does Pastor Armstrong define this? Finding satisfaction in the life that you have rather than in the life that Jesus desires you to have while carrying the identity of Christian.

6. What are the marks of a modern self-satisfied Christian? Answers may vary.

7. Christ holds being on autopilot against us. What does self-satisfaction do to spiritual growth? Stops it.

8. Historically, Ephesus the city declined. They didn't repent, and Jesus followed through with His warning. What did these historical consequences look like? The harbor filled in, and the seaport became landlocked.

9. Each letter ends with what? Encouragement to the individual believer. They do not lose salvation despite their consequences as a group.

10. No matter what goes on in the church or the world, what is true for the individual believer? The future of the individual believer is secure.

11. How does this letter represent the first church age? Starts at Pentecost. Acts 2—the early church was very aware of their first love (Jesus) and very attentive to Him, likely because they had a sense that Jesus would return pretty quickly. Then He didn't, so they had to figure out a new plan. The historical church of the first century mirrors this letter. The apostles were alive and doing their job. It was an impressive time of works, miracles, and gospel spread. They persevered both Jewish and Roman persecution.

12. What is the biblical definition of a Christian? One who has the indwelling of the Holy Spirit.

13. How did the first century church end up? Self-satisfied.

14. What exactly did this look like? They built the church like Romans—just for the sake of building it.

14. How did Christ purify the church at the end of the first century? He allowed sustained, unchecked persecution of the church at the end of the first century, which purified the church, leaving behind the believers who understood what it means to be a slave of Christ.

SESSION SEVEN ANSWERS
REVELATION 2:8–11

Overview

1. What are the three complementary interpretative methods? Literal/ historical, universal, prophetic.

2. What does the number seven symbolize? 100%.

3. What do these seven letters represent as a unit? The church age.

4. These letters seem not to fit into the prophetic meaning, so why are the letters here? Jesus provided these letters to reveal the history of the church after the fact, as a countdown clock of sorts to the end.

5. How do these letters give us confidence in God? If He can steer history so precisely as indicated in these letters, we can confidently believe that He is in control, even to (and of) the end.

Letter to the Church in Smyrna

1. The name of each city has meaning. What is significant about Smyrna? Transliteration of the word for myrrh, a substance associated with death and embalming.

2. First-century Roman law mandated what sort of worship, and who was the exception? Emperor worship, Jews were the exception.

3. Smyrna serves as a center for persecution of Christians. Which church father was martyred there? Polycarp.

4. Jesus assigns which element of His nature to this church? His understanding of death

and its lack of power over them.

5. What is Jesus' promise in this letter? Death is no impediment to obedience; there is life after death.

6. What was the cultural consequence of refusing to worship pagan gods as required by the government and workers' unions? Poverty.

7. What is the "synagogue of Satan?" They were Jews in name only. They missed the work and person of God. They're Jewish by DNA, but they are no people of His as they don't worship the Lord in truth.

8. "Children of God" is a biblical statement that refers to whom? Those who have been born again by faith. We are *not* all children of God. We are all children of Adam.

9. This understanding leads you to what? What you believe about Jesus.

10. Jesus notices their persecution and poverty. What does He *not* say? That He'd remove it. Their poverty, turned to work for the glory of Christ, their ability to earn treasure in heaven.

11. What is Christ specifically reminding this church of? See your life in light of eternity. Don't get caught up in what you have here; doing so sacrifices your treasures in heaven.

12. How can the church of Smyrna make the most of their situation (verse 10)? Don't fear death; enter suffering with confidence.

13. What is God's primary concern for you here on earth? Your holiness.

SESSION EIGHT ANSWERS
REVELATION 2:12–17

Overview

1. What is Jesus' goal for the church? Perseverance and obedience through affliction, maximizing their heavenly reward.

2. How were Roman prisons different than our modern prisons? They weren't places of provision or confinement. Trials happened very quickly, and punishment was carried out swiftly.

3. This time period of ten days' imprisonment is consistent with what? The Roman Justice System.

4. What is the symbolic significance of the number ten? Testimony.

5. So what is Jesus communicating symbolically? The church will have a time of

testimony, and He encourages them to make the most of it.

6. What is the key? Face your trials faithfully.

7. What does faithfulness in this context refer to? Not salvation—salvation is in no way dependent on *our* faithfulness; faithfulness refers to our behavior, holding to our witness.

8. What is the reward for their faithfulness? The crown of life.

9. What does the crown of life symbolize? In every single case, crown refers to an *earned* reward, not salvation.

10. What is the substance of the reward the crown symbolizes? An inheritance in the land when you return with the coming physical kingdom and a role in the government.

11. How does one earn a crown of life? Faithful endurance of persecution and martyrdom.

12. In reference to the race imagery referenced in 1 Corinthians 9:24–25, who are you competing against to earn your heavenly crowns? Yourself.

13. What promise does the letter end with? Those who overcome will not be hurt by the second death.

14. What is the prophetic value of the letter? There were ten periods of Roman persecution under ten Roman emperors, 100AD–313AD.

Letter to the Church in Pergamum

1. What does the name Pergamum signify? Married to a powerful institution or fortress.

2. What is the historical background of Pergamum? Seat of authority for the Roman province of Asia, including the "right of the sword." Had a huge library, Hellenistic culture, strong artistic and intellectual presence.

3. What is the symbolic significance of a two-edged sword? Judgement and correction.

4. What was Pergamum like spiritually? Very dark, even had a cult of Satan.

5. What is the historic significance of Balaam? He was a legitimate prophet but also a corrupt, greedy man, Numbers 22.

SESSION NINE ANSWERS
REVELATION 2:18–29

Overview

1. How do Peter and Jude use the phrase "the way of Balaam?" To refer to anyone who has replaced the love of God with the love of money.

2. What is the "error of Balaam?" Loving money so much one turns to a form of spiritual prostitution.

3. In what false teachings did Pergamum's Balaams encourage the church? Eating meat sacrificed to idols and sexual immorality.

4. What does the biblical phrase "tickling ears" refer to? People who tell or teach us what we want to hear, exterior stimulation that approximates the spiritual stimulation.

5. What three things are a recipe for "tickled ears?" A shepherd who cares more about his/her earthly comfort than your eternal comfort; encouraging the pursuit of your lusts, whatever they may be; a congregation more concerned with gratification of the flesh than eternal spiritual blessing.

6. What did the Nicolaitans teach? Creating distinctions within the church body, a class structure within the church.

7. What does it mean to "make war with the word of His mouth?" Jesus threatens to end the church that strays from Scripture by "cutting off the head."

8. What is the significance of hidden manna? Contrasts meat sacrificed to idols; obedience would result in provision.

9. What is the significance of the white stone? It was a physical testimonial practice employed by the medical school in Pergamum to show what they'd healed people of. Jesus turns this around to symbolize a testimony of eternal spiritual healing.

10. What stopped the persecution of the second era of the church? Constantine's battlefield vision in AD 313.

11. At that point, what powerful institution was married to the church? Roman government.

12. What were the consequences of institutionalizing Christianity within the Roman government? Infant baptism, mass, often forced, conversions, and a huge influx of pagan practices into the church—syncretism, priests, statues as objects of prayer, suddenly the majority of the church at large were not born-again believers.

13. So what three things resulted from this explosive "growth" of Christianity as the state

religion? Idolatry within the church, cult practices, and heresy.

14. How does Jesus say He will respond if they don't repent? He'll end it with a sword.

15. Historically, how did Jesus "end it with a sword?" He ended the Roman empire, therefore ending the institutionalized church.

The Letter to the Church of Thyatira: Roman Empire Church 313–600AD

1. What is the possible meaning of "Thyatira?" Unending sacrifice, odor of affliction.

2. Who was the primary god worshiped in this area? Apollo.

3. Again, what was the conflict between union work and Christians? Union membership required to work, idol worship required for union membership.

4. What is the significance of "eyes like a flame of fire" (Revelation 2:18)? Piercing discernment; Jesus sees it all.

5. What is the significance of "feet like burnished bronze" (Revelation 2:18)? Fires of judgment testing for purity.

6. Combined, what do we learn about Jesus? Christ has perfect judgment and the authority to render it righteously.

7. What does Jesus have to say positively about Thyatira? They're getting better and better at good works, and they love each other well.

8. What's the catch with good works? It can't be divorced from the truth of the gospel.

9. Who was Jezebel? Phoenician wife of King Ahab of Israel's Northern kingdom; synonymous with an evil-hearted, manipulative woman leading weak men.

10. What's the difference in Pergamum's and Thyatira's false teachers? Pergamum's Balaam was an ill-intentioned *believer*. Thyatira's Jezebel is an ill-intentioned *unbeliever*.

11. What judgment does Christ proclaim over Thyatira? Pestilence.

12. What will the physical evidence of Christ's judgment (illness in Thyatira) speak of? Jesus is still in charge.

13. What does the morning star signify? Jesus himself.

14. What does Jesus promise the church at the end of this letter? Authority to rule in the coming kingdom with Jesus himself.

15. What period of history does this letter represent? That in which the church was dominated by the Roman Catholic institution; it rose out of the ashes of the Roman

empire itself; the church transitioned from an institution of government to being the government itself.

16. This era began in AD 600 and continued for how long? Over 1,000 years.

17. How do we see a judgment of pestilence on the Roman Catholic Church? The black plague descends, beginning in Constantinople and Rome, the centers of the church; the plague wiped out the priesthood and led to a shunning of gatherings, i.e. mass. Helped gave rise to the Reformation.

SESSION TEN ANSWERS
REVELATION 3:1–6

Letter to the Church in Sardis

1. What are the three interpretive methods? Literal, universal, and prophetic.

2. What is the meaning of the name Sardis? The escaping ones, remnant.

3. Summarize what you learned about the historical city of Sardis. Capital of Lydian province. Commercial center known for dying wool. Built on a mountain, virtually impregnable.

4. What does seven signify again? 100%.

5. What do the "seven spirits of God and the seven stars" of verse 1 represent? The whole of God's Spirit and all of the churches.

6. What is Christ's assessment of the historical church of Sardis? It's a legitimate church, but it's weak. It has faith but no works.

7. How do we fulfill the purpose of faith: glorifying the Father? Good works.

8. Who alone is the judge of whether or not our works have met His expectations? God the Father.

9. What was the church in Sardis satisfied with? Faith alone, being a beacon of truth.

10. How does Sardis compare to Thyatira? They're opposites.

11. What is the whole point of good works? Creating inroads for opportunities to share the gospel.

12. What does Jesus mean by His admonition to "wake up" in verse 2? Come out of this stupor of ignorance and apathy and rediscover the mission of the church.

13. What is the fundamental truth of church life at work here? Churches who focus inside their walls lose their purpose and eventually die, and churches who take the

gospel outside their walls grow.

14. What is Jesus' recipe for strengthening the church? Remember what you've received and heard; if you remember the moment you first experienced your salvation, you have all you need to go out and share it.

15. What is the consequence for Sardis if it doesn't awaken? Christ will come like a thief in the night; they'd find themselves in an empty house if they did not wake up.

16. What is Jesus's encouragement to the individual believer? Consequences to the church as a whole do not threaten the salvation of the individual believer.

17. What is the significance of a white garment? A picture of those who are saved.

18. What is the picture of the unbeliever? Naked, unclothed.

19. So what, then, is the significance of soiled and unsoiled garments? It is a symbol of believers because clothes—whether they are soiled or unsoiled—refer to the quality and content of a believer's testimony. The condition of the garment refers to the condition of a believer's witness.

SESSION ELEVEN ANSWERS
REVELATION 3:7–13

Overview

1. Summarize Pastor Armstrong's explanation of the phrase "I will not erase your name from the book of life." Names cannot and will not be erased. This is an example of a Jewish poetic style that emphasizes a truth by negating the opposite.

2. When does the historical era of Sardis begin? 1517, the Protestant Reformation.

3. What is the prophetic significance of the name Sardis (the escaping ones, the remnant)? The faithful escape the heretical Catholic church to form protestant churches.

4. Why was the Protestant Church at this time considered the true church? It brought back solid doctrine and the true gospel.

5. What is the often-overlooked consequence of the Protestant Reformation? The abandonment of evangelism and diminished emphasis on works of charity. They corrected much of the heresy in Catholicism, but they overreacted when it came to good works because the works-based salvation doctrine of Catholicism was so distasteful.

6. What historic event gave rise to the beginning of the denominations we know today? Treaty of Westphalia ended state-mandated Christian faith and allowed freedom of Christian practice.

Revelation

7. How does Jesus' admonition to "wake up" align with church history? State-sanctioned Protestant denominations have died out, and the "dissenters" took the gospel global.

8. When does the age of Sardis end? AD 1648, with the Peace of Westphalia.

Letter to the Church in Philadelphia

1. What does Philadelphia mean? Brotherly Love.

2. Summarize what you've learned about historic Philadelphia. Founded by king of Pergamum. Smaller. Prone to earthquakes, so they lived outside for a time. Bred a culture of determination and persistence.

3. What do the attributes of Jesus in this letter point to? The centrality of His mission and message of the church; when Jesus goes before you, He can open any door.

4. What is the significance of "the key of David?" Jesus is the one to grant access to the temple, and therefore atonement or forgiveness, as well. He is the one who controls salvation.

5. What is true if you have a heart to reach the lost? Christ is with you, for you, and goes before you.

6. What is important about knowing that Christ is the only one who opens and who closes doors of gospel opportunity? You don't carry the weight of ministerial or evangelistic failure; there's no reason not to try because the outcome isn't your responsibility, only the trying.

7. What does Philadelphia best model to the church at large? Evangelism.

8. It's important to note that Philadelphia, alongside Smyrna, receives none of what from Jesus? Condemnation.

9. How does Philadelphia's faithfulness differ from Smyrna's? Smyrna maintained a faithful identity (internal) while Philadelphia maintained a faithful message (external).

10. What do these churches have in common? As persecuted churches, they maintain the strongest witness.

SESSION TWELVE ANSWERS
REVELATION 3:14–22

Overview

1. What does persecution do for you? Refines and equips you to do Christ's work.

2. How will Jesus protect His church from persecution? He converts the persecutors.

3. What phrase tells us that we are justified in reading Revelation prophetically? Verse 10: the persecution will affect "all who dwell on the earth"—this is larger than Domitian's persecution of Christians, so we know the statement extends beyond the first century.

4. What does a crown represent? Eternal reward for a faithful life of service to the Lord.

5. What does Jesus mean when He admonishes us to not let anyone steal our crowns? Rewards come to those who finish the race; you can't earn a crown if you quit early.

6. What promise does Jesus leave the believers with? Their eternal future is unshakeable.

7. Prophetically, what years does the age of Philadelphia span? Missionary church—1648 to about 1900.

Letter to the Church in Laodicea

1. What is the significance of the name "Laodicea?" People ruling; judgment of the people.

2. Summarize what you learned about the historical city of Laodicea. Self-reliant culture. Known for banks, wool, medical school. Wealthy Roman city, commercial and administrative center.

3. How does Jesus' reference to the deeds of this church differ from his references to the deeds of the other churches? For the other churches, He was concerned about the quality and quantity of the deeds as they reflected on Him. In Laodicea, His concern is how the deeds reflect on the believers themselves.

4. What spiritual conditions are represented by the physical conditions of verse 7? Blind to spiritual truth; wretched means unclean, unbeliever; poverty means not sharing in the riches of Christ. Naked means outside the covering of Christ's atonement.

5. What has blinded the Laodicean church to their spiritual poverty? Their earthly wealth.

6. How can a church be unbelieving? The physical trappings of church exist, attended by both believers and unbelievers.

7. Is it possible for people to accurately determine the spiritual "state of dress" of any other person? No.

8. What does the presence of unbelievers in the church cause? Apostasy and compromise.

9. So what is the significance of hot and cold? Self-aware believers and unbelievers.

Revelation

10. What's the problem of the lukewarm state? The unbeliever is unable to recognize what they don't have (Jesus).

11. Why does Jesus use the spitting out metaphor? It's culturally appropriate. They had a poisonous, lukewarm river that the medical school used as an emetic.

12. Jesus doesn't offer any commendation to this church. What does He offer instead? He invites them to faith—salvation

13. So prophetically, what era does the church of Laodicea represent? Ours.

14. What does apostasy mean? To stray or fall away.

15. Is the individual or the corporate church the issue here? The corporate church.

16. How does the shift to an apostate church happen? The majority within the universal church shifts from believer to unbeliever.

17. What are among the signs of the end times according to 1 and 2 Timothy? Prominent and prosperous false teachers; access to serious luxury, attaching food choices to spiritual states; the list of negative traits in 2 Timothy becomes the rule rather than the exception.

18. Where did the church go wrong? Two bedrock beliefs were lost at the end of the nineteenth century: the rise of biblical criticism from within academia which moved away from literal biblical interpretation, unity matters more than truth; the rise of evolution weakened confidence in Scripture in general and creation in particular. It's easier to retreat from a literal interpretation of Scripture than to fight strong cultural norms like evolution.

19. When does the age of Laodicea end? When the "things after these things" begin.

SESSION THIRTEEN ANSWERS
DANIEL 2:1–11

1. Why did Jesus embed a prophetic meaning in Revelation 2–3 that couldn't possibly be understood for centuries? The letters weren't given so the early church could know its future; they were given so that the church of the last days would awaken to their circumstances and recognize the importance of the events in their time.

2. Do we know when exactly the end of the Laodicean church era will end? No.

3. What does an "age" signify? A long, finite, time; it has a beginning and an end, and the transitions between subsequent ages are themselves noteworthy.

4. What is the significance of the term *last days*? It signals the end of an age and the transition to a next one. Sometimes this "last days" period can last a long time.

Answer Key

5. According to the writer of Hebrews, what event signaled our entrance into the last days? Jesus has appeared and the canon of Scripture is complete. There are no more segments of revelation yet to be revealed. The end could come at any time, and we've been waiting for 2,000+ years.

6. We now have a series of questions:

What is this age called, what will it be like, and why did it start (Luke 21:24)? Times or age of the Gentiles; Jews will be persecuted by Gentiles, and Gentiles will "trample" Jerusalem; The age begins when Jews lose control of Jerusalem and begin to endure persecution—it's in the book of Daniel, which serves as the backstory of Revelation.

7. So why are we reading Daniel? It explains the backstory of Revelation, the beginning of the age of the Gentiles, and the content of that age historically

Daniel 2:1–11

1. Summarize the context of this story in Daniel 2. Babylon attacks Jerusalem, and it falls. God gave Nebuchadnezzar permission to attack and conquer Jerusalem, but Nebuchadnezzar didn't know that. But God decides to fill him in by means of a dream interpreted by Jewish Daniel.

Session Fourteen Answers
Daniel 2:12–39

Daniel 2:25–39

1. What sort of work did Nebuchadnezzar enlist Daniel into? He was numbered among the wise men.

2. What time does Nebuchadnezzar's dream tell of? The future after 600 BC, our present age.

3. What pattern do we observe about the materials of which the dream statue is made? They decrease in value as they increase in strength and brittleness.

4. What is significant about the nature of the dream and its interpretation? It could only be given by God and interpreted by His representative; it's a clear example of God actively moving in the lives of men to shape history.

5. By God's decree, what is Nebuchadnezzar's domain? The entire physical world. God gave him the authority to rule over the entire world and everything in it, but Nebuchadnezzar didn't exercise it to its fullest extent.

Revelation

6. What do the various sections of the statue represent? Successive rulers/ empires/ kingdoms; also a timeline, the passage of time.

7. How do we know this dream represents the beginning of the age of the Gentiles? Nebuchadnezzar was the first to rule over Jerusalem and enslave Jews, and it's not returned to a sovereign, peaceful, un-persecuted state since.

8. What are the criteria for being a kingdom represented by the statue? Gentile kingdom (never Israel); most dominant power of their day; have to defeat their predecessor; trample/ control/ invade Jerusalem in addition to Babylon.

9. What is the second kingdom, and how is it less valuable than the first, Babylon? Medo-Persian empire; they won by sheer numbers, not necessarily skill, and their law/ rule wasn't as absolute as Babylonian.

10. What is the significance of the statue's crossed arms? Two nations, the Medes and the Persians, working together to rule one empire.

11. As far as God's role was concerned, how did the Medo-Persian empire differ from the Babylonian empire? God gave Nebuchadnezzar absolute authority, but there's no indication that God gave any of the successive rulers the same authority, despite the fact that they did indeed conquer in accordance to God's plan.

12. What is the third, bronze kingdom? Alexander the Great's Hellenistic Greek empire; he had limited power. He had a strong military that forced the hand of the city-states politically.

13. What is the significance of the bronze on the statue encompassing the thighs (a physical split)? After Alexander died, his empire was divided in half and ruled by his generals, east and west. It created a schism in thought and language that has never rejoined.

SESSION FIFTEEN ANSWERS
DANIEL 2:40–45

1. Why does Daniel gloss over the second and third kingdoms? They don't really matter; the point is the last one.

2. How is the fourth kingdom different from the other three? Rather than building a cohesive empire, they break up and recombine over time, working together to keep Israel from regaining its status.

3. When does the fourth kingdom begin? 63 BC, Rome.

4. Why can people not single out an ending date for the Roman empire? It never really ended in a formal sense. It broke apart, but it wasn't replaced.

5. What exactly succeeded the Roman Empire? The Holy Roman Empire, dissolved in 1806; followed by continually shifting borders throughout the Eastern Hemisphere.

6. What is the point of all of this national upheaval from a prophetic perspective? It's providing for the age of the Gentiles.

7. What phrase best describes the fourth kingdom? Imperialistic-democratic alliance.

8. What is the last portion of Nebuchadnezzar's dream representative of? A new kingdom not connected to prior Gentile kingdoms. It doesn't arise and replace its predecessor. It puts an end to the age of the Gentiles and begins a new age with a new sort of kingdom.

9. Why can this stone not be another Gentile nation? It ends the age of Gentile prominence. It has to be, by the nature of the Gentile/ not-Gentile dichotomy, a Jewish kingdom established by God Himself to exist eternally.

10. What is an altar? A place of sacrifice.

11. What is the purpose of sacrifice? Atonement.

12. What is the significance of uncut stones in Deuteronomy 27? It's a theological statement about who does the work of atonement: God alone.

13. When we pull together all the symbolism from the final portion of Nebuchadnezzar's dream, what conclusion can we draw? What is Daniel prophesying? The second coming of Christ.

SESSION SIXTEEN ANSWERS
DANIEL 7:1–8

Overview

1. Why are we reading outside of Revelation over the next several sessions? Other books in the Bible contain vital background information.

2. What transitional event moves us from the church age (the things that are) to the next age (the things after these things)? There won't be a church anymore.

3. What again is the age of the Gentiles? Israel's period of judgment on earth. A period of history in which Israel remains subjected to Gentile powers. Jewish people scattered and exiled, and Jerusalem being trampled and controlled by Gentiles.

4. What will signal the end of the age of the Gentiles? All these sanctions against Israel will be reversed.

5. What exactly will the reversal of these sanctions look like? Jesus will return and

Revelation

establish a kingdom (not peace in the Middle East). His kingdom will be Jewish and will regather Jews to their land and protects and sanctifies Jerusalem.

Daniel 7:1–10

1. What part of the dream in Daniel 2 is the focus of the dream in Daniel 7? He's revealing more details about the fourth kingdom, the bottom portion of the statue.

2. Rather than a timeline, what do these animals symbolize? The nature of the kingdoms represented by the statue. The winged lion represents Babylon, the bear represents the Medo-Persians, and the four-headed winged Leopard represents the Greek empire. Again, the fourth kingdom gets the most attention as represented by the last beast.

3. How does the fourth beast break the pattern? It's a collection of different things and nations that accomplish God's purpose in concert. It's not about any single nation. Rather, it's about a collective alliance of nations against Israel. This fourth animal doesn't even track with any known animal; it's just scary. Its prominent feature is a profusion of horns.

4. What is the historical norm of kingdoms in the world? Only one to a handful. The whole modern understanding of 200+ sovereign nations is the aberration of history, not the rule.

5. What is the pattern we need to recognize? The one who comes at the end (the little horn) resembles the one who comes at the beginning (Nebuchadnezzar).

SESSION SEVENTEEN ANSWERS
DANIEL 9:1–5

1. What in Daniel 7 parallels the uncut stone in Daniel 2? Verse 9: The end of age happens when the Ancient of Days is seated on His throne ruling in judgment.

2. What is the chief reason Daniel 7 exists? The ten horns refer to the ten toes of the statue. End of the age of Gentiles. To explain the fourth and final kingdoms.

3. What do the horns represent? Kings/ leaders.

4. At the end of the world, how many rulers will there be? Ten.

5. Where else do we find this same usage of the word *time*, and what does it represent? Revelation, three and a half years equals time (one year), time (two years), and half a time (six months).

6. What has to happen to our present-day world for it to fulfill the prophecy we see here? Some sort of cataclysmic geo-political event resulting in the emergence of only ten

Answer Key

ruling powers, from which a single ruler will gain dominance for three and a half years before Jesus comes back and destroys him.

7. What is important to pull from this? We can't identify the Antichrist today because we aren't down to ten global ruling powers. Christ's second coming is not going to happen until these things happen first.

8. How did Pastor Armstrong apply dates to the kingdom sections of his diagrams? Using the precise dates when rulers conquered Jerusalem.

9. Who is the primary subject of the events of Revelation? Israel.

Daniel 9:1–2

1. By the time Daniel reaches the ninth chapter of his book, what kingdom (Daniel 2) is he living in?

2. At what point is Scripture self-evident to humanity?

3. How is Leviticus 26 connected to Jeremiah 25?

SESSION EIGHTEEN ANSWERS
DANIEL 9:3–3, 20–27

1. How did Daniel misinterpret this period of 70 weeks? He anticipated the age of the Gentiles and the coming of the Messiah.

2. How do we know Daniel has made this misinterpretation? He immediately responds as Leviticus 26 commands in confessional prayer.

3. What do we learn about the Abrahamic covenant? It's unconditional, but the timing is dependent on confessing their own sins and recognizing they crucified their own Messiah.

4. How does God correct Daniel's understanding? He sends Gabriel.

5. What is "the Holy Mountain of God?" God's kingdom.

6. What is weeks literally? Sevens—490 years.

7. Are these "years" counted in the same way we count them? No.

8. What implies a break or pause in the counting? The transitional language between verses 26 and 27.

9. What ends the "pause" and resumes the counting? A covenant with Israel allowing them to worship freely until the rise of that eleventh horn/ leader gains power.

10. Where is the church? In the pause. The pause is the church age.

11. When does God's focus shift from the salvation of Gentiles to the resolution of Israel? When the full number of those who will be saved is met.

12. What is the purpose of the first 70 years? Letting the land rest.

13. What is the purpose of the subsequent 490+ years? The six outcomes listed in Daniel 9:24.

14. What is eight the number of? New beginnings.

15. What is our role in this timeline? We're the reason the counting pauses, the reason it starts or stops.

SESSION NINETEEN ANSWERS
REVELATION 4:1–4

Overview

1. What again are the three characteristics of the age of Gentiles? Israel subjugated to Gentiles, Israel scattered into Gentile lands, and Jerusalem conquered by Gentiles.

2. How does the remainder of Revelation (chapters 4–22) relate with Daniel 9 (weeks/sevens)? Revelation 4–22 describes in detail the final seven of Daniel's vision.

3. How should we refer to this final seven, the seventieth seven? The Day of the Lord, the time of Jacob's (Israel's) Troubles (for the effect of purification), Tribulation.

Revelation 4:1–4

1. What is the symbolic effect of repeating something three times in Scripture? To the fullest extent.

2. In heaven there will be no doubt about what? God is worthy of all honor, glory, and praise.

3. What do we know about the *when* of this scene? It follows the church age.

4. What does chapter 4 focus on? God the Father.

5. What is jasper an ancient name for? Diamonds.

6. What does the vision of Revelation 4–5 center on? God's throne.

7. What do elders in white robes signify? Human beings clothed in righteousness, leaders specifically.

8. What is suggested by the fact that these elders do not appear in earlier visions? They weren't there yet.

SESSION TWENTY ANSWERS
APOLOGETICS FOR THE RAPTURE

1. What do the (whiteness purity) of the garments represent? Works of the saints.

2. What do thrones represent? Ruling authority.

3. What do the crowns represent? Earned reward, future inheritance.

4. What do the elders represent? Human leaders.

5. What is the significance of 24? All leaders. Twelve means government/ leadership; doubling completes or emphasizes a concept. So, 24 refers to all of the leaders.

6. What is the significance of the entirety of the Holy Spirit being in God's throne room in this vision? It means His indwelling Spirit is no longer present on earth.

7. What is the conclusive proof of this being true of the end of the church age (take notes over the next several minutes as Pastor Armstrong constructs an argument for the rapture of the church)? "The coming of the Lord"—not Christ's second coming to establish His kingdom. Jesus comes back long enough to collect His Church. John 14 promises something different in addition to what Daniel prophesies. The second coming of Christ isn't right around the corner, but the "coming of the Lord" isn't dependent on anything; He'll collect His bride whenever He so desires.

SESSION TWENTY-ONE ANSWERS
THE DAY OF THE LORD VERSUS THE COMING OF THE LORD

1. What do we learn about the resurrection from Hebrews? No saint receives the kingdom without the rest of their group; glorification happens in unison with cohorts in a single moment.

2. What are the implications of the coming of the Lord in John 14? We all receive glorified bodies at the same time, and we receive our eternal rewards in the moment of judgment, another.

3. What all happens in the same moment at the Coming of the Lord? Resurrection and Judgement for the purpose of assigning rewards.

4. What is the "Day of the Lord?" The Tribulation

5. How do we know the Day of the Lord (Tribulation) follows the Coming of the Lord (Rapture/ Resurrection)? Second Thessalonians assures us we can't experience Tribulation because the rapture hasn't happened yet. Also, the "lawless one" is restrained by the presence of the Holy Spirit on earth as He indwells believers.

6. Why does Jesus use the metaphor of preparing a home for us to explain the waiting period before His return to claim His bride (the church)? Because it mirrors ancient Jewish marriage traditions. The length of a betrothal is determined by how long it takes the groom to build a home for his bride. The bride had no idea how long it would take, so she waited ready for as long as it takes. The leaving of the bride gives her family a week's notice to get the party ready.

7. So what is Jesus waiting for? He's waiting for the Father to tell Him His bride (the church) is ready (complete—has all the people it's going to have).

Session Twenty-Two Answers
Revelation 4:5–8; 5:1–14

Overview

1. What do we find in Leviticus 26? The penalties specified for not allowing the land to rest and for general disregard of the Old Covenant. God prophesies their disobedience at this point.

2. Why does the Tribulation happen? Because of the Old Covenant (Mosaic) requires consequences for lack of adherence.

3. What does God have for His actions? Reason, purpose, audience, outcome.

4. What is the accurate biblical term for what is popularly known as the rapture? The Resurrection.

5. What event ends the age of the Gentiles? Jesus's return (Revelation 19); the Tribulation is part of it.

6. What topic is described in Revelation 6–18? The last seven years of the age of Gentiles, the seventieth seven.

Revelation 4:5–8

1. What sort of creatures surround the throne in this passage? Cherubim, the highest class of angelic beings.

2. What are the three classes of angelic beings? Cherubim, Seraphim, and angels.

Answer Key

3. What is the purpose of cherubim? They serve as guardians to the glory of God.

4. What do we learn about the glory of God in Ezekiel 10, right before Nebuchadnezzar attacks? They escort the glory of God from the Jewish temple to heaven, where it has remained since.

5. How is Ezekiel 10 connected to Revelation 5? It serves as a preamble.

Revelation 5:1–14

1. Where does the focus shift from this point on in Revelation, and how is He pictured here? To Jesus, as a slain Lamb with seven horns and seven eyes standing next to the Father.

2. What is Father God holding? A completely sealed scroll (seven seals).

3. What is the significance of the scroll having writing on both on the inside and the outside? Traditionally, land deeds were one of few types of scrolls that had writing on the back/ outside. The deed was sealed to prevent tampering, and a summary was on the outside along with records of transference. The judge was the only one who could open the seals, and after doing so, he'd have to make a new deed, even if the terms were kept the same for it to be legal and valid.

SESSION TWENTY-THREE ANSWERS
REVELATION 5:1–14

1. What is the purpose of John's description of a land deed? He's alluding to the physical land of Israel, currently deeded to Gentile control, which will be returned to Jewish ownership at the end of the age of Gentiles.

2. Who had the authority to break seals on a land deed? The judge—Jesus.

3. What are the qualifications for being a mediator between God and man in the case of this land deed agreement? Able to represent both parties fairly.

4. What specifically qualifies Jesus to act as mediator and judge? His resurrection.

5. How does John convey Jesus and His authority to rule on earth? A resurrected Lamb with seven horns and seven eyes. All authority, all discernment. Rules via the Holy Spirit, which He's sent back out.

6. How has Jesus made Himself worthy to judge the world? He defeated the enemy and his only weapon: death. By the means of His death and resurrection, Jesus approves himself worthy to both God and man.

Revelation

7. What role do the prayers of the saints play in God's throne room? They are part of the substance of worship in God's throne room.

8. What is the role of a priest, and how are we priests? An intercessor between God and man, we intercede to God on behalf of the world.

9. Why can chapter six be frustrating? It says a lot without much detail; it leaves the reader with lots of questions. But the answers are found elsewhere in Scripture.

10. What is the significance of the quoted portion of Isaiah 2? Who is the audience for the events of Revelation 6? The whole earth. Isaiah 2 sets up God's judgment of the whole earth, a day of reckoning.

SESSION TWENTY-FOUR ANSWERS
COVENANTS AND CONSEQUENCES

1. Who is the focus of the Tribulation, despite its affecting the whole world and rightly so? Israel.

2. What pattern do we see emerging from these Old Testament passages? A great destruction is coming both because of and for Israel, but God will preserve a remnant of Israel.

3. How will God preserve a portion of Israel without breaking the Law? Jews who profess faith in Christ remain Jewish but are no longer under the Law. Jews who persist in unbelief in Christ remain accountable to the Law.

4. What do the blessings of obedience outlined in Leviticus 26 mirror? The reality of the kingdom.

5. What does it mean for the covenant to be national in nature? It's all or nothing. Any member of the nation acts in disobedience, then the nation as a whole gets all the consequences.

6. From what point of view do we need to understand the events of the Tribulation? They're specific, outlined in Scripture. They're methodical and controlled. It's not random chaos.

7. How do Jews escape the penalties of the Law encompassed in the Tribulation? Faith in Christ. That's how God preserves a remnant of the Jewish people—He saves the ones who come to believe. The other way to escape the penalties is for the nation of Israel as a whole to repent of both their own sin and specific sins of their forefathers.

8. How does Jesus's first coming, effectively for the Gentiles, avoid being an abandonment of His people, the Jews? He came after 69 sevens of punishment. The Jews as a nation don't receive Him until the end of the final seven, the end of the

Tribulation.

SESSION TWENTY-FIVE ANSWERS
SIGNS OF THE END OF THE AGE PART ONE

1. What is the purpose of the Tribulation? To bring the nation of Israel to a place where it recognizes that Jesus was and is their Messiah.

2. What is the event is always imminent, that no one knows the day or the hour? The rapture.

3. How do we know the rapture occurs prior to the Tribulation? Why is the church exempt? The age of Gentiles, the church age, must end before the Tribulation can begin, and the church isn't accountable to the Old Covenant, so it isn't accountable for the consequences of breaking it.

4. The end of the church age is unknowable. The beginning of the Tribulation is knowable and signaled by the establishment of a covenant on earth. Are there signs of the coming of the end of the age? Answers may vary.

5. What did the disciples mean when they asked Jesus for the time of His coming? They didn't know or understand He was leaving yet; they were asking for signs of His kingdom coming or of His coming into power.

6. What two features do scholars who misinterpret these passages look over? Jesus adds a question—what *not* to look for, and He answers out of order.

7. What are we *not* to look for? There are always going to be wars, rumors of wars, and pretenders claiming to be Jesus.

8. How can we be certain we will not miss Jesus's second coming? We'll be with Him then.

9. When the disciples asked about the end of the age, what specific period of time are they asking about? The seventieth seven—the Tribulation.

SESSION TWENTY-SIX ANSWERS
SIGNS OF THE END OF THE AGE PART TWO

1. How is "nation against nation" different from "wars and rumors of wars?" Nation against nation refers to world wars; wars and rumors of wars are generally just regular wars.

2. What makes a sign-worthy famine? More common, more severe, more frequent. Reaching to unexpected areas.

Revelation

3. The final sign is earthquakes. Summarize what you learned about the trends of earthquakes. Answers may vary.

4. What new sign do we learn of in Ezekiel 20? A regathering of Israel in their land.

5. What sign do we learn of in Malachi 4? Elijah will return before the Tribulation begins to resume and complete his ministry of restoring the hearts of Jews to orthodoxy.

6. What is a critical element of the beginning of the Tribulation? Rebuilding the Jewish temple and resume sacrifice in it. The political agreement allowing worship to resume begins the seven-year Tribulation.

SESSION TWENTY-SEVEN ANSWERS
REVELATION 6:1–4

Revelation 6:1–2

1. How can the Tribulation be broken down into sections? First half of Revelation 6–9, mid-Tribulation Revelation 10–15, Great Tribulation Revelation 16–19.

2. What is the popular term for what happens with the first four seals? The four horsemen of the apocalypse; the horses are both literal and symbolic.

3. In the first seal—the white horse—who is the unnamed rider (Daniel 9:27)? The Antichrist.

4. Summarize the symbolism surrounding the white horse and its rider. He's a military or political leader who threatens much violence (effectively) before he has the ability to see it through. He's working throughout a period of time to acquire power and rule. He has the power to broker an agreement to make peace in the Middle East that allows for Jews to resume orthodox worship.

5. What do we know about the Antichrist? The prince who is to come, and he's of the people who destroyed the temple (Romans)—so he's a Gentile. He denies Jesus as Lord—in direct opposition to Jesus. He's controlled by the deceiver in a unique way separate from the way all unbelievers are led by the deceiver (the spirit of the antichrist). He will claim to be god, eventually claiming to be *the* god in the Jewish temple, at which point he replaces the Jewish sacrificial system with worship of himself.

6. What restrains Satan and therefore the Antichrist? The presence of the Holy Spirit on the earth. Satan can't present an Antichrist when people still exist who recognize Jesus as Christ.

ANSWER KEY

Revelation 6:3–4

1. The second seal- the red horse- who is the rider, and what does the horse represent? Still the Antichrist. Now he accomplishes the violence he's threatened. He literally begins World War III.

2. Despite the havoc the Antichrist will bring, who is in control? Jesus.

SESSION TWENTY-EIGHT ANSWERS
REVELATION 6:5–8

Overview

1. What is the purpose for studying Revelation? To explain to both the church and the world what's coming to exhort them to escape it by choosing Jesus.

Revelation 6:5–6

1. What is the symbolism associated with a black horse and scales? Modern scales means justice; Ancient scales refers to monetary value, commerce. He will have an economic effect on the world indirectly by means of his war. Inflation. The black horse symbolizes the indirect death of many because of war and its consequences.

2. Summarize what you've learned about the denarius and its value. One denarius equals a day's wage. First century, it'd buy 12 quarts of wheat or 18 loaves of bread. In the Tribulation, one denarius equals a day's wage, one quart of wheat or 1.5 loaves of bread. A loaf of bread will cost something like $60.

3. While the Antichrist acts in the world for these things to occur, who is the driving force behind all of these occurrences? God. He's acting to accomplish good, but He's using turmoil to do it.

4. What is a possible significance of the exclusion of wine and oil from the inflation? The physical land of Israel will be removed, to some degree, from this set of consequences.

Revelation 6:7–8

1. How does this horse and rider depiction break the pattern, and what is the significance? Hades is introduced as following, and the rider holds nothing in his hand. It portrays an ultimate effect.

2. What is the significance of the ashen horse? Death. Ashen means a pale green here. Lots of death: 25% of the world dead. By today's population, this will be something like

Revelation

two billion people.

3. What are the deaths mentioned in verse 8 a culmination of? All four seal judgments associated with the horses.

SESSION TWENTY-NINE ANSWERS
REVELATION 6:9–17

1. Historically, who served as a birth pang to the Antichrist? Hitler. The Antichrist will be similar but worse.

2. How does seal five break the pattern? No horse or horseman, only in heaven. No looking down at the earth.

3. Why is it significant that the saints in Revelation 6:9 are disembodied souls? They became believers *after* the rapture on earth and were subsequently martyred. They're referred to as Tribulation saints, and they literally endure hell on earth.

4. Why isn't John invited to "look" in the discussion of the fifth seal? It refers to the tone of the entire seventh seven, not a moment. Being a Christian will be a dangerous thing in the Tribulation, and the full number of martyrs won't be reached until the end of the Tribulation.

5. What is the significance of the dead from the fourth seal going to Hades? They're unbelievers.

6. Where do the dead from the fifth seal end up? Under the altar in heaven.

7. What do the dead in both the fourth and fifth seals have in common? Their deaths are indirectly caused by the Antichrist and instigated by Jesus.

8. What does the sixth seal represent, and how does the sixth seal represent a shift in the nature of the judgments on earth? Supernatural calamities and destruction. They become increasingly supernatural in nature, evidencing the judgment of God.

9. Summarize what you've learned of the physical calamities in the sixth seal judgment. Black sun (plunging temperature changes > hurricane force winds > earthquakes). Red moon. The stars (asteroids/ meteor) fall to the earth. Mountains and islands *move* (complete obliteration).

10. What happens among people as a result of supernatural judgment? They recognize both God and the Lamb are judging. They have someone to explain to them.

ANSWER KEY

SESSION THIRTY ANSWERS
REVELATION 7:1–17

1. Is the book of Revelation organized chronologically? No. Things overlap.

2. How does John indicate overlapping content? He gives specific time references or context references.

3. How do we know the events of chapter 7 precede the events of chapter 6? There're no physical judgments or evidence on them on earth.

4. What is the significance of the detail that the Lord stopped the wind and therefore the natural water source? God is enacting judgment via natural means prior to the seals. This natural judgment is a contributing factor to the effects of the Antichrist on the world.

5. What is the significance of the term *bondservant* in the New Testament? Believers.

6. What is the significance of sealing? Being born again.

7. Who are the 144,000 witnesses? The new generations of believers born again after the rapture all of Jewish descent, taken in equal number from each of the 12 numbers.

8. Which tribe is missing from among the 144,000 and why? The tribe of Dan. They first introduced idol worship; this is the consequence.

9. What do we learn about the 144,000 from Revelation 14? They'll be virgin, male, Jews.

10. What is the significance of 12? Governing. God ruling through men.

11. Is this number of 144,000 symbolic? No. There will be exactly that many virgin, male Jewish converts, chosen specifically and saved miraculously by God.

12. What is the purpose of the 144,000 witnesses? They become the evangelists of the Tribulation.

13. There's a cause and effect relationship between the salvation of the 144,000 and the multitude of every tribe, tongue, and nation. What is it? The 144,000 are the evangelists who lead a worldwide movement that reaches people everywhere.

14. Where do these saints in heaven come from? They're martyred in the Tribulation. Very few believers live until the end, and that's a good thing for them.

15. How do the judgments all fit together? Like Russian nesting dolls. One hides inside the other. The seven bowls fit inside the seventh trumpet, and the seven trumpets fit inside the seventh seal.

Session Thirty-One Answers
Revelation 8:1–7

Overview

1. Why might chapter 7 be placed at this point in Revelation? It will serve as encouragement to the believers enduring Tribulation.

2. What is the opening of the seventh seal? The seven trumpet judgments.

Revelation 8:1–4

1. What is the significance of the moment of silence in heaven? It serves to underscore the awe of what's coming.

2. Why is the length of the pause vague? The number isn't significant. It doesn't require greater attention as would be indicated by precision.

3. Trumpet judgments one through three affect what? They affect the physical earth.

4. Trumpet judgments four through six, the woe judgments, affect what? The physical bodies of those on earth.

5. What is the symbolism associated with a trumpet? A warning of impending judgment

6. At what point of the Tribulation will the seal and trumpet judgments play out? Seals one through six and trumpets one through six will finish up before the "mid-Tribulation" begins.

Revelation 8:5–7

1. How does God warn the world that the trumpet judgments are coming? Another earthquake.

2. What is the first trumpet judgment? Hail of fine and blood, burning up one-third of the earth and everything growing in it.

3. What do the judgments of Revelation loosely resemble? Exodus.

Answer Key

SESSION THIRTY-TWO ANSWERS
REVELATION 8:8–13, 9:1–6

Revelation 8:8–9

1. What meaning should we apply to the idea that one-third of the earth is destroyed? It's a continuous section. One-third of the land becomes uninhabitable.

2. What does the fact that John doesn't quite have the words to describe what he sees hit the water in Revelation 8:8 indicate? It's definitely supernatural in nature.

3. How do we know this particular passage is literal? The details of blood killing fish and capsizing boats.

4. Why is God cutting off patches of the globe? Over the course of the Tribulation, God will narrow the focus the world down to just the Middle East. He's forcing migration to the location of the final showdown.

5. What does Pastor Armstrong interpret to be that first chunk of land and water to be affected by the first and second trumpet judgments? North and South America and the Pacific Ocean, each exactly 30% of the land and water masses on earth today.

Revelation 8:10–11

1. What would the best interpretation of this "falling star" named Wormwood be? A symbolic interpretation of that falling star is an angel, and the name indicates a fallen angel or demon.

2. Who sends Wormwood, and what is his purpose? God sends a demon as an instrument of His judgment, acting according to the destructive nature of the demon.

3. What does Wormword accomplish? He poisons one-third of the fresh water across the world.

Revelation 8:12

1. How do we interpret this reduction of light by one-third? The sun and moon are each blotted out for a consecutive one-third of each 24-hour period.

2. What is the result of this particular judgment in a physical sense? A new ice age.

3. What's the overall theme of these judgments in their effects on the earth? It becomes increasingly inhospitable to human life.

Revelation 8:13

1. What does the term *mid-heaven* signify? They numbered "heavens" to indicate layers of atmosphere. First the sky. Second is space. Third is God's throne room.

2. So there's an eagle flying in outer space speaking a message. What is the figurative significance of this aspect of the vision? An angel is sent to circle the earth and proclaim a warning of impending woe associated with the last two trumpets and all seven bowl judgments.

SESSION THIRTY-THREE ANSWERS
REVELATION 9:1–12

Revelation 9:1–6

1. What entity executes the fifth trumpet judgment? Another demon, Apollyon or Abaddon.

2. To what is Abaddon given the key? The bottomless pit, sheol.

3. Summarize what you learn about the three sections of sheol. It has three sections: Abraham's bosom (faithful dead; they've been restored to heaven by this point), hell (unfaithful dead; they stay there), demon prison (for those who were *too* disobedient by mating and creating Nephilim. They're the worst of the worst of demons; and God sets them loose in this judgment to torment the unsealed.)

4. What are some significant guidelines about the commission of the demons in this judgment? It has limits and directions; God is still in control. This is the first time there's an exception to any of the judgments, and that is not a principle that extends to any other judgments.

5. What is the significance of the sealed in this judgment and who does it include? The sealed are the faithful, sealed by the Holy Spirit. It includes the 144,000 and any of their converts.

6. Summarize the torment these demons will cause. Five months of ongoing physical pain via scorpion stings. But they'd have no hope of an end because they wouldn't be aware the judgment has a limit. But God will supernaturally intervene so that no one can die in this five-month period. So immense physical suffering with no hope of an end.

Revelation 9:7–11

1. How do we know these "locusts" are supernatural rather than natural? They emerge

from the pit and have characteristics no known "locust" possesses.

2. Why is this passage often misinterpreted? People start grasping for any conceivable earthly object that will fit the description here. But this passage is supernatural. There's nothing wrong with it being bizarre.

3. So what do we know to be true of these locusts? They're a demonic horde of terrifying, previously unknown form whose sole purpose is to inflict pain and torment on the unfaithful.

4. How does God reveal His grace in this judgment? He gives the unfaithful a glimpse of what their eternal fate will be if they die without repentance. And God graciously suspends death for this period to give them time to change at its end.

5. What is the symbolic significance of the number five? God's grace.

SESSION THIRTY-FOUR ANSWERS
REVELATION 9:13–19

Overview

1. What is the fifth trumpet judgment? Physical torment by locust-demons.

Revelation 9:13–19

1. Who is the chief actor in the events of this woe, and how does this affect the interpretation of this passage? God; the judgment is supernatural in nature.

2. What do we know about the bound angels released in verse 14? They're excessively violent and terrible, and God bound them intending to set them loose at this point in time and let them do as they will.

3. What interpretive principle do the numbered horsemen remind us of? We take them literally unless clearly indicated otherwise.

4. Summarize what we can learn about the horsemen? They are *not* the Chinese army. John knows what he saw: men on horses wearing armor. They are a demonic army. They kill one-third of the world through supernatural means; no indication of symbolism.

5. About what does Joel 2 prophesy? The Tribulation.

6. What do the demon army do to the land? Burn it up and leave it desolate.

7. Describe the Eden connection to the sixth trumpet judgment. The demon army sees the world before them as Satan saw Adam and Eve in the garden: enemies ripe for destruction.

Session Thirty-Five Answers
Revelation 9:20–10:7

Overview

1. What is the latter half of Joel's prophecy confirmation of? The supernatural nature of the army in addition to supernatural events in nature as they proceed.

2. What is the significance of one-third of the population dying? It will touch everyone on earth, whether they die themselves or not.

3. For the unbeliever, what is the death of those they know and love? It's a wound with no relief.

Revelation 9:20–21

1. Is the Lord using this suffering to bring more to faith? No. The remaining hearts are hardened permanently.

2. How many of those who survived this sixth judgment are faithful? Zero.

3. What does this judgment reveal about the nature of calamity in relationship to salvation? Calamity doesn't bring people to Christ. Only God does that, and sometimes He uses calamity to do it.

4. What is faith based in? A gift that comes directly from God.

5. Summarize what has happened in the first three and a half years of Tribulation. One-third of the earth is uninhabitable, and one-third of the fresh water is undrinkable. A new ice age has come, and about 50% of the people on earth who were alive at the beginning of Tribulation are dead.

6. How do we know the events of mid-Tribulation are so important? Six chapters of Revelation deal specifically with the events of mid-Tribulation.

7. In the sense of how time passes, how do we understand the events contained in Revelation 10–15? They're a collection of events and circumstances that occur simultaneously at the midpoint, and there are time cues in the chapters themselves to indicate these events are not a series but rather a single compound, complex event.

Revelation 10:1–7

1. How do we know this angel is good and not fallen? Positive descriptors.

2. How do we determine the identity of this particular angel, and what passage of

Scripture does it allude to? He's carrying a little scroll or book while being huge himself. He's loud, too. His identity is revealed in Daniel 12.

SESSION THIRTY-SIX ANSWERS
REVELATION 10:8–11

Daniel 12:1–9

1. What is the context for Daniel 12? Daniel has just spent time prophesying about the Antichrist, or the midpoint of Tribulation.

2. Who arises at the midpoint of Tribulation? The archangel Michael.

3. How do we know the second half of Tribulation will be worse than the first? Jesus refers to it as the "Great" Tribulation in Matthew 24.

4. Who was the first and only (for a long time) to know what happens in the second half of the Tribulation? Daniel.

5. When will Daniel's sealed prophecy be revealed? In the last days, after the advent of the Messiah.

Revelation 10:8–11

1. What is the little scroll the angel gives John? Daniel's sealed prophecy from Daniel chapter 12.

2. When will the events of the little scroll take place? When the seventh trumpet is blown (the bowl of judgments).

3. What is the significance of John eating the scroll, its taste, and how it sits in his stomach? Jesus and His coming kingdom is sweet, but the process required for it to happen is bitter.

4. What defines the midpoint of Tribulation? The Antichrist breaks the covenant that allowed traditional Jewish worship to resume, so he ends sacrifice.

SESSION THIRTY–SEVEN ANSWERS
REVELATION 10:11–11:6

Overview

1. Who is the main character of Revelation 11–14? The Antichrist.

Revelation

2. How do these mid-Tribulation chapters indicate that they refer to this midpoint? Time cues are included.

3. Why does God have Daniel write the scroll that John is given to reveal? To clearly illustrate the connection between Daniel's prophecies and John's Revelation.

4. In the sense of a timeline, how would we plot the mid-Tribulation events of Revelation 11–14? They all go in the middle; they're relatively simultaneous.

Revelation 10:11–11:2

1. What do we know about the inhabitable portion of the world and its inhabitants? The world has essentially shrunken down to the Middle East, Israel and the surrounding area, and the population is a mere fraction of what it once was.

2. What do we learn at the outset of chapter 11? There is once again a physical Jewish temple in Jerusalem.

3. What are the three points of the instructions to not measure the Court of the Gentiles? They focus our attention on three things: the temple exists and is in proper use, the age of the Gentiles isn't over yet, and we're now at the midpoint (42 months left to go).

4. What's the significance of these things being true? To some degree, the land of Israel must have been preserved to some extent so that the temple can operate, but God's greater plan is still ongoing.

Revelation 11:3–6

1. Which two characters do we meet in this passage? The two witnesses or prophets.

SESSION THIRTY-EIGHT ANSWERS
REVELATION 11:3–6

1. What two things does John intentionally connect? The temple operation and the ministry of the two witnesses.

2. What part of our Tribulation timeline describes the ministry of the two witnesses? The first three and a half years, the same time that the temple is in operation.

3. What is the purpose of these two witnesses' ministry? To both convict and condemn the world of sin.

4. How are these witnesses described? Wearing sackcloth, traditional mourning garb and they have supernatural defense powers: breathing fire and calling down plagues.

ANSWER KEY

5. Who are these witnesses? The two olive trees and lampstands in Zechariah 4.

6. What do the oil and lampstand represent in Zechariah's vision? The Spirit of God.

7. What is the role of Zerubbabel in the vision? He represents people used by God to accomplish His purposes.

8. Who are the two olive trees representing? Two men who have a worldwide ministry. The men described in Revelation 11.

9. Why are the witnesses hated so much that they need supernatural self-defense? They have the power to make life on earth even more miserable, including stopping rain for the duration of their ministry.

10. What might these witnesses be preaching? The end of the world, the judgments as they happen.

11. What is the role of these two witnesses in the overall story of Revelation? They narrate the happenings of the events, leaving no possibility of missing the point. They're the visual causes of the judgments Jesus enacts, so they're blamed for *all* of the scroll and trumpet judgments. God intends for the world to focus on them to make for a clear explanation and source of judgment events.

SESSION THIRTY-NINE ANSWERS
REVELATION 11:7–19

Revelation 11:17–10

1. Summarize what we learn about the two witnesses in this section. They die. Their bodies are put on display.

2. What is the significance of the reference to Egypt and Sodom? Depravity and idolatry.

3. At this mid-Tribulation point, how would Jerusalem be described? It's a Great city in that it's big. But it's depraved and idolatrous.

4. How does the world react to the witnesses' deaths? They display the bodies for three days and throw a party to celebrate.

5. What is the role of the "beast" in all this? He's the hero who slayed the villains.

6. How are the two witnesses connected to the temple in this period? Their ministry is located in the temple. Their presence protects the temple from aggression throughout judgment. When they're defeated, so is the temple.

Revelation 11:11–14

1. What happens to the two witnesses after three and a half days, and what is the significance of these events? They're resurrected and called to heaven, which displays God's approval of these men and their actions. At this point, Zechariah's prophecy of a worldwide ministry is fulfilled.

2. Are the witnesses operating in the first or second half of the Tribulation? Second.

Revelation 11:15–19

1. What does the seventh trumpet represent? The seven bowl judgments.

2. Why might the saints in heaven be so excited about God's kingdom on earth? They've regained their earthly bodies, which are designed for life on earth, not in heaven.

3. How does this section fit on our Tribulation timeline? It's a preview of the second half of Tribulation. The bowl judgments play out starting in chapter 16, and this is just the preview or foreshadowing.

SESSION FORTY ANSWERS
REVELATION 12:1–5

Overview

1. What narrative function do the two witnesses serve in the storyline of the Tribulation? They narrate the first half.

2. What are the events of mid-Tribulation? The final act of this age that set off the end of this age and the beginning of the next.

Revelation 12:1–5

1. How do we approach interpreting signs in Scripture? Signs are a convenient tool to represent real-world events in a figurative manner that allows for layered meaning.

2. What mistake do Bible students often make? They mix up the sign with the physical event and thereby misinterpret Scripture by failing to translate the signs.

3. What are the two signs that open chapter 12, and how do we know they are in fact signs? The pregnant woman and the child. We know they're signs because John says so.

4. What do we learn about the son in verse 5? Rules with a rod of iron, Psalm 2:7–9. Baby means Messiah, but not baby Jesus. Ruling Messiah.

5. What do we learn about the woman? She has a sun and moon under her feet, and a crown of 12 stars on her head. Genesis 37:5–10. Joseph's dreams communicate his relationship with his family. Jacob is the sun, moon is Rachel, and stars are his brothers. This is the only other place this symbol appears. So the woman's crown of stars and the sun and moon point to the people of Israel, and paired with the woman, the nation of Israel.

6. Who is the red dragon, and what does he do? Satan. He causes one-third of the angels to fall, creating his demon army.

SESSION FORTY-ONE ANSWERS
REVELATION 12:6–12

Overview

1. Summarize the big picture view of Scripture's story as explained in the beginning of video 41. Answers may vary.

2. What do the signs and symbols of this passage teach us about Satan? They explain how Satan's tactics changed after the cross and will change again at mid-Tribulation.

3. Where is the symbol of ten horns explained? Daniel 7.

4. What does Daniel's fourth beast represent? The imperialistic-democratic alliance of the modern Gentile era. At the end of the age of the Gentiles, the world government will eventually be ten kings sovereign over the whole world.

Revelation 12 *Expands* on Daniel 7

1. What is the governing structure of the world at the midpoint of Tribulation? Ten kingdoms/ districts, seven rulers; all of them serve as pawns of Satan ruling the kingdoms. Satan is the god of this world.

2. Genesis 3:15 is the *protoevangelion*. What does this mean? The first gospel; pre-gospel gospel.

3. Satan is *not* omniscient, so he couldn't possibly know who the Messiah would be. So how did he approach his mission to thwart the Messiah and world redemption? He's done everything he possibly could to derail God's plan by attacking anyone who could possibly be or produce the Messiah.

Revelation 12:6–12

Revelation

1. What is the significance of 1260 days? Mid-Tribulation time cue.

2. What happens to the nation of Israel at mid-Tribulation? They're taken to a place of safety and provision to wait out the second half of Tribulation.

3. Here we read about the heart of the mid-Tribulation moment. What is it? A war in heaven. Satan loses, and he and his demons are permanently barred from heaven. They may have fallen in the very beginning, but they've had access to God's throne room up until this point.

4. What does the passage in Job teach us about sin? It gives Satan fodder to accuse us before God.

5. Where is the only other place Satan could go after being barred from heaven? The earth. It's all that's left.

6. What effect does this permanent banishment from heaven have on Satan? He realizes at this point that he simply can't win. His punishment/ doom is coming, and he knows it. He's confined to earth, and he can't leave.

SESSION FORTY-TWO ANSWERS
REVELATION 12:13–17

Overview

1. Summarize Satan's response to his banishment from God's throne room. He focuses all his attention on the people on earth. He knows his punishment is coming, and he's desperate to do anything he can to thwart God's plan.

2. Why does God choose to banish Satan at this point? It forces Satan into his role in the Great Tribulation, as God had planned from the beginning.

3. Who is the target of Satan's aggression at this point, and how does he respond? Anyone who follows Jesus or is Jewish by birth is martyred.

Revelation 12:13–17

1. Why does God rescue Israel? He must preserve a believing remnant of Jews on the earth to keep His promises.

2. What does the symbol of being borne on eagles' wings indicate? God provides a supernatural means of escape, just as He did in the exodus.

3. Where does Israel go, who is included, and how do we know this? Jesus described their flight in Matthew 24:15–21. This escape is for Jews who believe in Jesus. It's a

test of faith. He's rescuing the *faithful*. Impregnable, high, on rocks. Will be able to be flooded (a wadi) and preserved from flooding. A sheep pen—a botzrah (bozrah)—i.e., Petra.

4. Why is the second half of the Tribulation called the "Great Tribulation?" Because of what *Satan* does, not God.

5. Since Satan can't attack the preserved remnant, who does he attack? The unbelieving Jews and the Gentile Christians. He martyrs most of them.

6. Does Satan martyr *all* of the unbelieving Jews and believing Gentiles? No. He preserves some.

SESSION FORTY-THREE ANSWERS
REVELATION 13:1–2

Overview

1. What is Satan's mission as described in Revelation 12:17? Making war with anyone left on earth who could remotely enjoy God's favor.

2. Who comprise the remnant? Believing (Messianic) Jews.

3. Why does the remnant represent a minority within the Jewish people? There is always a smaller subset of the Jewish people who recognize the Messiah or who would be considered an Old Testament saint.

4. So who comprise the persecuted of Tribulation? Believing Jews (protected), Unbelieving/ orthodox Jews (unprotected, they keep the Law of Moses but deny Jesus), Believing Gentiles (unprotected, God never promised to protect any group of Gentiles at any point.), and one more group we'll learn about next week.

Revelation 13:1–2

1. What does the repetitive use of symbols indicate to the discerning reader? A building story. The meanings don't shift. They build.

2. Who becomes Satan's primary agent on earth, and how has he been portrayed up to this point? The Antichrist. The beast. The rider of the four horses.

3. What does the rising of a beast from water indicate, and how do we know this to be true? The symbol of a beast indicates a world-dominating Gentile power. It parallels the beasts of Daniel 7.

SESSION FORTY-FOUR ANSWERS
REVELATION 13:3–4

Overview

1. How is the beast of Daniel 7 similar to the beast of Revelation 13? Chimera, multiple heads, horns, crowns, blasphemous names.

2. The Revelation 13 beast combines elements of the four beasts of Daniel 7. How is this significant? The Revelation beast is the embodiment of the age of Gentiles; he's the climactic leader of the age of the Gentiles.

3. The beast of Revelation 13 coincides with what element of Daniel's vision in Daniel 7? The little horn that supplants three other horns.

4. Which historical figure prefigures the Antichrist? Nebuchadnezzar.

5. Whose power does the Antichrist possess? Satan's.

6. How might the beast acquire such power? He becomes one with Satan.

7. Where are the symbols of the heads, horns, crowns, and blasphemous names explained? Revelation 17.

Revelation 13:3–4

1. Who is the slain head representative of, and when will we learn more? The Antichrist himself, Revelation 17.

2. What happens to the slain head—the Antichrist? He resurrects.

3. How does the Antichrist resurrect? Satan indwells him.

4. What's the result of his resurrection? The world worships him. Unilateral idolatry and devil-worship.

SESSION FORTY-FIVE ANSWERS
REVELATION 13:5–18

Overview

1. Explain the role and actions of the Antichrist. Murdered. Resurrected. Kills the witnesses. He presents himself as a counterfeit messiah. He's imbued with Satan's power. Ends traditional Jewish worship in the temple (because he replaces the need for sacrifice); he becomes god of the earth. Persecutes Gentile Christians and unbelieving

Jews.

Revelation 13:5–10

1. What do the Antichrist's words and actions accomplish? Set the whole world against God. He speaks arrogance and blasphemy against God for the whole of the latter half of Tribulation.

2. Who helps the Antichrist wage war against unbelieving Jews and Gentile believers? Those who worship him. Everyone outside the groups of unbelieving Jews and believing Christians.

3. If someone chooses to worship the Antichrist, is it possible at that point for them to ever be saved? No. It's unpardonable.

4. In terms of faith, what's significant of this mid-Tribulation moment? Humanity is clearly divided between those who choose Jesus and those who choose the Antichrist. There's no new faith from this point on. Those who are saved at this point are saved. There will be no more evangelism, or any added to the number of the saints.

5. Will there be any rebellion or resistance against the Antichrist? No. John says to accept your lot. You can't escape the persecution of the Great Tribulation.

Revelation 13:11–14

1. What is the symbolic significance of this second dragon-lamb beast? He speaks for Satan as his prophet. He can do signs and wonders *only* in the presence of the Antichrist.

2. What is significant of the False Prophet's limited power? It reinforces that Satan is *not* God. Satan is limited. He's neither omnipresent nor omniscient.

Revelation 13:15–18

1. What's significant about the False Prophet's image of the Antichrist? It's a classic tactic of Satan to focus worship on the physical rather than the spiritual. It allows people to worship Satan even when he's not physically present.

2. What is the abomination of desolation from Daniel 12? The image or icon of the Antichrist.

3. What does the Antichrist require of his followers to counterfeit God? The mark of the beast. He seals his followers.

4. What is the significance of the number 666? The most sinful man.

Revelation

5. Can you "back into" the number of someone's name? No.

6. So what is the purpose of this information? God is providing a warning to the unbelieving Jew not to fall for the Antichrist. They'll be the only ones capable of decoding the warning.

SESSION FORTY-SIX ANSWERS
REVELATION 14:1–5

Overview

1. What is the trigger event for mid-Tribulation events? Satan is cast down from heaven.

2. About how long is the mid-Tribulation "moment?" A few days to a few weeks. A relatively short period.

3. At the close of this mid-Tribulation moment, what is the primary human dilemma? Take the mark and live now but be doomed for eternity. Or refuse the mark, die now, and possibly inherit eternal life.

4. Describe the fourth group of persecuted in the Tribulation: who are they, and when will they be killed? The 144,000 Jews. They will all be killed by the end of the mid-Tribulation moment.

Revelation 14:1

1. What is the significance of Jesus standing on Mt. Zion at mid-Tribulation alongside the 144,000 Jewish martyred evangelists? To preserve the established timeline must be figurative.

Revelation 14:2–5

1. Where are the 144,000 and what are they doing? They're singing a song only they know in the throne room of God.

2. So what is the symbolic significance of Zion? An Ascendant Israel. The physical kingdom of Israel in glory. It's a place in heaven that will come down to earth at a later point.

3. What does "purchased" mean in this context? They've been saved from death by faith and brought to heaven.

ANSWER KEY

SESSION FORTY-SEVEN ANSWERS
REVELATION 14:6–11

Overview

1. Who were these 144,000 witnesses? The firstfruits for God. The most ripe, best fruit. The Law calls for the faithful to return the first and the best back to God.

2. What is the concept of firstfruits outside of the agrarian context? They're the first and the best, and they're given for Jesus.

3. So why are the 144,000 the first and the best, and what is their reward? The first converts after the rapture. They're evangelists who lived pure lives, models of obedience, and were instruments of revival. Their early martyrdom preserves them from the suffering of the second half of Tribulation.

4. The 144,000 and the land of Israel were preserved or sealed from judgment in Revelation 7. What happened and why? God removes their sealing at the mid-Tribulation point because they've fulfilled their purpose; evangelism is done. God allows their martyrdom as a reward for their faithfulness to preserve them from greater suffering. They serve as examples for the martyrs of the second half of Tribulation.

Revelation 14:6–7

1. What does this heavenly messenger preach? An eternal gospel; there's only ever been one gospel: the righteous will live by faith.

2. How is this angelic declaration a fulfillment of Matthew 24:14? The gospel never has been or ever will be dependent on human beings. The angel will share the gospel with everyone left alive at this point. Then Christ is on His way back.

Revelation 14:8–11

1. What is the message of the second angel? Babylon has fallen.

2. What is the significance of Babylon in this context? The kingdom of the Antichrist.

3. What's the message of the third angel? Those who take the mark are destined for eternal torment in hell.

4. What does this passage teach of hell? Place of suffering. Burning (heat) without ceasing. Wrath of God. No rest from punishment.

5. Why are the people who take the mark doomed to suffer forever? They're suffering

eternally for *who* they are, not what they've done. They've refused to be born again, so they're stuck in a sinful state forever with no hope of redemption.

SESSION FORTY-EIGHT ANSWERS
REVELATION 14:12–20

Overview

1. What is Pastor Armstrong's response to those who would say there is no eternal punishment or hell? Scripture is abundantly clear: hell is real, and it's horrible. Those who deny hell remove the need for the gospel and show themselves to be unsaved- false teachers.

Revelation 14:12–13

1. Who is the speaker in verse 12, and what is its purpose? It's John providing commentary on the words of angels and the Lord.

2. Why is martyrdom a blessing in the Tribulation? They escape the misery that will be life in the Tribulation.

3. What is the hope of the Christian? Resurrection. Eternal life after death.

4. What is the perseverance of a saint? Maintaining a faithful witness despite life's circumstances. The ability to suffer and die well.

5. What reward do these martyrs earn? Glorified bodies, governmental responsibility, material reward.

Revelation 14:14–16

1. Who is the people depicted in these verses? Angels. One at least is humanoid. Angels are messengers and reapers.

2. How does this section connect to the mid-Tribulation moment? It's illuminated by Daniel 7. The angels are reaping souls at an alarming rate made possible by the Antichrist's persecution campaign.

Revelation 14:17–20

1. What is the significance of the reaping symbology here? Deaths of believers. Then comes death and judgment for the unbelievers.

Answer Key

2. How does verse 20 fit into the overall timeline of Tribulation? It summarizes the deaths of all humans on earth. This verse serves as a preview of the end.

3. Since the numbers here are so specific, what sort of literal reality might it represent? The force and momentum of a wave of blood that goes through the Kidron Valley after God executes a mass judgment of unbelievers.

4. What is a simple summary of the latter half of the Tribulation? Believers are rooted out and martyred. The Antichrist does his thing. Life is relatively peaceful for the unbeliever.

Session Forty-Nine Answers
Revelation 15:1–4

Overview

1. Why is the second half of the Tribulation relatively unaddressed in the Bible? It's not really complicated. There's a lull in active judgment. Believers are persecuted and martyred. Everyone else has a relatively peaceful few years.

Revelation 15:1–4

1. All of Revelation 15 represents what sort of symbolic significance? It's a sign.

2. According to Daniel, what are the outcomes of this final set of judgments? To finish the transgression, to make an end of sin, to make atonement for iniquity, to bring in everlasting righteousness, to seal up vision and prophecy and to anoint the most holy place.

3. Who are these final judgments for? Unbelieving Israel and everyone else left on earth at this time (unilaterally wicked at this point).

4. What are God's intentions for these judgments? To refine Israel and bring them back to true worship of God.

5. Who stands on the glassy, fiery sea, and what is their victory? Martyrs; death is their victory. They've withstood the testing of Tribulation.

6. What sort of eternal perspective should every believer maintain? They never loved their physical life more than the Lord.

7. What is the purpose of singing the song of the Lamb? Heralding the approaching return of Jesus.

8. What is the purpose of singing the song of Moses? God deals with His rebellious

children by way of *strong* discipline (Deuteronomy 32), and He gives them fair warning of what that discipline will look like (Exodus 15).

SESSION FIFTY ANSWERS
REVELATION 15:5–16:6

Overview

1. How are the songs of Revelation 15 a sign, and what do they signify? Sung by believers to believers to communicate Christ's imminent return and rule, and He alone is righteous and holy (worthy to rule).

2. What is the purpose of these songs, and how do we know? To encourage the remaining believers and Jews on earth; it seems to be sung in a manner those on earth can hear. God is faithful and mighty to save. He is in control.

Revelation 15:5–8

1. How do we know there is a physical tabernacle in heaven? Hebrews indicates our earthly tabernacle and worship implements are patterned after those in heaven. Ezekiel and John both see it in their visions.

2. How does the Bible often describe God's wrath? Something poured out or filled up—contained in a cup.

3. What's the significance of God's wrath being contained in a bowl rather than a cup? First time in Scripture; a greater measure of wrath.

4. What is the significance of entrance to the heavenly tabernacle being inaccessible? Christ cannot intercede for humans during the bowl judgments. Grace and new faith are no longer available.

Revelation 16:1–11

1. What do we need to know about Revelation 16–22 before we begin studying it? Complex, overlapping events, not necessarily occurring in the order they're presented. Cause/effect relationships between the various events.

2. What pattern exists among the bowl judgments? These latter judgments are specifically targeted on unbelievers. God's wrath is discerning and precise.

3. What significance can be attributed to "loathsome" sores? They'll cause serious, unprecedented sort of damage to flesh.

Answer Key

4. What greater significance attaches to the sea and fresh water turning to blood? Sea navigation becomes impossible. So does drinking water. Supports the argument that these things occur right at the end of the latter three-and-a-half-year period.

SESSION FIFTY-ONE ANSWERS
REVELATION 16:7–16

Revelation 15:7–11

1. How does darkness create pain? It's similar to God withholding His presence from Jesus on the cross. It's both physical and spiritual darkness. What's left on the earth is not only pitch black but left to the mercy of the enemy.

2. As a whole, what are these bowl judgments a pattern of? Hell.

3. What does an evil, unrepentant heart do? Blaspheme its creator.

4. What is the significance of the direct parallels between the bowl judgments and those of the Exodus? They clearly indicate God's intention to free Israel from slavery (to sin in this context) and deliver them (to the kingdom in this context).

5. How do these first five bowls fit into the larger picture of the Great Tribulation? These judgments show themselves as plagues that physically recreate hell on earth.

How do the latter two bowl judgments set themselves apart from the previous five? The first five judgments kick off the war of Armageddon, and the latter two are His means of directing the flow of this war.

6. Summarize what you've learned about the War of Armageddon. The details are described discontinuously throughout chapters 16–19. Beginning with the fact that the war of Armageddon isn't a single military engagement but rather a series of events over weeks. It takes place in a series of locations and involves many different groups and characters. As usual, Revelation will give us the broad outline of the events of the war and how they relate to the bowl judgments. But crucial aspects of the story lie outside Revelation in other books of the Bible, particularly in the Old Testament prophets.

Revelation 16:12–16

1. What does the sixth bowl accomplish? It dries up the Euphrates, previously turned to blood. It creates a path for the kings (world leaders under the Antichrist) to wage war from Babylon. It prompts the Antichrist and his prophet to send out demon messengers to amass their armies to wage war against God in Har-Megiddo (the hill of Megiddo, the reference point at which the armies will muster).

Revelation

2. What does removing all water from earth facilitate? Desperation. Satan and those left on earth know they have nothing left to lose, and so they take the war to God. God accelerates the timeline of their rebellion to accomplish His will.

3. Will those left on earth recognize that Christ's return and their judgment is imminent? No. The few remaining believers will see it. The Jews will see the signs. The unrighteous will not know what hit them.

SESSION FIFTY-TWO ANSWERS
REVELATION 16:17–21

Overview

1. Where does the Antichrist amass his forces and why? The Jezreel valley north of Jerusalem. It's strategic for attacking Jerusalem/ Petra.

Revelation 16:17–21

1. What is the impact of the earthquake of the seventh bowl judgment? *Everything* is leveled. Mountains, islands, structures, everything.

2. In the big picture of God's judgment, what is the role of this last bowl judgment? The last of God's wrath is poured out. It's finished.

3. What sort of hailstorm accompanies the earthquake? Hundred-pound rocks falling from space. Literally everything is leveled/ destroyed.

4. Somehow people still survive. What is their response to these disasters? They blaspheme God.

5. What is the purpose of this last bowl judgment? God destroys every remaining Gentile structure. All that's left is Jerusalem and the mountain under it.

6. What is the "great city" of verse 17? Babylon. It's greatly damaged but not completely destroyed.

7. What are the two major themes of the Bible? The destruction of Babylon (antagonist) and the redemption of Christ (protagonist).

8. Why does Babylon get so much attention in this section of Revelation? The home of Sin, the site of Satan's attack on God in Eden. Ground zero. Satan's home base. Source of idolatry (tower of Babel). First kingdom to conquer Israel under Nebuchadnezzar—kicks off the age of the Gentiles.

9. What is idolatry? Any idea of a way to get to God other than Jesus and believing it's

possible.

SESSION FIFTY-THREE ANSWERS
REVELATION 17:1–8

Overview

1. When you hear the word *Babylon*, what should you think? God's instrument of discipline for His people.

2. Summarize what you've learned about false religions as they relate to Babylon. All of them. Satan introduces more options to undermine the truth that there's only one true path to God.

3. Symbolically, what is the direct opposite of Babylon? Jerusalem.

4. Symbolically, what are East and West? Good, west; Evil, east

5. What must happen to physical and symbolic Babylon in order for Christ's rule and reign on earth to be as it should? The physical end of Babylon is the symbolic and literal end of evil. End of idolatry, evil, sin, Satan and his minions.

6. What do Revelation 17 and 18 describe? God's judgment of spiritual Babylon, chapter 17, and God's judgment of physical Babylon, chapter 18.

Revelation 17:1–8

1. What does the harlot of Revelation 17 symbolize? Spiritual Babylon, idolatry, false religion. She's the mother of all false religion.

2. How does the symbolism of world leaders with the harlot of Babylon play out? World leaders use false religions to amass power. It's addictive as both stimulus to flesh and sedative to mind.

3. Which beast does the harlot ride? Where have we seen this beast before, what does this image symbolize, and who is it? Revelation 13:1; the Antichrist. There's a shift here at the end of the Tribulation. The Antichrist, idolatry, spiritual Babylon, evil; they're all united into one being/ force at this point in time.

SESSION FIFTY-FOUR ANSWERS
REVELATION 17:9–18

Overview

1. At this point in Tribulation, how many false religions are left in the world? There is one—the Antichrist's.

2. Summarize the reviews of the two beasts and their symbology. Satan controls the whole world. The beast and one of its heads each respectively represent the Antichrist.

Revelation 17:9–14

1. What does the phrase "to those who have wisdom" signify? You need to know both history and the Bible, specifically the Old Testament.

2. Summarize the explanation of the symbols in this passage. Mountains/ heads/ horns mean kings. Mountain/ head number seven means Antichrist. They're sequential rulers of the age of the Gentiles as described in Daniel 7, ending with the Antichrist. The ten horns are the ten kings of Tribulation. Antichrist is king number eight after his resurrection. This beast in Revelation 17 represents the *entire* age of the Gentiles, God's work to accomplish His purpose to bring about the restoration of His perfect world. The time cues for these leaders specifically reference the timeframe of John's life. Each of these rulers perpetuated false religion/ spiritual Babylon.

Revelation 17:15–18

1. What impact does the seventh bowl judgment have on false religion? Satan systematically eliminates all false religion (belief and physical edifices) outside the one that worships him.

2. How does this fit into the plan of God? God uses these evil rulers to clean house for Him. They cleanse the world of false religion, leaving only one supreme enemy for God to defeat Himself.

3. What remains of spiritual Babylon at the close of Revelation 17? Nothing. The only false religion left is that of Satan, the Antichrist, and his false prophet.

ANSWER KEY

SESSION FIFTY-FIVE ANSWERS
REVELATION 18:1–3

Overview

1. What is a good image of the way the seventh bowl judgment plays out? A domino effect.

2. What will Babylon be or become in the Tribulation? Physically returned to its former glory, set as the chief adversary of God's people and city.

3. At which points of history do Babylon's spiritual and physical power coincide? Eden, Babel, Nebuchadnezzar, Antichrist.

4. Revelation 17 describes which phase of God's destruction of Babylon? The spiritual Babylon, the systematic destruction of false religion, Satan's kingdom.

5. What is the effect of Satan consolidating his physical and spiritual power during Tribulation? It's easier for God to defeat them. God allows evil to "get its way" for the purpose of aligning history/ events to His will for His purposes.

Revelation 18:1–3

1. What's the significance of the phrase "after these things?" The events of chapter 18 are caused by those of chapter 16, the bowl judgments.

2. How does chapter 17 fit into the sequential narrative of Revelation? It's an interruption to provide the backstory of the spiritual battle happening alongside the physical.

SESSION FIFTY-SIX ANSWERS
REVELATION 18:1–8

Revelation 18:1–3

1. What will remain of Babylon? Nothing. It's leveled, but it will exist. It will become a prison for demons during the thousand-year reign. It's a place of death. Forever uninhabited by any but unclean scavengers.

2. Why must these passages of Isaiah and Jeremiah refer to an event still yet to come? The fall of Babylon to Cyrus didn't involve this sort of destruction.

3. Are the animal habitants of Babylon as described in Revelation 18 literal? No, they're a figurative depiction of demons.

Revelation 18:4–8

1. Who does God give warning of impending judgment on Babylon? Jews and believers. His people.

2. Where has God previously given this same warning? Jeremiah 51.

3. Where will those who flee Babylon go? Jerusalem.

4. What is the purpose of this physical destruction of Babylon? Payback for the millennia of animosity toward Israel.

5. What will be the two-stage destruction of physical Babylon? As the Antichrist's army marches toward Jerusalem, men will attack the city left vulnerable. What these raiders do not destroy, God will destroy supernaturally.

SESSION FIFTY-SEVEN ANSWERS
REVELATION 18:9–24

1. Where do we find the details of the destruction of Babylon? The Old Testament.

2. What is this "spirit of the destroyer?" An invading army that sweeps in like a rushing wind.

3. What region does "Leb-kamai" or "heart of my adversaries" reference? Mesopotamia.

4. What are the modern equivalents of the nations mentioned in Jeremiah 51? Turkey, Armenia, Southern Russia, and Iran/ Persia.

5. Why would an army attack Babylon, the devil/ Antichrist's headquarters, and what do they accomplish? It's defenseless. God inspires a coup to fulfill Isaiah and Jeremiah. They destroy the city and everyone/ everything in it.

6. How long does it take for Babylon to fall, and what does this indicate? It falls in an hour, and that must be supernatural.

7. How can all of the blood of prophets and saints be blamed on this one city? It's Satan's headquarters. It represents his work in the world. Substitutionary punishment in the same vein as substitutionary atonement.

8. What is the Antichrist's reaction to the fall of Babylon? The Antichrist realizes his last chance of rebellion is defeated. God is pressing the Antichrist to continue and attack Jerusalem. He has nothing left to lose.

ANSWER KEY

SESSION FIFTY-EIGHT ANSWERS
REVELATION 19:1–10

Overview

1. What part of the Bible tells us the most about Christ's second coming? The Old Testament.

Revelation 19:1–5

1. What does the phrase "after these things" indicate? A cause-and-effect sequence of events.

2. How does the fall of Babylon pave the way for Christ's return? The opposition to His rule is quickly disappearing.

3. Where will we be when the events of Revelation 19 occur? We'll be part of that singing multitude.

4. At this point, where is the believing church? In heaven with the Lord.

5. What is worship? The natural expression of any child of God who recognizes the power, wisdom, grace, and goodness of God. Any outward expression of glorifying God. Worship is demonstrative.

Revelation 19:6–10

1. Who is the bride of Christ? New Testament church term for the church saints, those baptized in the Spirit by faith in Jesus. Those living between Pentecost and the Rapture.

2. What is significant about the period of the church, the bride of Christ? God's Spirit always dwells somewhere. This is the only period in all of history in which God dwells in human hearts rather than a building or object.

3. Why does God use the metaphor of a wedding? To provide a clear picture of how things will happen. The order of end time events directly correlates to traditional Jewish wedding procedures.

4. What is the connection between the Passover of Matthew 26 and the wedding feast of Revelation 19? Jesus saves the last cup of Passover for the wedding feast between Him and His bride in the kingdom. We'll finish the Passover and kick off the wedding feast at the same time.

Revelation

SESSION FIFTY-NINE ANSWERS
REVELATION 19:6–10

1. What is the bride of Christ clothed in? Their righteousness as represented by clean, fine, white linen.

2. Who are the guests at this wedding feast in heaven? Old Testament and Tribulation saints, present in spirit form.

3. What's significant about John's interaction with his escort angel? The angel rebukes John's act of worship.

4. Summarize stage three of Armageddon. Centered between Jerusalem, the Mount of Olives, and Bozrah. Two of the seven kings allied with Antichrist turn on him and attack Babylon. Meanwhile, the Antichrist and his army marches on Israel. He meets no resistance along his path except in the area around Bozrah, modern-day Jordan (where the Jews are ensconced in Petra).

5. In between stages two and three, where are the Antichrist's forces? Some are in Jezreel, outside Jerusalem, and a remnant is outside Babylon.

6. Who does Antichrist target with an attack at this point? Bozrah. The Jews protected there. The Lord defends them.

8. In the Antichrist's next move, where does he move his forces and why? West of Jerusalem because of his anger at the fall of Babylon.

SESSION SIXTY ANSWERS
ISAIAH 29:1–7

1. What is stage three of the War of Armageddon, and what triggers these actions? Movement or attacks on Bozrah and the West side of Jerusalem, triggered by the fall of Babylon.

2. How does Antichrist mount his attack of Jerusalem? Via rudimentary means. A stone wall is adequate defense again. He mounts a siege followed by an invasion culminating in hand-to-hand combat.

3. How does God use Antichrist's military maneuvers to accomplish His will? He's luring Antichrist and his army into position for judgment and defeat.

4. What is Ariel? Another name for Jerusalem.

5. How do the people in Jerusalem defeat Antichrist's forces? They pray for God to save them, and He does by supernatural means.

Answer Key

6. What brings the Jewish people to this point of crying out to the Lord? They have experienced the real effects of these battles that have concentrated them in Jerusalem. They have been purified by fire.

7. How does the Lord supernaturally defend Jerusalem? He makes it enticing but impossible to conquer. He'll cause both the attacking army and their animals to be confused and blind.

8. Who all does the Lord defend? Those in Jerusalem proper in addition to the faithful camping north of Jerusalem in the land of Judah.

9. Which Old Testament event does this battle mirror? The Assyrian assault by Sennacherib on Hezekiah's Jerusalem.

10. Is there much of an actual battle in this war of Armageddon? No. Jesus defeats all without the Antichrist's maneuvers resulting in engagement.

Session Sixty-One Answers
Stages One–Three of Armageddon

1. Summarize stage one of Armageddon. Sixth bowl—God creates a path by drying up a river, and The Antichrist moves his forces to Jezreel.

2. Summarize stage two of Armageddon. Invaders destroy Babylon. Seventh bowl.

3. Summarize stage three of Armageddon. In anger because of Babylon's destruction, Antichrist besieges Jerusalem medieval-style. The Jews cry out in repentance to God, and He fights on their behalf. Antichrist also besieges Bozrah/ Petra with his remaining forces that had been stationed at Babylon.

4. What is the purpose of Tribulation? To finish transgression, to make an end of sin, to make atonement for iniquity, to bring in everlasting righteousness, to seal up vision and prophecy, and to anoint the most holy place.

5. How is the Mosaic Covenant connected to Tribulation? Tribulation is the consequence for the Jews breaking the covenant. It applies to all Jews forever as a unit, except those who escape the penalty of the Law by saving faith in Jesus, thereby grafting that individual Jew into the bride of Christ.

6. How do the events of Tribulation lead the Jews to repentance? They recognize the consequences of Deuteronomy 29 being fulfilled in their time. They therefore understand how God is calling them to respond.

7. Jesus set the terms for His return. What where they? What prompted His return? The Jews as a nation would call out to Jesus and embrace Him as the Messiah.

SESSION SIXTY-TWO ANSWERS
ISRAEL'S CONFESSION AND SALVATION

1. What must Israel remember or confess for God to forgive and restore them according to the Abrahamic covenant? Each individual Jew must confess their sin and their need for Jesus—individual saving faith. And this confession must also happen at a collective national level as they confess national sin from time past until present, including rejecting their Messiah.

2. What does "all Israel" in Romans 11:26 mean? At some point in history, every Jew alive on earth at that time will be saved all at once, triggered by their recognizing Jesus as Messiah as a collective nation.

3. What specifically fulfills the Old Covenant? Israel's collective, national repentance and acceptance of Jesus.

4. How does Israel reach a point where every living Jew is of a mind to confess Christ simultaneously? Because God can do anything and calling hearts to saving faith is His business. He softens their hearts and creates circumstances that lead to this conclusion.

5. Describe the infiltration of Jerusalem as a part of stage three of Armageddon? Antichrist makes it inside the walls and takes half the city amid much pillaging. The other half will stand. God lures Antichrist in. Antichrist's actions leave the Jews he doesn't kill terrified, and this creates the pivotal moment of faith for Jews.

6. Why has Satan always made his target the nation of Israel? Their collective calling on the Lord through saving faith in Jesus is what brings about the physical kingdom. If Satan can remove the group that will call out to Jesus and bring about His kingdom, theoretically, Christ will not return, and Satan will maintain his rein on earth forever.

7. How does this national moment of saving faith come about? God moves among them by His Spirit, resulting in national mourning. They recognize that they'd killed their Messiah, and they do not expect salvation at this point. But this national repentance results in moving the nation, as a whole, under the new covenant of grace in Jesus.

SESSION SIXTY-THREE ANSWERS
REVELATION 19:11–16

Overview

1. What does Zechariah's list of kinds of Jews coming to saving faith indicate? No group or strata holds out. All families, employments, education, etc. Every. Single. Jew.

2. What do Psalms 79–80 express? The collective repentance of Israel as the Antichrist invades Jerusalem.

3. How long does the siege of Jerusalem last before Christ returns because of Israel's repentance? Three days. The Spirit pours out on that third day, the Jews repent, and Jesus comes back.

Revelation 19:11–16

1. In what form does Jesus appear at this point? His heavenly, glorified form—Revelation 1.

2. What will be Jesus' name at this point? We don't know, but it won't be Jesus.

3. Why does it matter that Jesus is riding a white horse? He comes as ruler.

4. Why is Jesus's robe dipped in blood? From trampling the winepress of God's wrath.

5. Who is the army in white linen behind him? Raptured/ resurrected saints. The bride of Christ. We ride in behind Him in victory.

6. There's a second army present. Who are they? Angels. A heavenly army.

7. What sort of events will directly precede Christ's physical return? It'll be pitch black. Then heavens will literally open, and Jesus will come through with us and the angels accompanying Him.

SESSION SIXTY-FOUR ANSWERS
ARMAGEDDON STAGE FOUR

1. At the close of the last session, what was the state of Israel? Crying out to Jesus and mourning that they've missed their chance for salvation.

2. Summarize how Joseph's story prefigures that of Jesus. Joseph given by his brothers into the hands of Gentiles, who, through gaining power via God's favor, he eventually rules over. His position allows him to save the brothers who wronged him. The Jews resented Jesus and gave Him into the hands of the Romans. Through His death and Resurrection, Jesus gained authority over the Gentiles, and at the end of the age of Gentiles, Jesus saves the Jews who wronged Him.

3. How does Jesus's initial rejection by the Jews play into God's larger plan? Their rejection provides a means for the whole world to be saved, not just Israel.

4. At the beginning of Armageddon stage four, where are the Antichrist's forces? Divided between Jerusalem and Bozrah, besieging both.

Revelation

5. Where does Armageddon stage four occur? Bozrah

6. What does the "satiated" sword of Isaiah 34 signify? God is ready to execute judgment.

7. Who does the fighting at Bozrah, and what is the result of this battle? Just Jesus. He alone destroys the Antichrist's entire force at Bozrah and shepherds the faithful Jewish remnant out of Bozrah into the desert.

Session Sixty-Five Answers
Christ's Final Victory

1. Where does Isaiah see Jesus coming from, and why is His robe dipped in blood? Bozrah. The judgment on Antichrist's army at Bozrah resulted in the blood on His garment.

2. Why does it matter that the Lord keeps emphasizing that He alone is fighting? God doesn't need any help. Vengeance is the Lord's; the faithful have *no part* in it.

3. Where does Jesus go after He conquers the attackers of Bozrah? Jerusalem

4. What state does Jesus find Jerusalem in? Pitched in heated battle. The Jews have lost hope in victory but have gained faith in their Messiah.

5. Who accompanies Jesus as He approaches Jerusalem, and where specifically does He go? He goes to the Mount of Olives accompanied by the remnant from Bozrah, the bride of Christ, and a heavenly army of angels.

6. Why does Jesus stay at the mount of Olives? He changes the topography of the city before physically engaging the enemy.

7. What does Jesus do to change the topography of Jerusalem, and what is this reminiscent of? He literally creates a gap in the actual Mount of Olives, and the Jews in Jerusalem flees through this new valley, much like Israel escaped Pharaoh via the Red Sea.

8. After Israel escapes Jerusalem, what does Jesus do? He enters through the same valley He'd just created to engage Antichrist himself and his armies. He literally flays Antichrist with the word of truth, and it accomplishes the destruction of the whole army, too.

9. What is the physical result of Christ's defeat of Antichrist's army? A blood tsunami that sweeps the Kidron Valley.

ANSWER KEY

SESSION SIXTY-SIX ANSWERS
RESOLUTION OF ARMAGEDDON

1. How did Christ defeat Antichrist's armies? With the sword of His mouth.

2. How does God clean up the carnage? He calls birds down to eat the carcasses.

3. What is the state of the world after the resolution of Armageddon? The earth is at rest from war. No more opposing armies exist. Jews alive believe. Some believing and unbelieving Gentiles are alive at this point, too.

4. What happens when a physical body dies? All the spirits it contains are released, human or otherwise.

5. Why are the Antichrist and the False Prophet thrown alive into the lake of fire (hell)? So that the released spirits are bound as the body is destroyed.

6. How is the Antichrist's fate different from that of His armies? He doesn't join his armies in hell. He passes on into the lake of fire, the final, permanent home for all unbelievers. He's the last to die but the first to face final judgment.

7. What is the lake of fire, and what do we know of it? It's the eternal destination of all unbelievers. It contains all of them in their resurrected bodies for eternal pain, punishment, and death.

SESSION SIXTY-SEVEN ANSWERS
THE 75-DAY INTERVAL

Overview

1. What is the 75-day interval? The interlude between Christ's return and the inauguration of His kingdom.

2. What does Daniel 9:27 teach about the Tribulation timeline? Seven-year period/Tribulation, marked by three specific events: Covenant made, Jewish sacrifices in the temple ended, and complete destruction of the Antichrist.

3. Where do we learn of the interval period? Daniel 12:11–12.

4. What is the purpose of the first 30-day period after Tribulation ends? Cleansing and restoring the temple.

5. What is the purpose of the final 45-day period after the "desolation is abolished?" Resurrect OT saints and Tribulation saints into their glorified bodies. Judge and reward those who will enter the kingdom.

The First 30 Days of the 75-Day Interval

1. What does Isaiah 65 describe? A world renewed, remade.

2. Why is the remaking of the earth a necessity at this point? The earth has been made completely desolate. It's uninhabitable, and Christ's kingdom is quite large.

3. Where will Christ live in His 1,000-year kingdom? His temple raised in Jerusalem.

4. What is significant about the fact that it takes 30 days to repair the world and cleanse the temple? Three means Godhead. Ten means testimony. It is a testimony of God at the center and the source of all things.

5. Where are Satan/ Antichrist and the False Prophet during this 30-day period? In hell.

SESSION SIXTY-EIGHT ANSWERS
REVELATION 10:1–4

The Latter 45 Days of the 75 Day Interval

1. Why 45 days? 9x5. 9 means judgment, 5 means grace.

2. Why can't God the Father be physically present on the earth at this point? Sin will still be present on the earth, so God can't be.

3. What is the mission of the angel sent to earth in Revelation 20? To bind Satan and cast him in the pit/ abyss for 1,000 years.

4. What is the abyss? It's the specific holding place for demons awaiting final judgment. It's like hell, but it's not the same place sinful humans go.

5. What time is Daniel referring to the resurrection of saints in Daniel 12? The period of time after Satan is bound, the 45-day period.

6. Who all is resurrected in this time period? OT and Tribulation saints. This is not for unbelieving people.

Revelation 20:4

1. Who remains alive in their natural bodies at this point? Tribulation Jews and any other survivors.

2. What are the implications of this for the population of earth? Sin remains. Marriage and children can still occur. Unbelievers can multiply naturally. They don't attain resurrected bodies at this point.

ANSWER KEY

3. Wat does the Old Testament teach about the nature of Israel during this time? They will all be believing and faithful and capable of keeping His law.

SESSION SIXTY-NINE ANSWERS
REVELATION 20:5

Overview

1. Describe the conflict in how the surviving Jewish people enter the kingdom. They seem to maintain the ability to marry, have conflict, and die, but at the same time, they'll be sinless as a nation.

2. So, what's the answer? Some of these passages reflect the Old Testament saints, and others reflect Jewish Tribulation survivors. But what is clear is that 100% of the Jews in the kingdom know the Lord.

Revelation 20:5

1. Who are the remaining dead to be resurrected after the 1,000-year kingdom? Dead unbelievers.

2. What will happen to Gentiles who survive Tribulation? They'll be brought before Jesus to be judged, based on faith alone, not works. He separates believers and unbelievers. Believers enter the kingdom, and unbelievers go to hell.

3. What is the context of the Matthew 25 passage? Among whom do these works of mercy occur? Tribulation believers/ survivors (sheep) and Tribulation unbelieving survivors (goats)

SESSION SEVENTY ANSWERS
THE 1,000-YEAR KINGDOM

Overview

1. What do we learn about the kingdom period from Revelation? Only that it's 1,000 years long.

2. What does the term *kingdom* mean in the Bible? It's defined in a four-step progression: promise, proposal, program, and place.

3. What was the promise? God will fix what Adam broke.

4. What was the proposal? Accept Jesus as King.

5. What was the program? Advances the coming kingdom, recruitment.

6. What is the place? The literal, physical kingdom.

7. What can we know for sure about the coming kingdom? It will be better and more enjoyable than what we enjoy now.

Kingdom 101: How Creation Changes

1. What did God curse as a result of Adam's sin, and what did the curse do? The earth itself, continually devolving from perfection.

2. What does God provide in His blessing of Noah? God allowed people and other animals to eat meat. There were no predator-prey relationships prior to this moment.

3. To what pattern is God restoring the earth? Eden.

SESSION SEVENTY-ONE ANSWERS
CHANGES TO NATURE AND ISRAEL

Overview

1. What sort of relationships will cease to exist in the kingdom? Predator-prey.

2. Where is heaven specifically? Wherever Jesus is.

3. What will animals be like in the kingdom? Present and peaceful, domesticated.

4. What will the land or plants be like in the kingdom? Fruitful without work.

5. How is the restored land a picture of grace? God will do all the work, and we will reap all the benefits.

6. What one part of creation is not restored to its state in Eden and why? The snake doesn't get its legs back. Satan hasn't experienced final judgment, and sin hasn't been eliminated. The memorial is still needed.

Changes to Borders and Geography

1. What happens to the physical boundaries of Israel? It expands beyond even its historical zenith.

2. What Gentile nation do we know will remain, what will it be like, and why? Edom. It'll be completely void. And the entrance to the pit, Satan's prison, will be there.

ANSWER KEY

SESSION SEVENTY-TWO ANSWERS
THE STATE OF ISRAEL IN THE KINGDOM

1. What other specific Gentile nation will remain in the kingdom? Egypt.

2. What will be the tallest mountain in the kingdom, and what will be on top? Mt. Zion will be the tallest, and the temple will be on top.

3. What other changes will happen to physical Jerusalem? Jerusalem will be on top of the mountains, and two rivers will now run out of it, east and west.

4. What is significant about the eastern river? It turns the Dead Sea to fresh water, and plants and animals will thrive in it.

5. What will happen to the land around Mt. Zion? It'll flatten out into plains.

6. Where will the center of government of the kingdom be? Mt. Zion, Jerusalem.

7. Why is it significant that nations will exist that require ruling? It implies sin will be present because laws will be necessary to govern right behavior.

8. Who will compose Christ's perfect government? Glorified saints.

9. Who will be the ruler over Israel, and who will be his lieutenants? King David. He gets his job back. The apostles will back him up. One per tribe of Israel.

10. What do we know about the place of Gentiles in the kingdom? Not much. We'll have nations governed separately from Israel, ruled by resurrected saints.

11. Which nation will have primacy in the kingdom? Israel.

SESSION SEVENTY-THREE ANSWERS
DAILY LIFE AND DEATH IN THE KINGDOM

1. What is the fundamental purpose of government? To be an instrument of God to punish lawbreakers and encourage good behavior.

2. How does sin enter the kingdom? The survivors of Tribulation who enter the kingdom in their natural bodies. Living Jews and Believing Gentiles.

3. What are the conditions for entering the kingdom? Righteousness.

4. What is significant about those in their natural bodies being able to repopulate the earth? Their children won't be born faithful. They'll still have a choice.

5. How will Christ rule in response to sin? He won't allow it to grow and cause harm. He'll contain it quickly and perfectly.

6. What will be the two classes of people in the kingdom? Glorified, eternal, sinless

saints, and those believers who'd survived the Tribulation and their descendants; sinful, temporal.

7. What does Isaiah 65 teach us about life in the kingdom? No infant mortality.

SESSION SEVENTY-FOUR ANSWERS
LIFE AND FAITH IN THE KINGDOM

1. What does Isaiah 65 teach us about life in the kingdom? No infant mortality; lifespan of 100+ years unless truncated by consequences of sin, being an unbeliever. No death from old age. Believers live on to the end of the kingdom.

2. What is the message God is sending by the details of death in the kingdom? The kingdom is meant to be enjoyed by believers.

3. When do kingdom believers receive their eternal bodies? We don't know. Sometime after age 100.

4. What will determine saving faith in the kingdom? Faith in Jesus and the word of God.

5. Who is allowed to enter into the temple courtyard? Believers on specific days.

6. What do we know is true because salvation remains the result of faith prior to the truth becoming self-evident? Jesus isn't out roaming the earth; He remains unseen. Our glorified appearance won't be much different than the normal human form.

SESSION SEVENTY-FIVE ANSWERS
OVERVIEW OF LIFE IN THE KINGDOM

1. Will the sinlessness of glorified saints lead people to saving faith? No.

2. What will it be like for the saints in the kingdom? We'll have the opportunity to work, form relationships, and live.

3. What does Isaiah 4 teach us about what life will be like for Jews in the kingdom? Perfect weather. Protected by the Glory of the Lord.

4. What will be different for Gentiles in the temple in the kingdom? They'll be allowed to serve inside it.

5. What will be the responsibility of believing Gentiles in the kingdom? To testify what they've seen in the temple. To share the truth when they go home.

6. What will be the punishment for failing to attend the festival of booths? Drought. He'll withhold rain from the offenders.

ANSWER KEY

SESSION SEVENTY-SIX ANSWERS
THE TEMPLE IN THE KINGDOM

1. Which prophet tells us most of what we know of the temple, worship, and sacrifice in the kingdom? Ezekiel.

2. Why are Ezekiel's dimensions significant? They clearly illustrate that this temple in the kingdom will be something larger than has ever existed before.

3. What is the significance of the great size of this structure? It houses a large government, but it also supports the worship/ sacrifice of a large number of sinful people. Reinforces Jerusalem as the center/ pinnacle of the world.

4. What is the symbolic significance of the building's various dimensions? It's a place where sin (six) meets grace (five).

5. How does the millennial temple differ from previous ones? It lacks a curtain or veil separating the holy place and the holy of holies from the rest of the temple. The only furniture that will remain is the table of incense.

6. Why are most of the temple implements no longer necessary in the kingdom? They pictured Jesus and salvation. The picture is no longer necessary now that the reality is present.

7. Why is the table of incense still present in the temple? It represents intercession to the Father, which will still be occurring on sinful humanity's behalf.

8. Where does the river emerge from the temple, and how does it flow? Its foundations. Flows through a channel in the temple, divides and heads out the East and West gates to meet the seas, one of which is the Dead Sea restored to life, a visible symbol of living water.

SESSION SEVENTY-SEVEN ANSWERS
THE GLORY OF GOD

1. What is Christ's physical location in the temple? In the holy of holies.

2. When did the *shekinah* glory of God depart the temple and why? He left right before Nebuchadnezzar conquered Jerusalem, the punishment for Israel's sin.

3. Where did God's glory go when it departed, and why does this matter? East to the Mount of Olives. Comes back the same way He left, both in the first century and in Tribulation in fulfillment of prophecy.

4. Where is the Glory of the Lord during the millennium? Permanently residing in the

holy of holies. His glory fills the temple.

5. How is Christ's entry to the temple symbolic? Christ entered once for all, which is symbolized by His entry into the temple through the east gate never to leave and re-enter. Jesus never leaves the temple because to leave and return would suggest He must continue to qualify Himself.

6. Because the East Gate is permanently closed, who uses this space? David makes it his office.

7. When will those in the kingdom be able to see Jesus? Feast days, Sabbaths, and new moons.

8. How are the seven feasts of Scripture symbolic? All seven pictured some aspect of Jesus' ministry of redemption. The first three feasts represent aspects of Jesus' first coming. The last three picture aspects of His return, and in the middle, is Pentecost. Pentecost represents the church period between the two appearances of Jesus.

9. Which two feasts survive to be celebrated purposefully in the millennium? Passover (representative of redemption through Christ's blood) and the festival of booths (representative of God dwelling among man).

10. Why does God create a one-way route through the temple? It forces you to pass the visible Glory of God.

11. What are unbelievers allowed in the temple, and what are they forbidden? They're required to sacrifice in the courts but cannot enter.

12. Why do Levites have a new job in the kingdom temple, and who will be its priests? They facilitated idolatry in the past, so they'll have a limited role in the temple as custodians. The descendants of Zadok shall serve as priests.

SESSION SEVENTY-EIGHT ANSWERS
THE MILLENNIAL KINGDOM

1. Who was Zadok? The high priest in the time of David who maintained loyalty to David, the King.

2. How will the role of priests be different in the kingdom? Levites will kill the sacrifices rather than worshipers, and Zadok's people will take on the rest of the sacrificial duties the Levites used to do.

3. If Jesus is back in the kingdom, why does the sacrificial system return? The existence of sin fundamentally alters the relationship between people and God. It necessitates a shield between sinful humanity and God's glory.

4. What were the two fundamental effects of sin on the human condition? Sin ruined our relationship with other human beings by corrupting our nature and making us enemies of one another, and sin ruined our relationship with God by incurring His judgment and making us deserving of His wrath.

5. How does the Lord cover the spiritual lack caused by sin? Provision of a covering in the blood of Jesus. Covered by faith in the promise.

6. How does the Lord cover the physical lack caused by sin? Killing an animal to make clothes. It's restoring relationships via physical sacrifice. God presided over it and was satisfied by it.

7. How do we currently participate in a physical sacrificial system? The Spirit of God resides in the individual believer. Our spiritual covering comes by faith in Christ. Our physical sacrifice is made in our bodies.

8. What does it mean to make a sacrifice *in our body*? It is a form of worship, it is done in God's presence, it cleanses our guilty consciences, and it is modeled after Christ's sacrifices. So as we sacrifice our pride and self-interest to show love for others, we restore fellowship within the body.

9. Where does God dwell in the kingdom, and what does that mean for sacrifice? In the temple again, so physical sacrifice in His presence again.

10. What is the role of the saints in this whole system? We will oversee rather than participate. In our glorified state, we'll have no need for sacrifice in our sinless state.

SESSION SEVENTY-NINE ANSWERS
REVELATION 20:7–9

The Final War of Gog and Magog

1. In our timeline, what follows the millennial kingdom? A seven-year period for the war of Gog and Magog.

2. What event begins the war? Satan is released from his prison and immediately resumes deceiving humankind.

3. What is the target of the war? Jerusalem, specifically the temple.

4. How does the war end? God comes down and consumes it all in fire.

5. Why was Satan bound in the first place? So that he would not deceive the nations any longer, until the 1,000 years were completed.

6. How does Satan provoke sin? Through deception and by provoking sin by tempting

Revelation

our flesh nature to act according to its desire.

7. What is Satan able to do, and what is he not able to do? He can deceive, but he cannot make us choose sin. That's on us.

SESSION EIGHTY ANSWERS
THE PURPOSE OF THE WAR OF GOG AND MAGOG

1. Summarize the interpretation and significance of 1 Corinthians 15:24–28. The purpose of creation is to exist under the sole rule of Jesus. Once Satan is abolished, the need for Christ's rule disappears, and this present world will disappear.

2. What is the purpose of the millennial kingdom? To give Christ His promised opportunity to rule and rein over everything.

3. How long is the earth ruled by sinful people? 6,000 years.

4. Why is Satan released? So that Christ can abolish His final enemy and so that the world can be remade. It makes 1,000 years of perfect rule possible because no ruler is necessary without an enemy.

5. What are the details of Satan's deception and this final battle? After being released, Satan deceives Gog and Magog into attacking Israel with a massive army, but God defeats the attackers with fires from heaven and Satan is "thrown into the lake of fire and brimstone" (Revelation 20:10).

6. Other than Revelation 20, where do we read of Gog and Magog? Only Ezekiel 38 and 39.

7. How much of Ezekiel is devoted to kingdom prophecy? The last 16 chapters of 48 total.

8. How are the chapters of Ezekiel organized? According to the covenant promises to Abraham and his descendants.

9. Who are Gog and Magog? Magog is a place relatively close to Eastern Europe/modern-day Turkey, while Gog is the title of the ruler of this place.

10. How was the area of Magog named? After Noah's grandson who settled there.

11. Who starts this war? God

12. Why is it significant that the war of Gog and Magog is fought with wooden weapons? There's no metallurgy or knowledge of warfare after the fulfillment of Isaiah's prophecy of converting swords to plows.

13. What conclusion do we draw from the key details presented from Ezekiel 38 and

39? It refers to Israel that exists in a state that will not be possible until the kingdom.

SESSION EIGHTY-ONE ANSWERS
THE RESOLUTION OF THE WAR OF GOG AND MAGOG

1. What does Ezekiel 38 tell us about the movement of Gog and his army? Motivated by opportunity and greed, Gog mobilizes a huge army to take Israel because it's got the best stuff.

2. Where do these thoughts of Gog's originate? Satan's deception and inciting lust/coveting.

3. In the kingdom, how will God demonstrate His faithfulness in keeping His promise to keep Israel safe from enemies? He lets the enemy out to create a threat against Israel, providing God an opportunity to show Himself faithful.

4. How is the war of Gog and Magog resolved? God strikes them down with fire from heaven. The army dies while Israel's peace will remain intact.

5. What happens to the fallen soldiers and their weapons? The weapons provide fuel for seven years, and they'll bury their bones in the valley of Jordan, so much so the whole valley becomes an impassable cemetery.

6. What's the significance of God's words to the animal kingdom in Ezekiel 39? God upends the world with a bookend. God sacrifices an animal for man at the beginning, and He sacrifices men for animals at the end. A final act of judgment to close out the age and set *all* things right.

SESSION EIGHTY-TWO ANSWERS
REVELATION 20:10–15

1. What will the seven years following the millennial kingdom most closely resemble? Eden.

2. What occurs between this seven-year interim and the new heavens and earth? The Great White Throne judgment.

3. Where does Satan go at the time of judgment? The lake of fire.

4. Where is this lake of fire currently? Somewhere in the heavenly realms, and it's currently empty.

5. Who will be in the lake of fire during the millennial kingdom? The Antichrist and his False Prophet.

Revelation

6. What is the purpose of eternal punishment? It's not a place of restitution or atoning...it's a *dwelling* place for those who are unable to enter into the presence of God.

7. What is spiritual death? Eternal death, being separated from the presence of God for eternity.

8. What are the two kinds of resurrection? One is for believers first and over a long period of time, starting with Christ and ending with millennial saints, and the second is for unbelievers, a single moment at the end of creation containing all who have ever been unbelievers in all creation throughout time.

9. Who sits on the Great White Throne and why? Jesus because all judgment has been given into His authority.

10. What disappears at the beginning of this time of judgment? The universe, all creation

11. Who will be present around the throne in this moment and for what purpose? All humanity of all time, some to be judged, others to observe.

SESSION EIGHTY-THREE ANSWERS
REVELATION 20:21

1. During the Great White Throne judgment, where exactly will we be? We don't know. We'll all be in our eternal bodies in nothingness, the void that preceded creation.

2. What are the two parts of human existence? Our soul/ spirit, which exists eternally, and our physical bodies, which exist temporally.

3. Who are the only two people who miss out on the Great White Throne Judgment and why? Antichrist and his prophet. They will be resurrected and cast into eternal punishment at Christ's second coming prior to the millennial kingdom.

4. What are the two areas of hell, and who resides there? Hell/ Hades—dead unbelievers; abyss/ sea—demons.

5. What is significant about the demons' words to Christ is Matthew 8? They anticipate the final judgment and know it's coming.

6. Why will bowing to Jesus at this moment of judgment not be sufficient for salvation? Faith doesn't coincide with sight. Jesus's Lordship will be self-evident at this point, rendering saving faith impossible.

7. What is in the Book of Life? The names of all believers, a family tree if you will, from all time. It's existed from time immemorial, prior even to the creation of the world or humanity in it.

ANSWER KEY

8. Why is the Book of Life present at the Great White Throne judgment? It's the evidence required to condemn the unbelieving to eternal punishment.

9. By what criteria are these unbelievers judged? Their deeds measured against the Law.

SESSION EIGHTY-FOUR ANSWERS
REVELATION 21:1–8

1. How are the unbelievers convicted at judgment? By their deeds.

2. What is the punishment of unbelievers? They are thrown *alive* into the lake of fire for eternal judgment.

3. After unbelievers are judged, what remains? The Godhead, angels, and saints in their eternal bodies.

4. What scriptural principle is on display by the rather vague content of Revelation 21–22? Progressive Revelation.

5. To what two chapters of Scripture are Revelation 21–22 closely connected and in what way? Genesis 1–2, parallelism.

6. What are two specific details we learn of the new heavens and earth? No sea at all, just land. New Jerusalem, delivered by God ready-made, waiting in the heavenly realm even now.

7. What is the counterpart of the new Jerusalem in Genesis? Eden.

8. What does Jesus say is the significance of the new Jerusalem? Jesus is finally done creating all things new.

9. Where does God the Father dwell in the new heavens and earth? Among men

10. There will be no tears, death, mourning, crying, pain—what does their absence signify? The lack of sin on the earth.

11. What is the message of Revelation to the present reader? Seek Jesus while you still can.

SESSION EIGHTY-FIVE ANSWERS
REVELATION 21:9–21

1. What is the capital of the new earth, and what do we know about it? The new Jerusalem. The complete fulfillment of all God has promised to us comes in that place.

2. In the new earth, to what will the "bride of Christ" refer and why? The city of New

Jerusalem itself because it's His dwelling place.

3. What is the shape of the City? A perfect cube.

4. What do we know about the earth at this point? Not much, only that there exists a mountain for John to stand on.

5. What is the purpose of the walls and gates of the new Jerusalem? To serve as a memorial of what God has done in the prior creation.

6. Why the focus on Israel in the new creation? Without Israel there is no entry. Without Israel, there are no covenants, no prophets, no Law, no temple, no Christ—so truly everyone enters through Israel.

7. What are the symbolic significances of 12 and 3? 12—God ruling through people, specifically Israel. 3—the Godhead, God as the source of all.

8. Who is memorialized in the foundations of the new Jerusalem? The apostles.

9. What is the purpose of John's description of the new Jerusalem? It helps us understand that it's real, it's huge, and it's amazing.

10. What is significant about the city's dimensions other than their large proportions? Multiples of 12. Memorializing God's work through men.

SESSION EIGHTY-SIX ANSWERS
REVELATION 21:22–22:5

1. Why will there be no temple in the new Jerusalem? God won't need it anymore because separation won't be required to remove sin from His presence.

2. What is the light source in the new heavens and earth? God Himself.

3. What will be noticeably absent from the new world? Night. Darkness.

4. Why specifically did God create water/ seas the first time? So it would be available to flood the earth later.

5. Why specifically did God create light and dark the first time? To measure time.

6. So why will seas and darkness be absent from the new earth? We'll no longer require judgment or a measure of time.

7. What does the Bible teach us about the passing of time in this creation? We're counting down until its end.

8. What is significant about the tree we see in Revelation 22? It's the tree of life, the same that existed in Eden.

Answer Key

9. Why did God forbid access to the tree of life in Eden? It would allow them to escape death of their mortal bodies. God had a better plan.

10. Why has the tree of life existed throughout various phases of creation? It is the mechanism of physical eternal life.

11. What is the purpose of the tree of life? To make a point and help humanity remain mindful of God's position and honor Him and His faithfulness.

Session Eighty-Seven Answers
Revelation 22:6–21

1. Why does God not reinstitute some aspects of the first creation in His second creation? He no longer needs physical illustrations of spiritual truths.

2. What was the purpose of the first creation? Because the creation must know sin and the judgment that sin requires to fully appreciate the love of God; We must understand that God is a God of wrath and judgment if we are to praise Him for grace and mercy and now in the new heaven and earth we will forever remember and praise God for His plan of redemption for our sake. It displayed the full nature of God.

3. What literary purpose does the final portion of Revelation 22 serve? An extended benediction.

4. What that knowledge, what are we to do in the meantime? Live with eyes for eternity, prepared for the Lord's return. Let the words of Revelation influence the way we live our lives today.

5. What is the only possible interruption to the path of the unbeliever? The Spirit bringing the person to saving faith.

6. Where is the lake of fire in physical relationship to the new Jerusalem? "Outside" the city.

7. Why does Jesus testify to His own identity? Jesus speaks in first person directly to the reader. It's unique, and He recognizes there will be doubt.

8. What is the invitation of Revelation 22? Come to faith in Jesus. Drink living water and join the saints of this book.

9. What is the warning of Revelation 22? Be faithful to the word of God. Don't change it. You remove words, and He'll remove you.

About the Author
Stephen Armstrong
Founder of Verse By Verse Ministry International

Stephen Armstrong was the founder and principal teacher of Verse By Verse Ministry International. He came to know the Lord in his early thirties, while serving as an Air Force officer. After becoming a believer, Stephen experienced God's call to learn and teach the Bible, so in 1997 Stephen left the military, found a job in Colorado, and began a self-directed course of study in preparation to teach the Scriptures.

As he devoted himself to study, Stephen developed a love for an in-depth, verse-by-verse style of teaching God's word, believing it to be the best means to persuade the unbeliever of the truth of the gospel and equip the saints for the work of ministry (Romans 10:17; Ephesians 4:14–15).

In 2001, Stephen received God's call to move to San Antonio, Texas, where he soon found opportunities to teach and preach in churches throughout the area. Despite having no professional religious training, in 2003 Stephen was called by God to lead a church-planting effort in the city as pastor of Living Word Fellowship.

That same year, he also founded Verse By Verse Ministry of San Antonio (later to be renamed Verse By Verse Ministry International) out of a desire to offer his unique style of in-depth Bible teaching for free to a worldwide audience. Stephen helped plant Verse By Verse Fellowship in San Antonio, Texas, in 2018.

Stephen passed away in January 2021, leaving behind a library of insightful Bible teaching and a ministry team committed to advancing the gospel worldwide.

About Renown Publishing

Renown Publishing was founded with one mission in mind: to make your great idea famous.

At Renown Publishing, we don't just publish. We work hard to pair strategy with innovative marketing techniques so that your book launch is the start of something bigger.

Learn more at RenownPublishing.com.

Made in the USA
Columbia, SC
01 September 2023